Free Trade
Risks and Rewards

Few public policy issues have stirred political passions on both sides of
the Canada/US border as free trade did in the late 1980s. Negotiated
between Canada and the United States in 1987, the Free Trade Agreement became the dominant issue in the November 1988 Canadian
federal election, perhaps the most dramatic and divisive campaign in
the second half of the twentieth century. Ten years after implementation of the agreement, the McGill Institute for the Study of Canada organized a major conference to renew the discussion of free trade and
consider its economic impact. It also marked the fifth anniversary of
the North American Free Trade Agreement by expanding the discussion to include the impact of NAFTA on Mexico, as well as the NAFTA
side agreement of the environment.

Free Trade provides a historical framework for ongoing discussion of
economic and environmental issues. While there is empirical evidence
on trade flows – they increased dramatically in both directions – the
debate on related issues continues. The impact of free trade on jobs
and manufacturing productivity, the effectiveness of dispute settlement, the growth of foreign direct investment, the absence of adjustment programs, and the consequences for social programs are all
issues for spirited discussion. *Free Trade: Risks and Rewards* is an important reminder of why the issue was so passionately debated at the time
and why it remains important.

L. IAN MACDONALD is a Montreal-based columnist and communications
consultant. He is the author of *From Bourassa to Bourassa: A Critical Decade in Canadian History* and *Mulroney: The Making of the Prime Minister.*

Free Trade

Risks and Rewards

EDITED BY

L. IAN MacDONALD

Published for the
McGill Institute for the Study of Canada
by
McGill-Queen's University Press
Montreal & Kingston · London · Ithaca

© McGill-Queen's University Press 2000
ISBN 0-7735-2114-3 (cloth)
ISBN 0-7735-2115-1 (paper)

Legal deposit third quarter 2000
Bibliothèque nationale du Québec

Printed in Canada on acid-free paper

McGill-Queen's University Press acknowledges the financial support of the Government of Canada through the Book Publishing Industry Development Program (BPIDP) for its activities. It also acknowledges the support of the Canada Council for the Arts for its publishing program.

McGill-Queen's University Press and the McGill Institute for the Study of Canada also acknowledge the support of the Department of Foreign Affairs and International Trade, Hydro-Québec, and the Royal Bank Financial Group.

Canadian Cataloguing in Publication Data

Main entry under title:
    Free trade: risks and rewards
    Proceedings of the conference Free Trade @ Ten, held in Montreal,
    Jun. 4-5, 1999.
    Includes bibliographical references.
    ISBN 0-7735-2114-3 (bnd)
    ISBN 0-7735-2115-1 (pbk)
    1. Free trade – North America – Congresses. 2. Free trade – Canada –
    Congresses. 3. North America – Economic integration –
    Congresses. I. MacDonald, L. Ian II. McGill Institute for the Study of
    Canada. III. Free Trade @ Ten (1999: Montreal, Quebec)
    HF1746.F73 2000   382'.71'097   C00-900238-3

This book was typeset by Typo Litho Composition Inc.
in 10/12 Baskerville.

Contents

viii   Contents

Preface

L. IAN MacDONALD

The *Free Trade @ 10* conference, organized by the McGill Institute for the Study of Canada, was a unique event in that it brought the people who made the history together with academics, business and labour leaders who assessed the impact of the Canada-United States Free Trade Agreement (FTA) and the North American Free Trade Agreement (NAFTA).

The tenth anniversary of FTA implementation and the fifth anniversary of the NAFTA provided an opportunity to examine the results of free trade, to appraise its impact and to look at the road ahead. In Montreal over two days in June, 1999, several hundred participants, including dozens of students from universities from all three NAFTA countries, did just that. This book, *Free Trade: Risks and Rewards*, is the record of the proceedings of the *Free Trade @ 10* conference.

The 10-year Canada-U.S. trade data and five-year trade flows among the three NAFTA countries indicate a dramatic increase in bilateral and trilateral trade over the period. In 1988, the last year before FTA implementation, Canada's merchandise exports to the U.S. were $101 billion. In 1998, merchandise exports totaled $271 billion, and while these are constant dollars, the inflation rate over the period was remarkably low. Over the first 10 years of free trade, Canadian merchandise exports to the U.S. increased by nearly 170%.

Similarly U.S. merchandise exports to Canada of $86 billion in 1988 rose to $203 billion in 1998, an increase of nearly 150%. Trade in services also more than doubled during the period, to Canadian imports of $32 billion and exports of $27 billion. Altogether, two-way trade in merchandise and services is now about $1.5 billion a day.

At the signing of the FTA, President Ronald Reagan called it a "win-win" for both countries, and the statistical evidence would appear to bear him out. As John McCallum, chief economist of the Royal Bank of Canada, points out in an economic impact study commissioned for the conference: "It would be quite a coincidence if the explosion of Canada-U.S. trade after 1989 had nothing to do with the implementation of the FTA in that year." As for the impact of exchange rates, with the declining Canadian dollar stimulating exports, McCallum notes: "The fact that Canadian imports from the United States exploded almost as much as exports to the United States indicates this is not just an exchange rate story."

But beyond the empirical evidence of trade flows, there are other issues on which a lively debate continues a decade after implementation. The impact of free trade on jobs and manufacturing productivity, the effectiveness of dispute settlement, the growth of foreign direct investment, the absence of adjustment in the transitional period, and the consequences for social programs, or lack thereof, are all issues for spirited discussion.

The starting point at the conference was the Royal Bank impact study, "Two Cheers for the FTA," published as a special issue of RBC's monthly newsletter, *Econoscope*, and re-produced as an appendix to this book. A panel of eminent economists from Canada, the U.S. and Mexico discussed the impact of the FTA and NAFTA, and while most of them were generally favourable in their comments, the conference heard one notable dissenting appraisal from Andrew Jackson, chief economist of the Canadian Labour Congress. All the papers and presentations from the economists' plenary are re-produced here.

The issue of free trade has stirred remarkable passions in Canada, and to provide historical context Michael Hart has written a retrospective, "The Road to Free Trade," commissioned by Bob Hesketh and Chris Hackett for their CD-ROM project "Canada, Confederation to Present" and re-produced with their kind permission. Professor Hart, of the Centre for Trade Policy and Law, was a senior adviser to Canadian FTA negotiator Simon Reisman and is the author of "Decision at Midnight" a gripping narrative of the FTA negotiations and the deal that very nearly wasn't.

In more recent times, the free trade debate was renewed with the recommendations of the 1982–85 Royal Commission on the Economic Union and Development Prospects for Canada, which was appointed by the Trudeau government and reported to the Mulroney government. It recommended a leap of faith and the *Free Trade @ 10* conference was indeed fortunate to have the Chair of that landmark commission, Donald S. Macdonald, deliver the opening address.

The conference then heard from James A. Baker III and Derek Burney, the two senior political officials at the table during those three remarkable days in October when the FTA was agreed to as the hands of the clock ticked toward midnight of October 3, 1987 and the expiration of President Reagan's fast-track authority to negotiate an agreement to be voted "up or down," without amendment, by the U.S. Congress. As Secretary of the Treasury and Chief of Staff to the Prime Minister, they had direct instructions from their principals and represented the political will to reach an agreement.

As for the making of the deal, and later the selling of it, the dynamic of the trade talks was re-created by a Canada-U.S.A. plenary where the Canadian side was represented by former Trade Minister John Crosbie, former trade negotiator Simon Reisman, former Deputy Minister of Finance Stanley Hartt, as well as William Dymond and Michael Hart, former senior advisers to the Trade Negotiations Office (TNO). Team U.S.A. was represented by former United States Trade Representative Clayton Yeutter, former Deputy Secretary of the Treasury Peter McPherson, and former senior negotiators William Merkin, Jean Anderson and Charles Roh. The transcript of that session does not do justice to the highly informative and entertaining interventions, particularly by Simon Reisman and John Crosbie, neither of whom pulled any punches.

Following the economists' plenary at the beginning of the second day, the conference heard from a panel of business and labour representatives who had varying assessments of the sectoral results and opportunities resulting from the FTA. Participants included Bombardier Chairman Laurent Beaudoin, Telesystem Chairman Charles Sirois, Hydro-Québec Chairman Jacques Ménard, Air Canada Deputy Chairman Lamar Durrett, BCE Chairman L.R. Wilson, and economist Jim Stanford of the Canadian Auto Workers.

A workshop on free trade and social policy featured critical presentations by Gérald Larose, outgoing president of the Confédération des syndicats nationaux (CSN), and Duncan Cameron, Director of the Centre for Policy Alternatives, while Guy Stanley, professor at l'École des Hautes Études Commerciales in Montreal, was more skeptical as to the supposed impact of free trade on social programs Another workshop on dispute settlement featured a practitioner's view by Simon Potter, an expert NAFTA panel member from Canada, as well as by Yvonne Stinson, a leading Mexican practitioner and former Trade Counselor at the Mexican Embassy in Ottawa. In a session on free trade and the regions, former Ontario Premier Bob Rae, a strong opponent of the FTA at the time, made a well-received presentation on getting beyond the old debates and dealing with the consequences of integration and globalization. This breakout was joined by former New

Brunswick Premier Frank McKenna, former Deputy Prime Minister Don Mazankowski on behalf of the West and Montreal management consultant Marcel Côté.

A keynote address by former President George Bush was the bridge to second day sessions on the NAFTA, featuring the three ministers who negotiated the 1992 agreement, Carla Hills from the U.S., Jaime Serra Puche from Mexico and Michael Wilson from Canada. The 1993 NAFTA side deal on the environment was discussed in a panel led by former Quebec Premier Pierre Marc Johnson, also former co-chair of the National Round Table on the Environment and the Economy. Participants included Victor Lichtinger from Mexico, founding Executive Director of the NAFTA Commission on Environmental Cooperation, David Schorr of the World Wildlife Fund in Washington, D.C., William Reilly, former head of the Environmental Protection Agency in the Bush Administration, and Jean Charest, leader of the Quebec Liberal Party.

The final plenary session was a look-ahead that featured presentations from Thomas d'Aquino, President of the Business Council on National Issues (BCNI) and Peter Watson, former Chairman of the U.S. International Trade Commission. The closing keynote was delivered by former Prime Minister Brian Mulroney, whose government negotiated both the FTA and the NAFTA on behalf of Canada.

Free Trade @ 10 was a memorable conference, and many people contributed to its success. First and foremost, Desmond Morton, Director of the McGill Institute for the Study of Canada. *Free Trade @ 10* began with a conversation when we were working together on another McGill Institute for the Study of Canada symposium, the widely praised *Giving the Past a Future* conference on the teaching and learning of history in Canada.

"What about a conference on the tenth anniversary of free trade?" he was asked.

"Who would come?" he asked, cutting right to the chase.

With Brian Mulroney and George Bush, and other leading participants in these important public policy initiatives, we had the makings of a significant event. The former Prime Minister and President readily agreed to waive their speaking fees, as did everyone else on the program.

But even then, the significant organizational costs of the conference could not have been met without the support of our sponsors and partners: Royal Bank of Canada, Hydro-Québec, Bombardier, CN, Power Corporation of Canada, Barrick Gold, Alcan, BCE, Nortel Networks and Imasco. Partners in *Free Trade @ 10* included the Department of Foreign Affairs and International Trade, the Government of Québec, BCE Media, Montreal International, Air Canada, the Renaissance Hôtel du Parc, *The Gazette* and *La Presse*.

We are most grateful to William Watson and the Institute for Research on Public Policy for the special issue of *Policy Options* magazine, published to coincide with the conference, featuring interviews with Brian Mulroney and John Turner on the issue that made the 1988 campaign as memorable as it was bruising, as well as several papers prepared for *Free Trade @ 10* which are re-produced in these proceedings. We are equally indebted to John McCallum, senior vice president and chief economist of Royal Bank of Canada, for the economic impact study which served as a baseline for many discussions.

Special thanks to Victor Lichtinger, former Executive Director of the NAFTA Commission on Environmental Cooperation (CEC), for his invaluable advice on NAFTA and the environment and for obtaining the participation of key Mexican officials.

A conference of the size and scope of *Free Trade @ 10* required significant logistical and communications expertise. Fortunately, we had both in Luc Pinsonneault, our logistics wizard, while on the communications side we had the indispensable support of Michèle Bazin, Johanne Denault and Sophie Langlois of GPC Concordia Communication, who provided unstinting public relations support and met the demands of media from the three NAFTA countries. The high end look and design of the conference were produced by Matthew Alapi and his colleagues at Mosaïc Design Communication in Montreal.

Most of all, the organizers of *Free Trade @ 10* are grateful to the staff of the McGill Institute for the Study of Canada, who put in many long and thankless hours in the preparation and staging of the conference. Heartfelt thanks to Suzanne Aubin, Lynne Darroch, Marie-Louise Moreau and Natalie Zenga.

Finally, we would like to thank Philip J. Cercone and the staff of McGill-Queen's University Press, particularly Joan McGilvray, for facilitating the publication of this book.

For myself, as the coordinator of the conference, and as editor of this book, it was a unique privilege to work on both. The results are there, and here, as part of the historic record, on a matter that mattered.

L. IAN MACDONALD is a Montreal-based columnist and communications consultant.

Introduction: An Historic Surprise

DESMOND MORTON

On June 4–5, 1999, with the generous help of corporate and individual partners, and drawing on friendships often developed around the FTA and NAFTA negotiations and in the opposition to them, the McGill Institute for the Study of Canada invited several hundred people to Montreal to look at *Free Trade @ 10*. For two days, guided by many of the principal actors, we reflected on two events which will, I am sure, be included in even the most summary histories of the countries affected. We recalled the circumstances and the expectations in which these agreements were born; with help from other colleagues from business, labour and universities, we analyzed their impact on the ensuing ten and five years and we tried to anticipate how trading relations in the new millennium will shape the future of Mexico, the United States and Canada, and generations whose lives and potential depend on the wealth nations create for their citizens and humanity in general.

Historians are accustomed to evaluating the importance of trade agreements, especially for Canada. Certainly there have been agreements before these ones, notably the Reciprocity Agreement that Lord Elgin helped to negotiate between the U.S. and the British North American colonies in 1854. Canadians remember the Reciprocity Agreement as the beginning of a golden decade that ended after the U.S. Civil War. Canadian Confederation was, in part, a substitute for free trade, but reciprocity remained a trophy that any Canadian politician would have been delighted to re-gain.

In time, of course, reciprocity changed reputation. Victorious in 1873, Liberals promised to revive reciprocity and Washington rebuffed them. Lacking any leverage in Washington, Sir John A. Macdonald's Tories returned to power in 1878 with protective tariffs. The National Policy (NP to its friends) delivered low-paying jobs, high prices and substantial Canadian fortunes. Much as high tariffs defined the Republicans, the NP defined Canadian Conservatism from Macdonald to Richard Bedford Bennett. They won for Macdonald in 1891 and for Bennett in 1930, and they helped John Diefenbaker in 1957. When Sir Wilfrid Laurier's Liberals announced a new reciprocity agreement in 1911, the Conservatives mobilized business and labour and drove Laurier from power.

A young minister who lost his seat in 1911 was William Lyon Mackenzie King. Almost forty years later, as Canada's most durable prime minister, King remembered 1911 well enough to threaten fellow Liberals that if they dared contemplate free trade with Washington, he would come out of retirement – perhaps even his grave – to campaign against them. A devout spiritualist, King may have haunted the conference but no one reported his shadow.

After 1935, many traditional U.S.-Canadian trade barriers faded, but free trade was barred from the Canadian political agenda. Indeed, before his astonishing sweep of the Canadian electorate in 1984, Brian Mulroney himself reminded voters that the argument had been settled in 1911. Like other lost causes, free trade survived in the academy and the extremities, espoused by economists like the late Harry Johnson and the brothers Wonnacott, or by the prairie farmers who voted CCF or Social Credit, and blamed the greedy capitalists of Montreal and Toronto for denying them free markets and cheap machinery.

For those of us who grew up in the West, far from the centre of Canada, these notions confirmed that we were far removed from reality. The real vision was reflected by Walter Gordon and the Royal Commission on the Economic Perspective in 1957. The same results were expected when another Toronto nationalist, by the name of Donald S. Macdonald, chaired the Royal Commission on the Economic Union and Development Prospects for Canada. The experts are always right, aren't they?

Sometimes the most obvious thing in the world is utterly invisible – chiefly because people have shut their eyes. But when old policies have failed, someone has to sneak a peek. As a new prime minister, that's what Brian Mulroney could do. He was lucky that most members of the Macdonald Royal Commission had done so too. Their report defied some old political taboos. But it was Mulroney's government, not a Royal Commission, that had to persuade Canadians. It was not easy. The 1988 federal election was as bitterly fought on a single issue as Canada's notorious conscription election in 1917. Canadian voters were given glowing promises and they were given much to fear. So far as voters ever reach informed decisions, Canadians re-elected a Mulroney government and therefore chose the FTA.

The FTA was a crucial turning point for Canada. The North American Free Trade Agreement five years later was another. On that much, supporters and opponents agreed. There was not much other common ground and perhaps there still isn't. But ten and five years later, the prime actors in the negotiations can remember what they thought they were doing and why. And those who have lived through those years have seen outcomes they anticipated and others they did not.

Historians, of course, are Cassandras. They know too much about the past to feel really good about the future. As in markets, what goes around comes around. There have been huge winners from what Michael Hart reasonably calls "orthodox economic thinking," but there are losers too, dispossessed from their own comfort and security by economic changes beyond their power to influence. History is written by winners, but it is often made by losers, avenging their fate. The Great Depression taught us the folly of protectionism; it and the war that followed told us that ordinary people also demand their share of security and hope. Their absence from the consumer market between 1920 and 1940 was as much a cause of the Great Depression as fiscal and market constraint.

History always has more than one lesson to teach, and some lessons are less convenient than others. At the McGill Institute for the Study of Canada, historical benchmarking is part of our mission. Thus, we commissioned a 10-year economic impact study of the FTA by John McCallum, senior vice-president and chief economist of the Royal Bank of Canada, which was presented at the *Free Trade @ 10* conference and which is published as an appendix to these proceedings, along with 10-year Canada-U.S.-Mexico trade flows compiled by the Department of Foreign Affairs and International Trade.

The conference was a unique opportunity to bring together actors and activists on one of the most significant public policy issues of our time – one on which nearly everyone had an opinion, informed or otherwise, and on which nearly everyone took sides. This book of the proceedings will not stir those passions anew, but it provides a useful appraisal from a conference which is now part of the historic record.

DESMOND MORTON is Director of the McGill Institute for the Study of Canada.

PART ONE

The Context

The Road to Free Trade

MICHAEL HART

The gulf between orthodox economic thinking and the intuitive notions of do-it-yourself economics is widest in the sphere of international economic relations in general and trade policies in particular. The professionals and those who think like them, are very much in a minority. Perhaps the sharpest difference between minority and majority lies in their respective conceptions of where national interests lie in international trade.

David Henderson, Innocence and Design

INTRODUCTION

In 1987 Canada signed and in 1989 implemented a bilateral free-trade agreement with the United States, concluding a quest of more than a century. Since then Canada has entered into free-trade agreements with Mexico (in 1993 as a result of the North American Free Trade Agreement), Israel (1996), and Chile (1997). At the century's end, Canadian officials were busy negotiating a free-trade agreement with the members of the European Free Trade Association (EFTA) and were actively engaged in discussing the potential for a Free Trade Area for the Americas (FTAA) encompassing all the countries of the Western Hemisphere except Cuba. Ministers have mused about the prospect of turning Asia-Pacific Economic Cooperation (APEC) into a free-trade forum and wondered whether it would not be possible to construct a trans-Atlantic free-trade area. Finally, Canada is a charter member of the 1947 General Agreement on Tariffs and Trade (GATT) and its successor, the 1994 World Trade Organization (WTO), both of which are committed to the liberalization of world trade on a multilateral basis.

It is not an exaggeration, therefore, to claim that Canada has become a certified free trader, ready to consider a wide range of opportunities to

Reproduced, with kind permission, from *Canada, Confederation to Present*
Creators: Bob Hesketh and Chris Hackett. Editorial chair: Rod Macleod
Publisher: Chinook Multimedia Inc.

translate political rhetoric into economic and commercial reality. Canada has become fully committed to maintaining an open and rules-based economy in return for which Canadian-based traders and investors can count on reciprocal access to a growing number of markets around the world. In the closing years of the twentieth century, Canadians can truly be described as free traders. They appear to have crossed the gulf between do-it-yourself economic intuition and economic orthodoxy.

Canadians were not always free traders. Indeed, for much of their history, Canadians were primarily interested in convincing others to allow Canadian goods free entry to their markets. There is little evidence that before the 1980s Canadian governments, and most Canadians, thought open or 'free' access to the Canadian market was desirable. Canada's attitude was similar to that of its trading partners. It has always been easy to convince governments of the virtue of opening up foreign markets. Opening up one's own market, however, is a much more contentious proposition. Throughout most of the nineteenth century and well into the twentieth century, therefore, Canadians strove energetically to gain freer access to the markets of Great Britain, the United States, and others and toiled just as energetically to ensure that the Canadian market would not be overwhelmed by foreign competitors. Canada's quest for free trade, therefore, had until recently a decidedly mercantilist cast to it and, not surprisingly, met with little success.

That there was such a quest may surprise some who think that free trade was invented by the 1984–93 Conservative government led by Brian Mulroney. Not quite.[1] Free trade, at least with the United States, was a constant theme in Canadian politics from the late 1840s through the election of 1911. By that time, Canadian manufacturers had become unalterably opposed to free trade and succeeded in sharing their concerns with the majority of the electorate. For the next 70 years, governments accepted that judgment and took a more perspicacious approach to the liberalization of trade with the United States and others.

By the 1980s, however, Canadian producers were ready to change their mind and accept the benefits of policies that economists could fairly describe as free trade. Producers' willingness to adopt free trade had been heavily conditioned by four decades of positive experience in negotiating agreements dedicated to a much more modest objective: gradual liberalization within the framework of a multilateral, rules-based regime. The successful establishment and progressive enlargement of that system from the mid-1940s through the 1980s, however, laid the foundation for the more radical quest for free trade with the United States and, increasingly, with others, that has dominated Canadian trade policy since the mid 1980s.

By the closing years of the twentieth century, Canadian barriers to the entry of foreign goods, services, capital, and technology, while not wholly gone, have reached levels at which they no longer constitute a major obstacle to trade and investment. Close to 40 percent of Canadians' total expenditures on goods and services are now supplied from outside the country. The barriers to the exports of Canadian goods, services, capital, and technology to the markets of the members of the Organization for Economic Cooperation and Development (OECD) – more than 90 percent of Canadian exports – have similarly become inconsequential. As a result, some 40 percent of Canada's gross national product (GNP) is now earned from exports of goods and services. The challenges for the future are to make that trade more secure, to spread the application of liberal trade rules and conditions beyond the members of the OECD, and to remove the remaining pockets of entrenched protectionism (most notably in trade in agriculture). Attaining these challenges has become increasingly realistic as a result of Canada's long experience in traveling the road to free trade.

EARLY BEGINNINGS

Canada has always been a trading nation. From earliest days, Canadians have relied for their livelihood on exports to bigger and wealthier markets. Initially, those exports were largely resource-based and often at very low stages of processing. Furs and fish, then wheat and forest products and, finally, metals and minerals were sold on world markets in exchange for machinery, consumer goods, food, and other products not readily available at home or available more cheaply from foreign sources.

From the earliest arrival of European settlers until the early nineteenth century there was, strictly speaking, no Canadian trade policy. Trade and economic activity in the northern half of the continent was regulated first by French and then by British officials implementing their respective colonial systems. It was not until the early nineteenth century that the sparsely settled northern colonies gradually gained a modest degree of self-government and began to regulate their internal economic affairs. Only then did a native Canadian trade policy begin to emerge.

Canada's colonial and sentimental ties to Britain and geographic ties to the United States ensured that the preponderance of the country's commercial relations would be with these two countries. As a result, much of Canada's trade policy, from its early pre-Confederation origins until well into the years after the Second World War, was forged in reaction to policies pursued by these two world powers, policies typically adopted without any thought, positive or negative, about their possible impact on Canada.

Throughout much of its history, Canada sought a special place for its products in one of these two markets or in both. The history of Canadian trade policy, therefore, is a record of the changing priorities attached to commercial ties with one or the other. The quest for special status was complicated by the trade policy and attitudes in vogue in these two dominant powers as well as by non-commercial sentiments and considerations. The latter often flowed from the fact that Britain and the United States were major powers with worldwide interests, responsibilities, and influence while Canada, rather self-consciously, worried about its self-image and identity. Only in the last 30 years, with the demise of the UK's economic power and the development of the United States as Canada's only major trade and investment partner, has Canada struck out across the Atlantic and Pacific in search of countervailing forces to the overwhelming influence of the United States. To date that search has brought only limited returns.

In Canada as elsewhere, trade policy had its origins in fiscal policy. The tariff was used primarily as a device for raising taxes and only secondarily as a means of protecting domestic producers. Trade policy thus developed as an offshoot of fiscal policy and the earliest record of trade policy making can be found in budget statements. The initial right of the colonists in Canada to raise their own taxes to pay for the administration of their part of the British Empire was one of the principal results arising from the disaster posed for British colonial officials by the American Revolution. Not until the 1840s, however, did Canadian politicians begin actively to address the trade policy challenge posed by their decisions about fiscal policy. The need to do so was made more urgent by the British decision in 1846 to adopt unilateral free trade, thus ending the special status long enjoyed by Canadian wheat, lumber, and other commodities in the British market.

FROM U.S. RECIPROCITY TO A 'NATIONAL' POLICY

Canada's initial response to Britain's provocative decision was to try to negotiate free access for Canadian resource products to the U.S. market, a quest that became temporary reality in 1854. With the Elgin-Marcy Reciprocity Agreement Canada secured free entry for its exports of resource products in return for granting the Americans navigation rights on the Great Lakes and fishing rights on the Grand Banks. The treaty has the distinction of being one of only three trade agreements to pass U.S. Senate muster between 1776 and 1934, when the current U.S. system of delegated authority for the negotiation of trade agreements was introduced. The United States, however, gained no trade concessions of any value and when the colonial legislatures further increased duties on U.S. goods, the die was cast for its abrogation by the Congress in 1866. Once the Civil War was over and southern free traders were effectively removed from congressional decision making, the treaty proved to have few friends and to serve even fewer interests.

The abrogation of the agreement added to the forces that led to Confederation in 1867, as the colonies that made up British North America agreed to establish a customs union to offset the loss of both British preferences and American reciprocity. In the years following Confederation, Canada repeatedly sought renewal of reciprocity, only to be told by successive American administrations that the only acceptable basis upon which Canadians could enjoy free access to the U.S. market was as members of the Union. As Secretary of State James G. Blaine raged in 1896, Canadians could not have the "sentimental satisfaction of waving the British flag, paying British taxes, and enjoying the actual cash remuneration of American markets. They cannot have both at the same time."[2]

Confederation came at the end of a period of strong, export-led growth, largely to the United States, as Canadian farmers, loggers, and other producers successfully exploited the growth in the U.S. economy, the Reciprocity Treaty of 1854, and the rise in U.S. prices during the Civil War. The first railroads helped further to boost Canadian growth. Unfortunately, the boom only continued another five or six years beyond Confederation. Bad times hit in the mid-1870s and lasted for the next 20 years. Canada's exports to the United States stagnated while those to the UK grew only incrementally. Domestic production was also sluggish. More people left Canada than came and many people concluded that Confederation was a bust.

Canada was not alone. The economies of other countries similarly floundered. By the 1870s the international economy had reached the zenith of the impact of the first industrial revolution and the British-led expansion of trade. Trade within continental Europe, between Europe and Great Britain, and across the Atlantic had grown steadily and trade policy had encouraged that growth. Britain's pursuit of unilateral free trade and the negotiation of a series of interlocking most-favoured-nation (MFN) trade agreements based on the Cobden-Chevalier Treaty between England and France in 1860 had encouraged that trade.

The period from the mid-1870s to the mid-1890s, however, was one of dislocation and slow growth everywhere but in the United States.

Not surprisingly, protectionist sentiments steadily mounted, exacerbated by nationalist passions released by nation-building policies in Germany, Italy, and elsewhere. These sentiments found expression in renewed imperial fervour in Britain. They fostered the gradual retreat from the liberalism embodied in the treaty system adopted in Europe in the 1860s. The treaties were not abandoned, but they were renegotiated and reinterpreted to provide new competitive advantages for domestic industries at the expense of foreign competitors. These protectionist sentiments were also reflected in the jingoistic policies pursued by Republican administrations in the United States, steadily raising the tariff and rebuffing Canadian efforts to renew the Reciprocity Agreement of 1854.

The response in Canada was the National Policy introduced by the Conservative government of Sir John A. Macdonald in 1878. It was built on the conviction that if others were not going to open their markets to Canadian goods, Canada would pursue what today would be called an import-substitution strategy. Canada would try to go it alone and develop a more self-reliant national economy stretching from the Atlantic to the Pacific.

Underpinning these developments were changes in the technology and organization of production. This is the period when steel making came into its own, fueling a revolution in production and transportation leading to the second railway boom, the development of steel hulls and steamships, the introduction of refrigerated ships and railcars, a quantum leap forward in the mechanization of production, and many other innovations which fundamentally altered the nature of the economy and to which international trade only adjusted gradually. Not surprisingly, this was a period of pessimism about the future. The transformation in the economy was not easy. It took time and it took adaptation. There was much pain as individuals and institutions had to adapt to new demands. Repeated rebuffs by the Americans of Canadian overtures to restore reciprocity added to Canadian pessimism about the country's economic future.

RENEWED PROSPERITY AND CHANGING ATTITUDES

By the early years of the new century, however, a renewed, upward trend was clearly discernible. Trade and production again grew rapidly. Barriers came down. The adjustments made during the period of trouble began to pay dividends, launching a new period of economic growth and internationalization. On the trade front, there was a revival in the treaty system in Europe. The United States Congress adopted the

Table 1
Trade and Growth in the Canadian Economy, 1900–1939
(in millions of current dollars)

Item	1900	1913	1922	1931	1939
Merchandise Exports	156	443	884	601	906
Merchandise Imports	177	655	745	580	713
Current account balance	-37	-408	-47	-174	+126
Net long-term capital movement	+30	+542	+237	+113	-136
Domestic investment	86	405	362	626	592
Steam railway mileage	17,656	29,304	39,358	42,280	42,637
Capital empl. in manufacturing	447	1,959	3,244	4,961	n/a
Population (000)	5,322	7,527	8,919	10,377	11,267

Source: A. E. Safarian, *The Canadian Economy in the Great Depression* Table 1, 22; F. H. Leacy, ed., *Historical Statistics of Canada,* 2nd ed; *Canada Year Book,* 1932 and 1946; Stovell, *Canada in the World Economy,* table 27.

Underwood Tariff in 1912, the lowest tariff in more than 50 years. At the outbreak of the First World War, trade barriers in both Europe and North America were at their lowest level in more than half a century.

In Canada, the economic boom was once again fueled by exports, including wheat from the newly opened Prairies, lumber, newsprint, and various agricultural commodities, as well as new investments in mining and manufacturing (See table 1). Immigration patterns reversed and the population grew rapidly. The Western territories were the main beneficiaries. Between 1871 and 1911, their population mushroomed from 75,000 to 1.3 million. By the turn of the century, therefore, Canadian producers began once again to clamour for better access to the U.S. and British markets.

THE SEARCH FOR IMPERIAL PREFERENCES

In 1896 Canadians put their trust in a new Liberal government led by Sir Wilfrid Laurier. Liberal policy preference had long been for freer trade with the United States. The party's experience over the previous 18 years in opposition, however, had taught it a healthy respect for pragmatism. Once in office, Laurier and his finance minister, W.S. Fielding, concluded that reciprocity with the United States was not to be. Instead, they sought to build a trade policy based on Canada's imperial connection. If Canadian goods could not gain a privileged status in the U.S. market, then they had to regain such status in Great Britain. Unfortunately, the British government was not prepared to abandon the policy of free trade it had adopted in the 1840s. Not until the 1920s did it finally relent when it gradually introduced the protectionist policies prevalent everywhere else, clearing the way for a comprehensive system of imperial preferences.

In the middle of this period – in 1911 – the Liberals made one last stab at reciprocity with the United States and succeeded, only to be rejected at the polls. Laurier and Fielding succeeded in negotiating an agreement with the Republican administration of William Howard Taft that was wholly favourable to Canadian interests. It provided for free entry of resources and the harmonization of tariff levels on manufactures. The tilt toward Empire over the previous 15 years, as well as the growth of a domestic manufacturing class dependent on high tariffs, had made reciprocity on any terms politically unacceptable.

The defeat of Laurier in the 1911 election confirmed for the triumphant Tories the value of the imperial connection and reduced the concept of Canada-U.S. reciprocity to that of a political albatross, not to be raised again in any serious way until the 1980s. As a result, Canada and the United States did not have a trade agreement between them from 1866 to 1935 and extended least-favoured-treatment to each other. Not surprisingly, growth in trade between the two countries, despite the pull of geography, slowed during much of this period. Instead, American entrepreneurs with an eye on the Canadian market satisfied their goals through branch-plant operations that may have helped to develop Canada, but created political headaches of their own in later years. Canadian agricultural and resource exports similarly found the U.S. market less than reliable and instead concentrated on British and other markets. With the exception of a few fisheries and similar agreements, Canadian officials did not need to develop any expertise in managing commercial relations with the United States because they did not amount to much. Not until 1926 did Canada set up a diplomatic legation of its own in the U.S. capital, relying until that time upon British representation.

By that time Canadian politicians, together with their colleagues in Australia, New Zealand, South Africa, and the West Indies, had convinced Britain of the value of a new system of imperial preferences, consolidated at the 1932 Imperial Economic Conference in Ottawa. Success in implementing imperial preferences, however, did not lead to the desired results. The importance of the British market had by then begun to wane. Despite the lack of reciprocity, the pull of geography had made

Table 2
Canada's Trade in Goods with Great Britain, the United States and the Rest of
the World Selected Years, Proportion of Total

Year	Britain		United States		Rest of World	
	Imports	Exports[b]	Imports	Exports[b]	Imports	Exports[b]
1870[a]	57.1	37.9	32.2	50.0	10.7	12.1
1880	47.8	51.2	40.0	40.5	12.2	8.3
1886	40.7	47.2	44.6	44.1	14.7	8.7
1891	37.7	48.8	46.7	42.6	15.6	8.6
1896	31.2	57.2	50.8	34.4	18.0	8.4
1901	24.1	52.3	60.3	38.3	15.6	9.4
1906	24.4	54.2	59.6	35.5	16.0	10.3
1911	24.3	48.2	60.8	38.0	14.9	13.8
1916	15.2	60.9	73.0	27.1	11.8	12.0
1921	17.3	26.3	69.0	45.6	13.7	28.1
1929	15.0	25.2	68.8	42.8	16.2	32.0
1933	24.0	39.0	54.0	32.0	22.0	29.0
1937	18.2	40.3	60.7	36.1	21.1	23.6
1939	15.2	35.5	66.1	41.1	18.7	23.4

Source: William L. Marr and Donald G. Paterson, *Canada: An Economic History*, 389.
Notes
a. Figures for Ontario, Quebec, New Brunswick and Nova Scotia only
b. Domestic product only

the United States a rising source of imports and of investment capital.
The slow decline of Britain as a world economic power had begun, with
the United States as the obvious replacement. Canadians were beginning to learn that proximity to the dominant political and economic
power of the twentieth century could be both an asset and a liability. Un-
questionably, the U.S. market offered attractive economic opportunities.
At the same time, however, U.S. attitudes sometimes made it difficult to
realize these opportunities while U.S. power and global responsibilities
could make it a difficult trading partner.

Economic times were also less than propitious. The first world war
had brought the boom of the opening years of the new century to an
end. The postwar period was one of economic stagnation, with only a
few short periods of economic growth on a global basis. Canada in the
1920s was one of the few bright spots. Nevertheless, during this period

a new set of momentous changes took place in the technology and organization of production.

The combined insights of entrepreneurs like Henry Ford and managers like Fredrick Taylor led to a revolutionary way of organizing the production of thousands of identical and relatively reliable but inexpensive products. The new methods involved learning how to organize a stable work force and complex machinery in order to produce thousands of copies of identical parts which could be assembled into a wide range of consumer products. It required learning how to take advantage of economies of scale, how to generate sufficient demand to make the investment required to make economies of scale profitable, and how to distribute the resulting products to a wide range of consumers. The answer lay in large corporations organized to develop and manufacture new products more efficiently than the competition, source the necessary raw materials, establish distribution networks, and develop and satisfy the necessary high, sustained demand.

This new type of industrial firm required a vast army of people with technical, administrative, and managerial skills as well as immense numbers of unskilled assembly workers. The key to reaping rewards was to manufacture on a very large scale and maintain demand for the same product for a considerable period of time.

In conjunction with these developments in industrial technology, processes, and organization, governments developed a typical set of new policies and programs. These reflected the widespread acceptance of what Jan Tumlir called the planning ideology involving political authorities much more closely in the structure and operation of the economy.[3] The combined demands of the First World War and the depression fostered an acceptance that governments had a role to play that would have been unthinkable in the nineteenth century. The state was more and more viewed as the source of wisdom and legitimacy while the collectivist urge increasingly saw the individual's well-being as subordinate to and dependent on that of the state. The consequences of the all-pervasive grip of this statism could be seen in the secularization of society and the decline in the influence of organized religion.

This change in political and social ideology, when combined with the move toward democracy and universal suffrage, had profound implications for domestic economic policies and for attitudes toward the establishment of a planned international economic order. It led to the modern mixed economy which accepts a significant role for government in guiding economic development at both the macro and micro levels. And it led to the interlocking arrangements which have underpinned the interdependence of national economies since the Second World War.

Initially, however, the transformation of the craft economies of the early twentieth century to the industrial economies of the middle of the century created much anxiety and disruption. The economic instabilities of the 1920s which led to the beggar-your-neighbour policies of the 1930s can in large measure be attributed to the dislocations flowing from Fordism and Taylorism. The initial response to the new economy of the 1920s and 1930s was to hunker down and try to export the problems of adjustment. It took a depression and a war to convince political leaders that there had to be a better way. That better way was built on a fundamental reversal in U.S. trade policy.

THE RENEWAL OF U.S. RECIPROCITY

Over the years, Canadians had learned that, strictly speaking, the United States did not have an international trade policy. Congress, to which responsibility for commercial policy had been assigned by the Constitution, regularly passed a tariff act which set the rates of duties to be charged on thousands of imported products. The tariff bill was an intensely political process involving the disparate interests of every member of Congress. It is thus not surprising that for most of U.S. history, tariffs steadily increased and U.S. trade policy became ever more complex and protectionist. Even when the need to balance protectionist interests against fiscal requirements gradually disappeared with the introduction of the income tax in 1913, tariffs mounted to even higher levels. They reached their zenith in 1930 with the infamous Smoot-Hawley Tariff Act, which brought tariffs on dutiable goods to an average of nearly 60 percent, substantially higher than tariffs anywhere else in the world.

U.S. tariffs were not only high but also autonomous, unaffected by any international obligations. Between 1776 and 1934, various presidents had attempted to negotiate tariff agreements using their treaty making authority. Only three of these efforts were ever ratified by the Senate and brought into force: an 1825 agreement with Hawaii, the 1854 Reciprocity Agreement with Canada, and an 1898 agreement with Cuba.

As the economic importance of the United States grew in the period after the First World War, the need for changes in U.S. trade policy became painfully apparent. They came in 1934 in reaction to the excesses of the Smoot-Hawley Act. Experience since 1930 had demonstrated that the protectionist and isolationist zeal symbolized by the Act had deepened not only the misery of the United States but also that of other countries. In response, U.S. officials devised a plan that took account of the limits placed on the president by the Constitution and the reality of congressional politics but that allowed the United States to adopt a reciprocal, non-discriminatory, bargaining tariff. They requested Congress to pass an act giving the president the authority for a period of three years to negotiate tariff agreements which would reduce tariffs by as much as 50 percent with any country prepared to provide reciprocal concessions. Agreements that satisfied these conditions would be self-executing and not require Senate ratification. Congress agreed and passed the Reciprocal Trade Agreements (RTA) Act, providing the president with a powerful new tool for reversing nearly a century of increasing U.S. protectionism and for allowing the United States to play a leadership role for the first time in international economic affairs.

Canada was among the first to take advantage of the new program. The ink on the 1932 agreements establishing imperial preferences was barely dry when Canada began and eventually succeeded in negotiating the long-sought-after reciprocity agreement with the United States. Initiated under Prime Minister R.B. Bennett and concluded under his successor, Mackenzie King, Canada quietly entered into a trade agreement with the United States in 1935 providing for most-favoured-nation treatment and modest levels of tariff reductions.

Canada followed up in concert with Britain in negotiating a more extensive agreement three years later by which time Canada had developed a team of experts with a solid base of experience in negotiating such agreements. During the 1937–38 triangular negotiations in Washington, Norman Robertson, one of the members of that team, candidly explained to his colleague, Lester Pearson, back in Ottawa: "Triangular trade negotiations ... are dreadfully difficult and discouraging ... I can get on with the Americans a damn sight more easily than with the English ... Our direct negotiations with the U.S.are the least of our worries right now. We can cope with them but not with God's Englishmen and the inescapable moral ascendancy over us lesser breeds."[4] Robertson thus reflected the large gulf that had been raised between Canada and Britain and the development of closer relations between the United States and Canada. Dana Wilgress, another member of that team, concluded 20 years later that "the successful outcome of the triangular negotiations of 1938 served to stabilize trade relations with the two chief outlets for Canadian products ... In reaching this goal Canada had won the respect and high regard of her trading partners."[5]

The achievement of Canada-U.S. reciprocity marked the beginning of a new era in the history of Canadian trade policy, the period of the professionals. Up until 1932, trade policy had been a highly partisan issue in Canada. Generally, the Conservatives had stood for high tariffs and the imperial connection, while the Liberals had preferred lower tariffs and the American connection, although both parties, when in power and circumstances warranted, had pursued the policy of the other. There was much more continuity in policy and administration than the rhetoric of electoral campaigns would suggest. During this partisan era, ministers and prime ministers themselves formulated the policy and then negotiated the agreements. Advice was sought from outside business and academic advisors. The role of the civil service was to transcribe and implement. From 1932, however, trade policy increasingly became the special preserve of a highly talented and homogeneous group of professionals who not only advised ministers and carried out their instructions but gradually came to dominate the process. One of the hallmarks of their approach was to work closely with the Americans and develop what became known as the "special relationship," a relationship which allowed Canadians frequently to sue for exemptions from U.S. measures aimed at others.

FROM RECIPROCITY TO MULTILATERALISM

One of the early fruits of Canadian-American cooperation was the successful conclusion of the General Agreement on Tariffs and Trade (GATT) in Geneva in 1947. From a Canadian perspective, it had the particular virtue of providing a set of rules and procedures for gradually liberalizing trade and resolving trade conflicts on a multilateral basis. Canada could pursue close relations with both of its major trading partners and not have to choose between them, as it had been forced to do during earlier periods in its history. In effect, the GATT became Canada's trade agreement with the United States and Britain as well as with the rest of the world.

After a slow start, the GATT succeeded in providing a regime consonant with the new business practices and governmental policies developed over the previous 20 years. The GATT allowed national firms in industrialized countries to take greater advantage of their economies of scale by finding foreign markets for their products, either directly or on the basis of foreign direct investment. The combined effect of advances in transportation, communications, and the reduction in trade barriers made it possible for companies to compete for much wider markets, face much stronger competition in the home market, and become increasingly specialized. The result was unprecedented expansion in global production, trade, investment, and prosperity. Increased international trade and competition in turn accelerated globalization or harmonization of consumer tastes and demand, setting the stage for further internationalization of the economy.

Canada's new multilateral trade policy rapidly became the mainstay of government policy and enjoyed remarkable success. Canadians participated in a world-wide expansion of trade and investment unprecedented in world history. In the quarter century from the founding of the GATT to the first oil shock (1948–73), the real value of world trade expanded by a factor of six, while world income quadrupled and population doubled. Canadian trade grew by a factor of seven, GNP by a factor of five, and population doubled. While exports remained largely resource-based, the domestic economy diversified, and more and more goods were exported at higher stages of processing. A wide array of imports enriched the lives of all Canadians. It appeared that Canadian trade policy was finally paying the kind of dividends that had long been sought.

The virtues of rules-based relations and the liberalizing bias of the GATT regime were, for most of the postwar period, offset to some extent by powerful interests in Canada that saw greater benefit in maintaining protection than in adjusting to competition. Thus, throughout the period, Canadian governments kept to a delicate compromise between the mercantilist interests of domestic groups, particularly manufacturers and eastern dairy, poultry, and horticulture producers, and broader national interest in rules-based, multilateral liberalization.

Not surprisingly, there was not always a congruence of interests between Canada and its increasingly important trading partner, the United States. Canada maintained protection that harmed U.S. export interests while the U.S. took measures that harmed Canadian interests. Canadians found U.S. protectionism particularly galling in the face of the overwhelming economic superiority enjoyed by the United States.

At the end of the war, as Canadian officials helped to establish the multilateral system, they flirted briefly with a bilateral free-trade agreement with the United States but in the end accepted the political instinct of Mackenzie King that such an agreement would not be politically acceptable. Within a few years this episode had been wiped from the record of institutional memory and multilateralism had been accepted as the only professionally sound policy. The 1965 Autopact and the defence production sharing arrangements with the United States, which gave the products of Canadian branches of some U.S. multinationals special status in the U.S. market, were regarded as special solutions to unique problems and in no way inconsistent with multilateral faith and practice. They were products of the "special relationship," the second pillar of postwar Canadian trade policy.

The auto and defence agreements added further to the continental direction of Canadian economic development. By this time, opinion in Canada was beginning to question the wisdom of such close ties to the

American economy. As if to prove the critics' case, President Nixon and his Treasury Secretary, John Connally, brought the special relationship to a crashing halt in 1971. Faced by a mounting drain of dollars caused by the Vietnam War and U.S. overseas investment, as well as U.S. responsibility as the reserve currency under the fixed-exchange regime of the International Monetary Fund, Nixon took dramatic action that effectively altered the postwar consensus on monetary cooperation. The various measures, including a ten percent import surcharge, hit Canada hard. Canadian officials trooped to Washington to explain that Canada should be exempted from the measures only to learn that they were considered a major part of the problem. There would be no exemptions and Canada would have to make its own adjustments. In case the point had been missed, President Nixon told the House of Commons the following year that he respected "Canada's right to chart its own course" – the United States would follow its own course and respect Canada's right to do the same. There would be no more special relationship.

Canada's ability to use quiet diplomacy to advance its trade interests had in part reflected the fact that during the first three decades after the Second World War, trade was much less important to the United States than to Canada. With few exceptions, American firms manufactured goods and produced services for American consumers, and American consumers relied almost exclusively on American goods and services. Competition in the United States meant competition among American firms. Abroad, American firms might compete with European, Canadian, and other firms, but more often on the basis of goods produced by American branch plants than on the basis of exports from U.S.-based plants. Until the 1970s, the value of neither American merchandise exports nor imports ever exceeded five percent of U.S. gross domestic product. The United States might formally have been the most open economy in the world during this period, but in terms of actual levels of trade, it was one of the most closed. Consequently, the number of special interests affected by Canadian and other imports was quite small, in part explaining why the State Department succeeded in subordinating U.S. trade policy to broader geopolitical considerations.

Trade played a much more important role in the Canadian economy, particularly trade with the United States. During the first decade and a half after the Second World War, growth in the Canadian economy might have been spurred more by domestic than foreign demand, but by the end of the 1950s, when most European currencies had returned to full convertibility and reconstruction in Europe and Asia had been completed, Canada was participating in a trade-led boom. For Canada, however, that boom was largely a matter of trade with the

United States (see table 3). Trade between Canada and Britain never recovered from the devastation of war, depression, and Britain's long attachment to a closed sterling area. By the time sterling was returned to convertibility in 1957, Canadians had developed a clear preference for American over British goods, and Britain had learned to rely more and more on European and other Commonwealth suppliers. In the following two decades, the Canada-U.S. pattern of close interdependence accelerated further, fueled by the effect of growing two-way investment flows.

The intensification of bilateral trade and investment naturally added to the potential for conflict. Canadians might not be considered "foreign" by most Americans, but to those who had to compete with Canadians either at home or in Canada, Canadians did not always measure up to American standards and, without representation in Congress, were fair game for either protectionist measures at home or some extraterritorial arm-twisting in Canada. Managing these tensions proved more a Canadian than an American challenge. Even during the heyday of the special relationship, Canadians had learned that any irritant in the relationship was usually considered their fault and required them to take appropriate action to fix the problem. By the early 1970s, Canadian vulnerability to U.S. actions had become acute, particularly as the long U.S. economic lead over its trading partners began to erode and U.S. firms learned that they would have to compete with foreign suppliers not only abroad, but also at home. Many were convinced that foreigners could only beat them on the basis of some unfair advantage, and Congress agreed by strengthening the U.S. unfair trade laws. The payments crisis that led to the Nixon measures of August 1971 may have been caused in large part by the outflow of U.S. investment as well as the cost of the Vietnam War, rather than by the inflow of imports or the paucity of U.S. exports, but American producers found it easier to blame foreign trade policies and practices. Congress agreed.

The world had become a much less predictable place. Soon after the crisis of the punitive Nixon trade and monetary measures, Canadian officials had to deal with Britain's decision to abandon the Commonwealth and join the new and exclusive European club. The increasingly urgent demands of developing countries further intruded into the cozy world of postwar multilateral institutions. The oil shock of 1973 similarly undermined confidence in the postwar policy consensus.

The Trudeau government's response to these changed circumstances, the Third Option, involving a "contractual link" with the European Common Market and "broader and deeper" relations with Japan, did not prove very successful. It had originally been conceived by Secre-

Table 3
The Direction of Canadian Trade in Goods, 1949–73

| | Exports (millions of dollars) | | | | | | |
| | Britain | | U.S.A. | | Rest of World | | Total |
Year	value	%	value	%	value	%	value
1949	701	23.5	1,521	50.9	767	25.6	2,989
1951	636	16.1	2,326	58.9	988	25.0	3,950
1953	656	15.8	2,458	59.2	1,038	25.0	4,152
1955	772	17.8	2,598	59.9	962	22.3	4,332
1957	734	15.0	2,931	59.9	1,229	25.1	4,894
1959	786	15.7	3,083	61.4	1,153	22.9	5,022
1961	909	15.8	3,107	54.0	1,739	30.2	5,755
1963	1,007	14.8	3,766	55.4	2,026	29.8	6,799
1965	1,174	13.8	4,840	56.8	2,510	29.4	8,524
1967	1,169	10.5	7,088	63.7	2,863	25.7	11,120
1969	1,096	7.6	10,211	70.7	3,137	21.7	14,444
1971	1,380	7.9	11,683	67.2	4,333	24.9	17,396
1973	1,588	6.4	16,671	67.2	6,562	26.4	24,821
IMPORTS (MILLIONS OF DOLLARS)							
1949	300	11.1	1,899	70.4	497	18.5	2,696
1951	417	10.2	2,846	69.4	838	20.4	4,101
1953	463	11.0	3,048	72.4	701	16.6	4,212
1955	406	8.9	3,283	72.3	854	18.8	4,453
1957	520	9.5	3,878	70.7	1090	19.9	5,488
1959	589	10.7	3,709	67.3	1,211	22.0	5,509
1961	618	10.7	3,864	66.0	1,287	22.3	5,769
1963	527	8.0	4,445	67.7	1,593	24.3	6,565
1965	619	7.2	6,045	70.0	1,969	22.8	8,633
1967	649	6.0	7,952	73.1	2,273	20.9	10,874
1969	791	5.6	10,243	72.5	3,097	21.9	14,131
1971	837	5.4	10,951	70.1	3,830	24.5	15,618
1973	1,005	4.3	16,502	70.7	5,818	24.9	23,325

Source: *Historical Statistics of Canada*, 2d edition, series G 389–400.

tary of State for External Affairs Mitchell Sharp in response to the 1971 Nixon measures and became an article of faith for some ministers and officials for the next dozen years, although in many instances it involved more rhetoric than action. Sharp came to have his own regrets, remembering that "the Third Option came to be invoked enthusiastically by the government and by others to support policies that were far more nationalistic than my paper had proposed, a consequence that I deplored."[6]

The dominance of the United States, the EC, and Japan during the Tokyo Round of GATT negotiations (1973–79), the seventh and, at the time, most complex, and longest of the postwar multilateral trade negotiating conferences, and their rejection of Canadian negotiating objectives, further suggested just how marginal a player Canada had become in the multilateral world. By this time GATT was seen by Canadian business leaders and politicians alike as a bogeyman preventing actions they saw to be in the national interest rather than as the best means for achieving Canadian goals. For years, Canada's trade policy had been synonymous with its industrial policy, but in the 1970s nationalist experiments such as the Foreign Investment Review Act (FIRA) and the National Energy Program (NEP) accentuated the growing gulf between those who preferred a more interventionist industrial policy and the trade policy professionals who continued to advocate a liberalizing trade policy.

As a technique for managing trade relations with the United States, the Third Option was also less than helpful. But then, as Robert Bothwell observes, "Trudeau was never very much at home with Americans, and never entirely came to grips with the significance of the United States in Canadian life."[7] Because trade with the United States continued to expand, issues and irritants in the relationship also grew. U.S. officials could appreciate Canadian anxieties about over-dependence on the U.S. market, but they did not appreciate some of the policy measures chosen, whether in the realm of investment (FIRA), energy (the NEP), or culture (various measures to increase Canadian content in publishing and broadcasting). All were considered confiscatory and discriminatory. The net result was a deterioration in Canada-U.S. relations. The Trudeau years not only saw an end to the "special" relationship of the 1950s and 1960s, but also witnessed the growing perception in Washington that Canada was becoming a "problem" country. There was no way that Canada could now count on the benefit of the doubt. Its friends were few and without influence.

Changes in the way Washington operated further undermined the traditional basis for managing trade and investment relations between the two countries. Exemptionalism not only did not work because Canada was no longer seen as an important and special partner, but also because the centres of power had changed. In the period from the 1930s through the 1950s, Congress had delegated its trade negotiating authority to the president, who in turn had relied on the State Department to execute this delegated authority. In pursuing its mandate, State often subordinated narrow commercial policy considerations to broader geopolitical interests. Canada counted on State's willingness to view matters broadly rather than narrowly to defend its interests and thus concentrated its resources on diplomatic channels in the State Department.

In 1962 Congress established a Special Trade Representative (transformed in 1979 into the U.S. Trade Representative) to be the principal executor of U.S. trade policy. The State Department lost its lead role and was reduced to just another agency participating in the policy formulation process, weaker than most because it lacked any domestic constituency of its own.

Finally, Congress began to reassert its role in the trade and economic policy-making process much more aggressively in the 1970s, at the same time as the traditional power-brokering system in Congress disintegrated. In the aftermath of the Watergate scandal and the rapid decline in the Imperial Presidency established by Franklin Roosevelt, power in Washington became even more decentralized. Canadian ministers and officials could no longer count on the State Department and the White House as centres of power that could be courted to help defend Canadian interests, nor could they rely on a few major figures on the Hill capable of applying the brakes when special interests got out of hand and sought measures clearly inimical to Canadian interests. As Allan Gotlieb, Canada's ambassador for most of the 1980s, observed, by the 1980s the Speaker of the House could deliver his own vote and little more.

Thus, while the 1971 Nixon measures may have symbolized the end of the special relationship, the handwriting had long been on the wall. Even if Canada had remained the most constant of U.S. allies, prepared to give Americans the benefit of the doubt in return for which Canada could count on its friends to defend its interests, its friends could no longer deliver what Canada needed. During its heyday, Canada dit not expect to win all its battles in Washington, but it had won enough of them in the more than 35 years since the two countries had entered into a reciprocal trade agreement to make the special relationship into a central canon for the conduct of bilateral relations. By the end of the 1970s it was clear there would be no return. Other means would have to be developed to ensure that Canada could defend its interests in the U.S. capital. It took a few years, however, for the full implications of these developments to penetrate official and business attitudes.

THE DECISION TO NEGOTIATE A BILATERAL FREE-TRADE AGREEMENT

By the early 1980s, Canada's economic dependence on the United States had reached new heights, while rules and institutions to underpin that degree of dependence had not kept pace. A growing array of irritants led to heightened anxiety among Canadian business leaders about the management of the relationship. Efforts to launch a new round of multilateral negotiations at a ministerial meeting of GATT in 1982 proved premature, leaving Canada in what was perceived to be an increasingly intolerable situation: heavily dependent on a single market but without sufficiently free and secure access to that market to make investment on the basis of a North American economy feasible (see table 4).

Not surprisingly, the early 1980s proved a difficult time within Canada's trade bureaucracy. While some Canadians advocated an interventionist and protectionist industrial policy, others had begun to consider once again the benefits of a comprehensive reciprocity agreement with the United States. The professional attachment to the multilateral gradualism of GATT was being squeezed between free-trade continentalists prepared to pursue a bilateral approach to achieve more open trade and stronger market disciplines, and protectionist nationalists, prepared to reverse the achievements of the previous 40 years by reintroducing interventionist policies. Multilateral gradualism was dismissed by many as dated and irrelevant, offering either too little (for free traders) or too much (for protectionists). Public debate focused on the economic, cultural, and political dimensions of competing views of Canada and finally forced first an internal and finally a national debate. Officials were forced to address the insistent demands of outsiders, whether bilateralists or nationalists, and, more fundamentally, to respond to the politicians and their immediate advisors.

It was not an easy task. Free trade had proven one of the most divisive issues in the history of Canadian politics. At least two elections had been fought on the issue, in 1891 and 1911, and the supporters of free trade had lost both. Little wonder, therefore, that the origins of the decision to negotiate with the United States in the mid-1980s lay more in professional than in partisan considerations. It was not part of the agenda of new Conservative Prime Minister Brian Mulroney, elected in 1984, nor had it played an important role in the agenda of the Conservative Party. Mulroney had categorically dismissed free trade during his successful leadership bid in 1983. It had been advocated by a number of prominent members of the party, including Finance Minister Michael Wilson and Justice Minister John Crosbie, but Crosbie had

Table 4
The Direction of Canadian Trade in Goods, 1973–86

Year	U.S.A.	Britain	Japan	EEC	ROW	Total
EXPORTS (MILLIONS OF DOLLARS)						
1973	16,671	1,588	1,807	1,552	3,203	25,461
1975	21,074	1,795	2,130	1,583	5,203	33,347
1977	30,319	1,929	2,513	2,727	6,018	43,506
1979	43,519	2,589	4,083	4,661	9,465	64,317
1981	53,667	3,321	4,487	5,379	14,040	80,895
1983	64,528	2,449	4,728	4,194	12,608	88,506
1985	90,417	2,409	5,707	4,273	13,338	116,145
IMPORTS (MILLIONS OF DOLLARS)						
1973	16,502	1,005	1,011	1,477	3,330	23,325
1975	23,641	1,222	1,205	2,074	6,573	34,725
1977	29,630	1,281	1,803	2,358	7,083	42,256
1979	45,571	1,928	2,159	3,691	9,521	62,870
1981	54,131	2,234	4,040	4,065	14,195	78,655
1983	54,103	1,810	4,409	4,150	11,114	75,587
1985	73,817	3,281	6,115	7,067	14,076	104,355

Source: Statistics Canada: *Summary of Canadian International Trade* (65–001).

failed in his leadership bid and Wilson did not place the issue at the top of his priorities. What mattered politically was that a number of other key Conservative goals lent themselves to a decision to pursue a Canada-U.S. free-trade agreement: one was a commitment to place Canada-U.S. relations on a less adversarial tone, and the second was a desire to reduce the role of government and allow markets to play a larger role in Canadian economic life. Finally, Mulroney and his ministers were prepared to accept the advice of officials and of other influential voices that free trade and better relations with the United States were not unrelated.

The result was the negotiation of a free-trade agreement with the United States, which generations earlier had been the goal of both Liberal and Conservative politicians but which had been quietly buried as an unattainable and unnecessary goal. As late as 1983, the professionals could still conclude that: "The free trade option has been a contentious issue throughout Canada's history, due less to economic considerations than to issues of sovereignty and self-determination. The evidence to date of the need to proceed is not convincing, nor does a call for free trade command broad support. Most assessments tend to highlight the economic advantages for Canada without taking full account of the costs or consequences both political and economic."[8]

This judgment was not sustained. Two years after a Liberal government released its review of Canadian trade policy dismissing the need for a free-trade agreement, a Conservative government decided to proceed, following the advice of a royal commission, a parliamentary committee, nine of ten provincial governments, and the great preponderance of business organizations.

The immediate catalysts to the decision to pursue free trade with the United States, then, were the conviction of business leaders that they needed a better way to defuse and resolve trade and investment disputes with the United States and the determination of senior officials to find a better way to manage Canada-U.S. relations. The FTA responded as much to a management crisis as to an economic imperative in Canada-U.S. relations. Officials responsible for both the broad spectrum of Canada-U.S. relations and the narrower commercial policy concerns of Canadian exporters to the United States were looking for a better set of rules which would level the playing field between the two sides. The most important element in the equation was not that trade would be free – although that obviously had some important ramifications – but that it would be governed on an agreed basis. The agreement would provide a set of rules that would be equally binding on the United States and the Canadian governments and contain procedures to ensure that these rules would actually be implemented. It would provide a way to regain the benefits of the lost special relationship, but on a more sustainable, contractual basis. The rules would also govern much more than trade in goods; economic relations had moved well beyond the basics.

NEGOTIATING FREE TRADE

The negotiations were the most public and controversial trade negotiations in Canadian history. For three years, they dominated the public agenda. The news media followed them with breathless attention. Pundits and commentators showed endless enthusiasm for dissecting every dimension, from the trivial to the profound. Cartoonists had a field day. The debate was sometimes enlightened and other times confused by a stream of articles, books, and conferences. On a daily basis, Canadians from coast to coast were beguiled and inveigled by a bewildering array of claims and counter-claims. The debate pitted brothers against sisters, divided fathers from sons, figured prominently in a series of provincial elections, and dominated the federal agenda. Experienced observers of the national political scene regularly concluded that the negotiations would be drowned in a sea of controversy, abandoned by a government that could only take so much.

In the United States, the negotiations hardly caused a ripple. Outside of a few politicians, lobbyists, and officials in Washington and a specialized academic and business audience in the northern tier of the country, no one was aware that the United States had any pressing interests in Canada or was pursuing a precedent-setting international agreement. For most Americans, Canada is really not a foreign country, and commerce between the two countries is perceived to be little different from trade between Michigan and Ohio. Even in Washington, the issue remained at or near the bottom of the priority list for most of the three years, surfacing briefly at moments of decision before being overwhelmed by yet another crisis in Central America or the Middle East. On the few occasions that it did surface, the caterwauling of special interests suggested it attracted more hostility than support. As the negotiations hovered between indifference and neglect, many experienced U.S. observers concluded that important as the negotiations might be, there was not enough American support behind them to bring them to a successful conclusion.

The pundits and pessimists in both countries, however, were proved wrong. The Canadian government stuck to its guns and determined that it had to have an agreement. Also surprisingly, both the U.S. administration and the Congress demonstrated that they were prepared to come to terms with the hard issues and to look forward rather than backward. In a dramatic series of events during the fall of 1987, political leaders from both sides hammered out a satisfactory package that had until then eluded the professional negotiators. With agreement came a new debate. No longer based on speculation and conjecture, the issues now turned on specific words and intentions. The result, however, was acceptance of the agreement in both countries and its implementation on January 1, 1989.

The debate in Canada on the merits of the FTA was in many ways a debate on the merits of deepening integration. It indicated that the compromises which governments now had to forge differed significantly from those that had animated the trade negotiations of the 1950s through 1970s. Then the debate had been largely between import-competing (read manufacturing) and export-oriented (read western agriculture and resource) producers. Echoes of old imperial sentiments and appeals to new economic nationalism added spice but were essentially secondary considerations. By the 1980s, however, Canadian producers were largely of one view. Even import-competing sectors accepted that there had to be significant restructuring if Canadians were going to compete in the global economy and that such restructuring could best take place within a framework of rules that allowed them to compete in a larger market, even at the expense of more competition at home. The new opposition came from a coalition of populist groups worried about a range of issues from Canadian culture and health care to environmental protection, gender equality, and other largely non-economic concerns. Each group believed its cause to be threatened by a more open economy as well as by closer economic ties to the United States. The debate pitted a corporate internationalist vision against a populist nationalist one.

From the perspective of those charged with managing Canada-U.S. relations, however, the intensity and far-ranging nature of the debate seemed at times to border on the bizarre. The claims and counterclaims on both sides of the divide attained an extravagance that insiders had difficulty appreciating. What made it particularly puzzling was that there seemed to be little appreciation that without a better set of rules and procedures, Canada's ability to promote and protect its interests in Washington would continue to deteriorate, leading in effect to precisely the kinds of outcomes opponents most feared. A well-conceived and implemented trade agreement might do more to protect Canadian sovereignty and freedom of action than the continued drift toward a continentalism without rules, i.e., a continentalism in which the United States called all the shots. The nationalist alternative of a sturdy Canada going its own way and cocking its snoot at the United States seemed hardly more reassuring.

RECIPROCAL FREE TRADE AND MUCH MORE

The FTA was meant to serve the twin objectives of enhancing and securing Canada's access to the U.S. market, with both objectives enshrined within a binding agreement. The price for meeting these objectives would, naturally, be to enhance and secure U.S. access to the Canadian market. Looking back now from the vantage point of 1999, many of the specific objectives Canadian officials identified in the early 1980s appear to have been achieved; their subsequent influence on corporate behaviour and economic performance was generally as expected: painful at first but more positive as the anticipated changes took hold. Economic analysis leading up to the FTA negotiations and immediately thereafter indicated that the Canadian economy would need to go through a period of painful adjustment but, to the extent that firms and governments alike would allow these adjustments to take hold, the economy would benefit in increased efficiency,

Table 5
Trade and the Canadian Economy, 1987–96

Year	Dom. Merch. Exports (millions of current dollars)	GNP at Mkt Prices	Exports/GNP (percentages)	Cdn Share of World Trade (percentages)
1987	121.4	535.2	22.7	4.0
1988	133.9	587.2	22.8	4.2
1989	134.8	629.3	21.4	4.1
1990	141.0	645.6	21.8	3.7
1991	138.4	654.6	21.1	3.6
1992	154.5	665.9	23.2	3.5
1993	176.8	688.9	25.7	3.8
1994	213.4	720.2	29.6	3.7
1995	248.4	749.8	33.1	3.5
1996	258.4	793.2	32.6	3.5

Source: Historical Statistics of Canada, 2d edition, G57, F75; IMF, *International Financial Statistics*, various years; Statistics Canada, *Catalogues* 65–001 and 13–201-xpb.

leading to more specialization and export-led growth. The FTA would not solve all the problems faced by the Canadian economy, including problems of fiscal profligacy, but it could help to address problems of industrial structure, productivity, and competitiveness.

Economic studies over the past few years suggest that the positive effects have begun to take hold, offsetting the earlier but expected negative effects.[9] Indeed, over the course of the past decade, Canada experienced one of the strongest periods of trade-led growth in its history. As shown in table 5, merchandise exports to all sources more than doubled at market prices. Total trade – exports and imports, goods and services – rose from less than 50 to about 80 percent as a proportion of GNP. The United States accounted for the preponderance of this trade, as it has for most of the postwar years. In 1997, in nominal terms, merchandise exports to the United States represented 82 percent of the total, while U.S. imports accounted for 67.5 percent.

Of course, there is always some ambiguity about measuring or assessing the impact of a major policy initiative. It is always difficult to isolate one factor and try to attribute specific changes in behaviour and performance to that factor. Nevertheless, there developed a pattern of behaviour and performance over the past decade which suggests a strong correlation between changes in Canada's trade and investment performance – both outgoing and incoming – and changes in trade and investment policy. The cause and effect relationship, however, is more difficult to determine. Did Canada pursue more outward-oriented trade and investment policies in response to changing trade and investment patterns or vice versa? Did policy changes lead to changes in the patterns or did changes in the patterns lead to changes in policy?

The relationships probably run in both directions and tend to reinforce one another. Policy changes have facilitated and sometimes even stimulated changes in trade and investment patterns. But even more often, changes in trade and investment patterns induced by technological and other factors have been instrumental in convincing governments to make the rules more responsive. The rules thus often catch up to changing reality and help to validate the direction of change. Changes in the intensity and nature of Canada-U.S. trade were placing inordinate strains on the management of the relationship. By catching up, the forces of proximity and technology were allowed to function more effectively and perhaps even accelerate what was already taking place. Because the technological changes were profound and policy changes had been resisted, the FTA was publicly perceived to have been a bigger deal than it probably was. On the other hand, continued resistance to the forces of technology and proximity would have had very negative results. Policy does matter.

FROM THE FTA TO NAFTA AND THE WTO

Within two years of the conclusion and implementation of the FTA, wounds that had only barely begun to heal were opened again as the United States and Mexico agreed to enter into their own bilateral free-trade negotiations. Faced with the Hobson's choice of standing aside and letting the new negotiations erode what had been painfully achieved only two years earlier or of participating and thus re-activating the bruising debate of the FTA, the government agreed it was better to join and use the opportunity to strengthen the FTA rules. The result was an even more comprehensive trade agreement covering all of North America. A new accession clause announced that the NAFTA regime could grow eventually into a western hemisphere trading system.

Concurrently, negotiations continued in Geneva to conclude the largest, most ambitious, and most comprehensive global trade agreement ever attempted. After eight years of labour, the negotiators produced a draft agreement almost 500 pages long. To that draft were added a long list of specific market-opening national commitments ranging from traditional tariff concessions to new commitments on agriculture, government procurement, services, and investment practices. Gaining the political support of the more than 100 participating governments proved even more difficult. The end of the Cold War and the waning of U.S. dominance complicated the political arithmetic of the negotiations and underlined the need for the emergence of a new equilibrium. A final push in the closing half of 1993 succeeded, however, in bringing the negotiations to a successful conclusion before the end of the year and before the end of U.S. negotiating authority. On January 1, 1995, the original 125 signatories of the new World Trade Organization ushered in a new era of multilateral cooperation and freer trade. Canada was a charter member of the new club, underlining that its achievement of bilateral free trade with the United States in no way diminished its commitment to global rule-making and liberalization.

THE IMPACT OF THE FTA ON CANADA-U.S. RELATIONS

Has the FTA worked as a tool for managing relations with the United States? Has it helped Canadians adjust to the demands of a more global economy? Yes, to the extent that Canadian governments have been prepared to use its rules and procedures. The existence of an international agreement does not mean there will not be conflict, only that there is a better basis for resolving conflict. The fact that there is a criminal code does not end crime, nor does the existence of courts stop civil litigation. Both the criminal code and the courts provide a more orderly, predictable, and just way of addressing conflict. They make it possible to bring a conflict to an end and resolve an issue. The same considerations hold true for international rules and procedures. A profound misreading of the FTA and the NAFTA led to many popular Canadian complaints about the rash of Canada-U.S. trade disputes in the late 1980s and early 1990s. The existence of rules and procedures does not end disputes, and in fact, may increase the number of issues that need to be resolved on the basis of rules using formal procedures. As John Holmes, Canada's diplomatic sage, noted, "What has been sought, after all, is not a formula for eliminating conflict but a more satisfactory process for resolving it, bearing in mind that the new agreement would probably multiply rather than diminish the number of conflicts."[10]

The agreement did at first seem to multiply disputes, as players on both sides of the border tested the will of the two governments to live by the new rules. Procedures under Chapter 19 dealing with anti-dumping and countervailing duty cases proved particularly popular and have continued to engage parties in all three countries under the

NAFTA. Under the FTA, a total of 35 cases were litigated, with a variety of results, some favouring Canadian parties, some American parties, but as William Davey concludes in his study of all the FTA cases: "The dispute settlement mechanisms of the [FTA] have worked reasonably well, particularly the binational panel review process. The basic goal of trade dispute settlement … is to enforce the agreed-upon rules. By and large, these dispute settlement mechanisms have done that.[11] Chapter 19, which was much less than Canada had originally sought, proved a pleasant surprise in reducing the cross-border temperature in trade remedy disputes, forcing administrators on both sides of the border to mind their Ps and Qs, and reducing the capacity of U.S. legislators to pressure tribunals to favour the home team.

The more general dispute settlement provisions of Chapter 18 of the FTA (Chapter 20 of the NAFTA) have been used less frequently but as usefully. A variety of difficult issues, including salmon and herring landing requirements on Canada's west coast, the application of automotive rules of origin, and the continued right of Canada to maintain high tariffs to protect supply-managed agricultural goods, have all been resolved with the help of high-quality panels and the procedures of the FTA or NAFTA. Additionally, the much improved multilateral procedures under the World Trade Organization are now available to help resolve conflicts, as in the issue involving Canadian restrictions on imports of split-run periodicals. In all of these cases, the application of clear rules within a set of binding procedures that ensure the equality of standing of both parties has greatly facilitated the management of relations between the two countries. Canada has not won all the cases, in large part because Canada's policies have been inconsistent with Canada's obligations. The purpose of dispute settlement is not to guarantee that Canada always wins but to ensure that issues are resolved on the basis of agreed rules and procedures rather than power politics.

The exception that would seem to prove the rule is the continuing saga of softwood lumber. Originally written out of the FTA, it has continued to bedevil Canada-U.S. relations for more than a decade and a half. Canada's current agreement to restrain exports of softwood lumber appears to have been based on a political judgment that while Canada had right on its side, the cost of proving this point, both economically and politically, outweighed the benefits of restraining the imports and thus ensuring peace in the industry for five years and keeping the scarcity rents in Canada. Reasonable people can differ about the wisdom of this political judgment and its long-term impact on the integrity of a rules-based approach to managing relations. With this single exception, the new era of more certain rules and procedures has proven its worth.

FREE TRADE AS THE NEW NORM

The Canada-U.S. FTA, as well as the NAFTA and much of the Uruguay Round, were negotiated while the Conservatives were in power in Ottawa. The FTA was bitterly opposed by the Liberals and the NDP. The Tories, however, saw their policies vindicated in their 1988 electoral triumph. Nevertheless, opposition to the FTA mounted during its first five years as the pain of adjustment to its requirements was compounded by the Bank of Canada's determination to wring inflation out of the economy. In the 1993 election Canadians expressed their displeasure and reduced the Conservatives to a corporal's guard of two MPs.

The new Liberal government, however, while still politically opposed to the FTA, did not follow through. Once in office it implemented the NAFTA and concluded the WTO agreement. New Trade Minister Roy MacLaren, who had been uncomfortable with his party's opposition to free trade, set out to prove that he was every bit as much of a free trader as his Tory predecessors. The FTA and NAFTA were followed by bilateral free-trade agreements with Israel and Chile, by enthusiastic participation in the Free Trade for the Americas initiative, in APEC discussions, in efforts to launch free-trade discussions across the Atlantic, and in the launch of negotiations with the remaining members of the European Free Trade Association. The Liberals sent out strong signals at home and abroad that a major divide had been crossed. Canada had become a free trader. With the exception of a few sectors such as dairy and poultry products, Canadian industry was considered ready to take on the world, at home and abroad.

A NEW ERA

The successful conclusion and implementation of the FTA, NAFTA, and WTO suggests that Canadian trade policy has entered a new phase with challenges that have yet to be fully grasped. Trade policy has for centuries been organized on the basis of the measures governments use at the border to define and defend national markets and national producers. Over the past century and a half, as a result of successful multilateral, regional, and bilateral negotiations, a rules-based international order has become a universally accepted part of both intellectual and intergovernmental discourse.

The success of that order in integrating national economies into a global economy now poses a new series of challenges suggesting the need for both a new trade policy and a new regime. Today we have a global economy, regional economies, and local economies, while the role of national economies is diminishing. Yet governance continues to be organized on the basis of national polity. The result is growing conflict between national political and international economic goals.

The full impact and implication of the global economic changes that are driving the demand for a new approach are, of course, not yet fully understood. Nevertheless, we can already discern an emerging agenda of new trade policy issues, including some related to substance (e.g., competition policy, environmental policy, product standards, subsidies, dispute resolution, and social policies) and others relating to form (e.g., global and regional agreements, various approaches to conflict resolution, and the nature and potential effect of international legislation). We are seeing not only the "end" of trade policy as it has been practiced for the past 50 years but also a new beginning attuned to today's changing circumstances and tomorrow's challenges.

As the production of manufactured goods becomes ever more disaggregated, varied, and sophisticated, the cost of developing and manufacturing new products has increased exponentially. More and more, the costs are concentrated in developing the product – both the product and the most cost-effective process by which to manufacture it – rather than in production, devaluing the labour content in many products and increasing the risk in producing it. Typically, labour and raw material costs now constitute less than a quarter of the final cost of a product.

These changes in manufacturing technology have led to massive adjustments within industrial countries. Unskilled or semi-skilled assembly-line workers – the core of industrial labour – are being replaced by highly skilled knowledge workers, capable of understanding and adapting computer-controlled machinery. We are also seeing a rapid acceleration in the globalization of production. So-called footloose industries which are not tied to particular locations, as are mines or sawmills, are looking for the most congenial place to invest, depending on the availability of the particular factors of production most important to that industry. Low-skill, standard-technology, labour-intensive manufacturing firms, for example, are locating manufacturing facilities where they can find the best combination of low-skilled labour and related factors – productivity, skill levels, labour laws, fringe benefits, access to inputs, and distribution networks.

In the closing years of the 1990s, as we stand on the threshold of a new century, the salient features of the Canadian economy, when placed in their global context, suggest the need for urgent attention to a range of critical economic policy choices. To quote James Gillies: "Canada has an open economy that depends heavily on international trade; imports large amounts of capital; runs a chronic deficit in its current account of the balance of payments; does not have an internationally competitive manufacturing sector, except in a few areas; imports most of its technology; has a high percentage of foreign ownership of productive resources; has over 80 percent of its trade with one country; and is losing market share for many of its major [traditional] exports because it has become a high-cost producer of its resources and their by-products."[12]

Many of these features developed as a result of the trade policy choices governments made during Canada's first 125 years. The choices made were in many instances beneficial. It is hard to argue with the fact that Canadians now enjoy one of the highest standards of living in the world, while controlling the second largest piece of global real estate with less than half of one percent of the world's population. Nevertheless, as Gillies and others have argued, these features can also become liabilities as Canadians adjust to the much more competitive and integrated global economy of the next century. If Canadians are to adapt their economy to the challenges of the next century, they will need to look again to trade and related economic policy choices. Making the right choices will require that they have a clear understanding of the choices made in the past and of the influence these choices have exercised on Canada's economic development.

MICHAEL HART is a professor at Carleton University's Norman Paterson School of International Affairs, a senior associate at the Centre for Trade Policy and Law (Carleton University and University of Ottawa) and former senior advisor, Trade Negotiations Office, Canada.

NOTES

1 The year before the Tories came to power, historian Jack Granatstein prepared a paper for the Macdonald Royal Commission with the catchy title of "Free Trade Between Canada and the United States: The Issue That Will Not Go Away," in Dennis Stairs and Gilbert R. Winham, eds., *The Politics of Canada's Economic Relationship with the United States* (Toronto: University of Toronto Press, 1985). To modern observers, much of that quest may have seemed like a far cry from the real thing, but it nevertheless proved an enduring theme in Canadian trade politics.

2 Quoted in Granatstein, "The Issue That Will Not Go Away," 18.

3 Jan Tumlir, "Evolution of the Concept of International Economic Order 1914–1980," in Frances Cairncross, ed., *Changing Perceptions of Economic Policy* (London: Methuen, 1981).

4 Quoted in J.L. Granatstein, *A Man of Influence: Norman A. Robertson and Canadian Statecraft 1929–1968* (Ottawa: Deneau, 1981), 74.

5 L.D. Wilgress, *Canada's Approach to Trade Negotiations* (Montreal: Private Planning Association of Canada, 1963), 13.

6 Mitchell Sharp, *Which Reminds Me ... A Memoir* (Toronto: University of Toronto Press, 1994), 186.

7 "Has Canada Made a Difference? The Case of Canada and the United States," in John English and Norman Hillmer, eds., *Making a Difference? Canada's Foreign Policy in a Changing World Order* (Toronto: Lester, 1992), 11.

8 Department of External Affairs, *A Review of Canadian Trade Policy* (Ottawa: Supply and Services 1983), 212.

9 Daniel Schwanen of the C.D. Howe Institute has provided the best continuing analysis of the trade impact of the FTA and NAFTA. In *Trading Up: The Impact of Increased Continental Integration on Trade, Investment, and Jobs in Canada* (C.D. Howe Commentary no. 89, March 1997), his third report, he concludes that 'the pattern of trade between the two countries has shifted roughly in the direction of pre-FTA expectations, and the competitive position of Canadian and U.S. producers in each other's markets has improved relative to those in third countries in many sectors that were liberalized under free trade.'

10 John Holmes, "The Disillusioning of the Relationship: Epitaph to a Decade," in Lansing Lamont and J. Duncan Edmonds, eds., *Friends So Different: Essays on Canada and the United States in the 1980s* (Ottawa: University of Ottawa Press, 1989), 313–14.

11 William Davey, *Pine and Swine* (Ottawa: Centre for Trade Policy and Law, 1996), 288–9.

12 James Gillies, 'Canadian Industrial Policy: Past and Future,' in Jerry Dermer, ed., *Meeting the Global Challenge: Competitive Position and Strategic Response* (North York: Captus Press, 1992), 60.

Interviews with Brian Mulroney and John Turner

WILLIAM WATSON

On Oct. 25, 1988, in one of the most famous exchanges in Canadian political history, Liberal Party leader John Turner told Prime Minister Brian Mulroney that in signing a free trade deal with the United States he had "sold out" the country. Does Turner still think that? How does former Prime Minister Mulroney evaluate the impact of the deal today? The following are edited transcripts of their conversations with *Policy Options'* editor William Watson.

WATSON: On the cover this month we're running a shot from your famous debate with John Turner in October 1988. In his book about that election, Graham Fraser says the last person who talked to you that night, whom he doesn't name, told you that you could sleep well because you'd won. Did you have that impression coming out of that debate?

MULRONEY: Well, I thought we had done well and when I woke up the next morning, I read most of the leading columnists in the country, who almost to a man and a woman said that I had won it handily. I wasn't surprised by that judgement because that was my view, too. But I was aware of the deep-seated antipathy to our position by most, not all, English-speaking members of the Ottawa press gallery. They not only were opposed to free trade, but they were opposed to the GST, they

Originally published in *Policy Options* (Montreal: Institute for Research in Public Policy, June 1999, 20, No. 5). Editor William Watson talked to Brian Mulroney and John Turner in April 1999.

were opposed to Meech Lake, they were opposed to me, they were opposed to our agenda. And so, I think what happened that evening – not to detract in any way from John's achievement – was that he exceeded expectations. You remember that they were trying to get rid of him during the campaign. You remember the putsch against him. He had been sick, his back was hurting, he was in terrible political shape and he came in there swinging … and I think he exceeded expectations and so, by that group, he was proclaimed the winner and then he went on to have some good days because the polls reflected what they were being told by the media, particularly in the *Toronto Star.*

But I wondered afterward why it was. He said absolutely nothing that I hadn't heard before that night, so I was intrigued by that, and I wondered why it was that people were impressed with him. Then it dawned on me that it was the first time that they had heard him, and were really listening to what was going on. And they heard for the first time that they were going to lose their pensions, they were going to lose their social security, they were going to lose their regional development, they were go to lose their identity, their language – there wasn't much they were going to keep – and that had resonance. Just look at where the vote went. From Cape Breton Island to any area of the country that depended directly on the involvement of the federal government, there was strong support for his view.

WATSON: Then you had to change campaign strategy and address that head on.

MULRONEY: Well, there was a poll sometime later that showed him about 11 points ahead and so, our campaign, which had been almost on cruise control because we started off ahead, had to adjust. You may remember, to go back, that we were in third place six or seven months earlier, and we brought it all the way back to first place by the first of October. Then the Liberals ran such a poor campaign that we were in a strong leadership position in the debates. When we fell behind after the debates, we went at it hammer and tong and turned it around, I think it was by the 11th of November, and then we really cleaned up between the 11th and the 21st.

WATSON: If we head backwards a year to September 1987, with three weeks left the negotiations were suspended. How close did we come to not having a deal?

MULRONEY: Very close. Because for us, things like the independent dispute settlement mechanism were key. These were deal-breakers, and there was some doubt whether we were going to achieve this. So, when I instructed Simon Reisman to pack it in and come home, I was deeply concerned that we might not prevail.

WATSON: You were ready to call it off?

MULRONEY: Absolutely. We either got the deal that we wanted or we wouldn't have one.

WATSON: I have the impression from reading histories of the talks that nothing happened for about a week and then it was informal contacts that finally got things going. How did you sweat out that week?

MULRONEY: Well, there was a lot of talking going on. I don't have any calendar in front of me, but my recollection is that we were moving towards the week of the IMF/World Bank meetings in Washington, and it was pretty clear that the only way we were going to get [a deal] was if Jim Baker took it over. And so I worked on that with George Bush and Ronald Reagan and I was quite confident that when Jim Baker took ... over completely that there would be a deal. And there was.

WATSON: You're a negotiator from way back. This wasn't just a bluff?

MULRONEY: Simon was brought home because what was on the table was unacceptable to us and I would have had no deal rather than a deal that was unacceptable to Canada. Because I could envisage the beneficial results that would flow to us from this deal, I was very troubled by what was going on. But when Baker got in, I thought we would get it back on track. In fact, as you'll remember, my argument with Baker and Bush was "That's fine, you just let me know and I'm going to call President Reagan and you're going to have to explain to him how you can do a nuclear arms reduction deal with your worst enemy and you can't do a free trade deal with your best friend." And neither of them wanted to have that responsibility.

WATSON: What was their reaction?

MULRONEY: Oh well, it was always, "No, no, no, no, Brian, don't do that."

WATSON: You yourself were something of a convert to free trade, were you not? In 1983 in the leadership campaign, you had opposed John Crosbie's proposal for a Canada-U.S. FTA and you made that famous comment about how if we opened up the borders, the Americans would shut down the branch plants and we'd lose part of our industry.

MULRONEY: There are two things there. First of all, in a short and highly politicized, highly controversial leadership campaign, you don't really always get the time to explain things. So, if you advance a cause – say a flat tax, by way of illustration – there are enough people in Canada resistant to change that they'll kill you on it within weeks. So you have to be careful during a leadership campaign because your adversaries will distort and deform pretty well everything you put out there. If you're the front-runner, you'll have nine or ten people shooting at you and you're the only one shooting back. And so there was a strategic reason to be prudent about free trade.

But there was also a substantive reason. My opposition was to untrammeled free trade, and that's because I didn't believe that we could achieve the independent dispute settlement mechanism, which had never been attained before. I was very doubtful about that. And without that, in my judgment, there could be no free trade agreement. What John Crosbie seemed to be promoting – and I say, seemed, because I wasn't sure – looked to be a comprehensive free trade agreement without an independent dispute settlement mechanism, and I was opposed to that. In fact, I told President Reagan from the beginning when we first talked about this in Quebec City that this was a condition *sine qua non* for us. So, if you look at the speech that I gave to the Conservative convention in June of 1983, I spoke very clearly about refurbishing the Canadian-American relationship and expanding our trade initiatives with them in a dramatic way. But I didn't want to be pigeon-holed during the leadership campaign. No, I wasn't opposed to free trade at all. I didn't think that we could get what we eventually got. I was wrong on that.

WATSON: You said recently that you thought the free trade agreement would be your principal political legacy. What's your evaluation of how the deal has worked?

MULRONEY: Well, I think to appreciate the value of anything you have to consider its absence. Where would Canada be today if Mr. Chrétien's and Mr. Turner's view had prevailed in 1988? There would be no Free Trade Agreement with the United States, therefore, no NAFTA, therefore, no GST, because they all go together. If their view had prevailed, which was essentially a Luddite view of Canada, then I think that Canada would be very ill-prepared for the new millennium and, indeed, would be playing catch-up everywhere. In fact, Paul Martin and Jean Chrétien would not be celebrating the elimination of the deficit because the deficit's been eliminated essentially by two instruments: by the Free Trade Agreement with the United States and by the GST. My view is, that after ten years during which our Canadian-American trading relationship has jumped to $575 billion a year in Canadian dollars, and with institutional arrangements that were the model for NAFTA and, in many cases, the model for the WTO, I think that, if you look at it, most people would consider it quite a significant success.

WATSON: How does the FTA tie in with the GST?

MULRONEY: The manufacturers' sales tax was a secret 13.5 percent tax on all manufactured goods in Canada. We were the only industrialized country in the world to have that. So, on the one hand we were entering into a free trade agreement designed to enhance our exports and to make Canada an exporting nation. On the other, we were secretly penalizing our exporters with a 13.5 percent tax. So, with the GST, we eliminated the 13.5 percent tax. The GST was a consumption tax which came off at the border and therefore, rather than being penalized, Canadian exporters were placed on an equal footing with the Americans. And so it was an essential part of the whole economic restructuring program. I think that probably explains in some part why Canada's exports as a percentage of GDP have gone from somewhere in the neighbourhood of 23 percent or 24 percent when we signed the free trade agreement to 41 or 42 percent today. That indicates the dramatic nature of the transformation of our economy.

WATSON: Has anything about the subsequent functioning of the deal surprised you?

MULRONEY: One thing I might mention is the whole productivity matter. I was quite startled when I saw some of the productivity numbers that came out earlier this year and, like most Canadians, I've been a little confused by conflicting data that has come out of the government. I look forward to that issue being clarified because to me, it's inescapable that if you do the kinds of things that we have been doing, that inevitably they must lead to two things: enhanced productivity and lower unit costs. And I cannot for the life of me understand how we came up with this data which indicates that we are falling further away from the Americans in terms of their productivity gains. Then I was really surprised to see some new data come out saying, "No, the first stuff was wrong." And I think that's it urgent that this be clarified.

I think the agreement's biggest achievement is the attitudinal changes it has wrought among Canada's political élites, and thinkers and doers, and movers and shakers. For example, it has made the Liberals believers. Every one of [their principal figures] voted against the Free Trade Agreement and yet now they're among its biggest supporters. They're promoting free trade everywhere. So it's turned out, I think, to be the right thing.

But if you believe in free trade, then you have to believe in open investment, you have to believe in deregulation and privatization. And so, these are the changes that we made because it all went together. It was a package of attitudes: free trade, getting rid of FIRA, getting rid of the National Energy Program, privatizing Air Canada, privatizing Canadair, privatizing Petro-Canada and so on. Deregulation and all of those things. And I look at it today, all of the things that I did are still in place. And so what began as a free trade agreement has wound up shaping attitudes, not only of my government and my party and people on the right, but it has forced the Liberals into a completely new set of policies which they adopted from us, and I commend them on that, because the alternative of where they were heading in their Red Book was to come in and to reintroduce Mr. Trudeau's policies, and none of that has taken place. It's the Mulroney government policies that are all in place and have shaped Canada as we begin the new millennium.

WATSON: Was that a matter of choice or of necessity for them? In 1988, the critics argued that if we tied ourselves to the United States and opened our economy to them, we would be forced to imitate them in many ways. Is it true that the FTA has, as it were, constitutionalized smaller government in Canada and a deregulating, privatizing philosophy?

MULRONEY: Yes, I think that's true. I think that the Free Trade Agreement has created a new mind set and a new code of comportment internationally in economic and monetary matters, within which we now have to operate. No, I think the Americanization – to the extent that there has been an Americanization of Canada – I think most people would agree that it has probably come from the Charter of Rights more than the Free Trade Agreement. The Free Trade Agreement has been a strong instrument of Canadianization, because when you strengthen the Canadian economy, you strengthen the public finances of a nation, then you Canadianize, you strengthen your sovereignty and a lot of people … well, the evidence is that our opponents have now endorsed all of this.

WATSON: Has the FTA reduced the allegiance that Canadian firms may once have felt to Canada? We read about corporate leaders who say tax rates here are too high for them to be profitable here, so they may have to leave.

MULRONEY: In terms of the attraction of industry, competitive tax rates are absolutely key and we're going to have to do more than we have done to make certain that, as the integration continues in this hemisphere, Canada recaptures its competitive position. I think that's being eroded now, and has been for some decades, compared with the United States.

WATSON: How about the view that in the long run, if we increase the North-South connection, we will reduce the East-West connections?

MULRONEY: I don't think that they're mutually exclusive. I think that if you look forward to the year 2005 if there is a Free Trade Agreement of the Americas, with 800 million people from Nunavut to Easter Island, probably generating something in the neighbourhood of 14, 15 trillion dollars a year in goods and services, involving 34 countries – which will be the largest, richest free trade agreement in the world. And Canada will have an absolutely key role at the very heart of that. And that is because we were the authors of the Free Trade Agreement with the United States and I'm very pleased about that.

————

WATSON: The cover of *Policy Options* shows you and Mr. Mulroney in an exchange from the leaders' debate in the 1988 election. What was that like? What are your memories of that night?

TURNER: Well, that was a pretty exciting night. It was probably one of the highlights of Canadian electoral history, where an election was really being fought on a specific issue that people could understand. So it was a highlight, emotionally, politically and, of course, in human terms.

WATSON: After the debate did you think that you'd inflicted, not a knockout blow, but a pretty substantial blow?

TURNER: No, I felt that I'd made the case against the agreement as I read it.

WATSON: During that debate, the phrase you used that prompted the famous exchange was that Mr. Mulroney had sold us out to the United States. Was that a phrase that you considered carefully or was it something that came up in the debate and were you surprised when he took such great offense to it?

TURNER: Well, by "selling out" I meant, as I explained in the debate, that once you yield the economic levers of sovereignty you eventually lose the political levers. So, it was inevitable that we would, as Canadians, narrow the scope of our independence as the years went by.

WATSON: Is that your view of what has happened under the deal?

TURNER: Well, my view of the deal is that it is not, nor was it ever, a free trade agreement, and this was my main argument against the document that was negotiated. Free trade means free trade. I believe in free trade. I felt that Canada had always negotiated more successfully multilaterally, within the GATT, the General Agreement on Tariffs and Trade, and now the World Trade Organization, than we ever could on a bilateral basis with a nation like the United States, ten times stronger than we were economically. And if you're stronger economically, you're going to make a better deal for yourself.

Now, it is not a free trade deal because under the dispute settlement mechanisms, if the United States challenges a Canadian export into the United States, the binational panel appointed under the mechanism has to apply American law "as it may be amended from time to time." In other words, the United States Congress did not yield its jurisdiction over trade. It still hasn't yielded its jurisdiction and it can change American trade law anyway it wants "from time to time" and we are bound under the agreement. That is not free trade.

WATSON: Of course, it works the other way around, that we can change our trade law as well.

TURNER: We can change our trade law as well, but that's not what concerned me primarily. Our exports can be cut as they have been in softwood lumber, as they may be in steel, as they may be in plastics.

The Americans did not yield jurisdiction. During the course of the negotiations, Lloyd Bentsen, who was then the chairman of the U.S. Senate committee on trade – he was the senator from Texas, later Secretary of the Treasury – Lloyd Bentsen came up with some of his colleagues from the United States Senate and I said to him, "Have I read the agreement properly?" He said, "You have, Mr. Turner. The United States will never, and I repeat, never yield its jurisdiction over trade. The Congress will never yield its jurisdiction." And I said, "Well, is there any way we can negotiate this down a bit?" And he said, "No, this is a take it or nothing deal, Mr. Turner."

And then I turned to the leading Republican on the other side of the aisle, who was up with him, I said, "Senator, you've heard what Senator Bentsen just said to me. Does that view carry the view of your party as well?" And he said to me, "Mr. Turner, Senator Bentsen is speaking to you today, not only on behalf of the Democratic party of the United States, but on behalf of the entire United States Senate." So I didn't misinterpret the agreement. The United States Congress has not yielded any jurisdiction over trade.

WATSON: Do you think it ever will?

TURNER: The United States Congress will never yield its jurisdiction over trade. In fact, I'm concerned that it may become more protectionist in the next few years because of imports coming in from Asia and other parts of the world.

WATSON: People have argued that the WTO may eventually cause countries to give up jurisdiction. You're not hopeful at all?

TURNER: Well, I have no quarrel with the World Trade Organization. I've always believed that Canada does better negotiating multilaterally than we ever would in negotiating bilaterally with the United States.

WATSON: The most obvious result of the deal has been the big increase in Canada-U.S. trade. Do you attribute that to the deal and are you impressed by that?

TURNER: Well, I'm delighted with the amount of exports into the United States, but let's examine why it happened. At the time of the deal, the average tariff on goods going into the U.S. was well below 10 percent. What's affected our trade figures has not been the trade agreement – which is not a free trade agreement, I repeat – but the exchange rate. The exchange rate has fallen 25 to 30 percent, and any economist who knows trade movements will tell you that the exchange rate is far more important than any tariff. It's the Canadian dollar that has accelerated the rate of those exports into the United States.

WATSON: Your argument that giving up the economic levers would eventually require you to give up the political levers – do you see an erosion of Canadian sovereignty towards the United States? Has that fear been fulfilled?

TURNER: Well, I think you're finding more of a north-south pole than we had before. You know, this country was not built on free market forces. This country was built east, west and north deliberately by resisting those north-south forces. We built a railway and then two railways. We built an airline and then two national airlines, and tried to build a national highway and a public broadcasting system from coast to coast, and a system of social security, ending in medicare, from coast to coast. We deliberately built this country east, west and north. Had we relied solely on free market forces, Sir John A. Macdonald and his successors would never have achieved much.

WATSON: Is there a time when a country becomes mature and doesn't need those mechanisms any longer, and can privatize Air Canada and so on and still have these east-west connections? Does an infant industry or an infant country ever grow up and take off these protective wraps?

TURNER: Well, we have some additional structural problems in that sense. We're a very decentralized country under our constitution. The provinces have very considerable jurisdiction over what we do in Canada. You couldn't find a more decentralized country. And a decentralized country has more trouble resisting these forces north-south under the trade agreement, or under so-called globalization. Plus the fact that we have the continuing instability of "Where is Quebec going to go?"

If I were a Frenchman, with a thousand years of France, behind me or an Englishman, with a thousand years of history behind me, or if I had the economic strength and strong nationalism of the United States, I wouldn't be quite as worried, but here we are, a fragmented nation, and with a problem in Quebec that we haven't solved.

WATSON: There is general agreement that the dispute settlement mechanism was the key to the deal. Neither country, as you say, has given up its law, but has the dispute settlement system helped depoliticize some of our disputes with the United States, or do you see it essentially as a fig leaf for the final negotiation of the deal?

TURNER: I have no quarrel with the dispute resolution mechanism. It makes sense to me, but we always did pretty well before [the FTA] with the same type of mechanism under the GATT in Geneva. But no, I have no quarrel with the dispute resolution mechanism. I think that's a good thing in resolving disputes between United States and Canada. My quarrel is that the panels' jurisdiction can be changed from time to time by any amendment the United States Congress chooses to make.

WATSON: Is there anything about the workings of the deal over the last ten years that has surprised you? Nobody has perfect foresight, of course. Have things happened as a result of the deal that you find a little puzzling?

TURNER: No, I predicted the softwood lumber situation, for instance. By the way, the lumber and forest industry was one of the industries that supported my position; they knew what was going to happen. So did the steel industry. The cultural problem that Sheila Copps is facing in magazines, that was predictable, because although culture was outside the scope of the agreement, the United States secured a clause that allows it, if Canada takes any cultural initiatives contrary to the spirit of this agreement, to take retaliatory action, and that's what's happening now in the magazine situation. I think one of the continuing unknowns is what is going to happen to Canadian water under this agreement.

WATSON: Do you think there's a chance there will be bulk exports?

TURNER: I think there's a chance that some day the United States will argue that water is within the scope of the agreement.

WATSON: What are nation-states going to do in this globalizing era? Do you see any way of getting around these forces that may be so hard on countries that are not as secure culturally or psychologically as say, Britain and France?

TURNER: I think that Paul Martin is taking some useful initiatives. We have to strengthen the international organizations, including the World Trade Organization, the International Monetary Fund, the World Bank. We've got to ensure that there are some minimal ethical and legal standards around the world so that the movement of capital and people and goods is supervised a little more by those who are democratically responsible. You can find out just what happens in a total free market by observing what's happening in southeast Asia, for instance.

WATSON: That requires governments to negotiate deals that interfere with internal affairs even more than standard trade deals will, does it not? There have to be international agreements about labour standards and so on and so forth. Is signing onto such agreements consistent with your emphasis in 1988 on maintaining Canadian sovereignty.

TURNER: It would depend on the issue. And the Canadian Parliament would have to look at every situation as it came up. I think we would be very reluctant to lower our environmental standards, say. But if the agreement were to raise other countries up to our standard, I have no problem with that. And these would be multilateral agreements, not bilateral ones.

WATSON: Will the U.S. Congress buy that kind of thing?

TURNER: Well, that's a good question. I'm sure they'll insist on their own labour standards and their own environmental standards. We have found that the environment is a sensitive issue that's not protected under the agreement. I think we have to be careful, but what we're talking about here is that you can't allow free market forces to run roughshod over national governments. You do have democratically responsible elected governments and what I'm saying is that if you allow free market forces to run absolutely free, you're turning the world over to big multinational corporations and I don't think the average Canadian would welcome that.

WATSON: If we go back to 1988, had things turned out differently in the election, would you actually have torn up the deal? What would your policy stance have been?

TURNER: Well, there's no doubt that "tearing up the agreement" was perhaps a flamboyant phrase. It's a lot harder to get out of this kind of agreement than it is to sign it, just as it's a lot harder to get divorced than it is to get married. Negotiating our way out of the agreement would be very difficult in today's circumstances with the United States. That's part of the problem, as well.

WATSON: Would you have been able to do it in 1988 or 1989?

TURNER: Perhaps. Remember that, although we lost the election, more people voted against that agreement, by voting for the Liberal and New Democratic parties, than voted for it.

WATSON: So the fear of political consequences wouldn't have been terrible but perhaps relations with the U.S. would have been damaged.

TURNER: In the short term.

WATSON: Still, you're hopeful we can survive, even though we've locked ourselves into this deal?

TURNER: I think we're going to have to negotiate very hard with the United States when they sidestep the agreement, as they have with quotas on our softwood lumber and so on. I think we're going to have to watch agriculture very carefully, perhaps our water. There are going to be issues that come up from time to time under which we're not going to be protected under the agreement because the United States is not bound in terms of changing its law.

WASTON: Do you see long-term dangers for our social policy? That was a great concern in 1988, medicare, pensions and so on.

TURNER: Well, you know there are still forces in the United States that would like to privatize our health care.

WATSON: They would like to privatize our health care?

TURNER: Well, you know, the Americans still operate under manifest destiny.

Leap of Faith

DONALD S. MACDONALD

I have been asked to give my remarks in my former capacity as Chairman of the Royal Commission on the Economic Union and Development Prospects for Canada which, in its final report of September 1985, recommended that Canada seek to enter into a free trade agreement with the United States under Article XXIV of the General Agreement on Tariffs and Trade ("GATT").

What the Commission recommended was more or less the treaty that came into effect ten years ago and whose tenth anniversary we now observe. The conference organizers have asked me to explain "why" and "how" the Royal Commission came to the conclusion that it was in Canada's best interests to reverse a policy that had stood for 100 years.

I propose to address the subject in three parts: firstly, to talk about the economics of the decision; secondly, to talk about some fundamental political concerns that have been an important part of Canadian thinking about our trade relations with the United States; and thirdly, to state some conclusions about the decision from the perspective of ten years on.

Firstly, I address the economic questions. From the very earliest settlement by Europeans of this part of the North American continent, the need to sell products into export markets has been an important reality. In the minds of the imperial sovereigns who sent the first exploratory expeditions, the hope of returns in gold, silver and valuable jewels may have been high in their expectations, but for those who settled down to make their lives in the newly settled territories, the exports were much more humble commodities: cod fish, furs, and as time went on, forest products. The newly created communities could not manufacture, or could not manufacture economically, many of the basic things they needed for their survival and so had to import to meet those needs. For much of Canadian economic history, the goods and services produced by more advanced economies could only be enjoyed by Canadians if, from our natural endowment, we produced and exported products based on that in which we had a comparative advantage.

As settlement increased, Canadians started to provide for themselves some of the products and services which heretofore they had purchased from abroad, but the Canadian firms which set out to do that faced fierce competition from outsiders, at first in the imperial homelands, and then in the United States.

A significant development in Canadian economic policy occurred with the creation of the National Policy Tariff introduced in 1878 by Sir John A. Macdonald. While the newly created Dominion of Canada continued its aspirations to be a major exporter of resource products, the National Policy Tariff created a set of barriers behind which Canadian manufacturing industries could be developed to serve the Canadian market. And that became the Canadian economic policy for the next 100 years: seeking tariff-free access for Canadian goods exported abroad, but maintaining a protected market for manufacturing here in Canada. There were always dissenters from that policy, elections were fought for and against it, but as the Royal Commissioners sat down to commence their work in 1982, that was the structural pattern that prevailed.

Let me pause for a moment and give a little background on the Royal Commission and why it was created. The original concern of the government of Pierre Elliott Trudeau (from which I had retired four years previously) in creating the Royal Commission was about internal trade between the Canadian provinces and inter-provincial barriers to it. These questions about the economic union had not been successfully dealt with in the constitutional discussions of the early '80's. The initial goal set for the Commission was to seek solutions to that set of problem. But as discussions evolved between the government and myself about the way to address that issue, it became clear that attempting to design a structure for internal trade could only be addressed when it became clear in what directions the Canadian economy itself was going. Hence, from what started out as the "Royal Commission on the Economic Union" also became one on "Development Prospects for Canada." The Order in Council creating the Commission did not specifically invite our examination of Canadian trade policy, although one of the recitals to the Order in Council stated as follows: "that significant changes are occurring in the world economy, particularly in the sphere of industrial activity, the utilization of natural resources and movement of capital within and among countries, changes which will have important consequences for Canada." With the invocation of changes in world economic circumstances, and Canada's dependence upon international trade, it was inevitable that trade policy should have a central place in our work.

That conclusion was reinforced as our work continued, both from the counsel of the able group of advisors that we had assembled, and significantly, from the responses that we were receiving from the public, both in written submissions and during the three months of public hearings. There came an inevitable conclusion: that paying our way by trading abroad based on our natural advantages in commodities, while maintaining a protected industry at home, could not continue; that to stand still within a hundred year old policy would merely assure economic stagnation, a condition which no spokesman from any point of the political or economic spectrum was prepared to advocate.

The alternative, to open up the Canadian market to international competition, had been advocated patiently for a long time by a succession of Canadian economists: John Young in the 1950s, Harry Johnson in the 1960s and, since then, by a group that included Ron and Paul Wonnacott.

The argument is one specifically of *scale*, that Canadian industry when confined to its own protected market could not attain the economies of scale, nor the varieties of product, nor the rate of innovation that it would be capable of if it had access to a broader market.

What was more, it became apparent from the words of the producers themselves, from the Canadian resource industries, that the comparative advantage which Canada had known in so many commodities on world markets would diminish over time. Canada would continue to be a major resource producer and seller but for a range of reasons, these industries would not be able to attain the same increases in returns which had contributed so much to the increases in standards of living that Canadians had enjoyed in previous decades.

Let me pick copper as an example. Canada had attained the status as one of the principal copper producers and exporters in the world. But the testimony of the copper industry was that this comparative advantage would diminish. There were richer deposits of the mineral than those in Canada to be found and developed abroad; the Canadian costs of mining and refining were higher than those in the other countries; and in some cases the deposits were closer to sea water and the costs of transportation to market were lower. There was also significant change on the demand side for copper. Whereas copper had been much used in electro-mechanical processes and in communications lines, that technology was being replaced by electronics and fibre-optic cables. Important changes in both supply and demand were therefore upon us.

An alternative to the existing industrial structure was therefore needed and our conclusion was that Canada should seek better access to a larger international market for value added goods and services, as well as for the products for which we already had favourable access. The best such opportunity would be by entering into a free trade agreement under Article XXIV of GATT with our neighbour, the world's largest and wealthiest economy.

What was more, that moment presented an unusually favourable opportunity to negotiate such an agreement: President Reagan was in full exercise of the powers of the office of President, and had declared himself in favour of such a free trade agreement with Canada among its other trading partners.

The economic question was not the only question that had to be addressed by Canadian policy makers. There was, is, and always has been a deeply felt concern among Canadians that to get too close to our large neighbour is to put at risk our sovereignty and independence. The noted Canadian journalist, Anthony Westell, had captured these Canadian sentiments in a sentence which we quoted in the report: "The desire to escape from U.S. influence, the desire to put distance between Canada and the United States, arises in large measure from fear of absorption by the U.S. and from jealousy of U.S. wealth, power and vitality."[1] That same set of concerns was before the Government of Canada in the foundation years of the nineteenth century. In introducing his National Policy Tariff in 1878, Sir John A. Macdonald laid stress on these political considerations, in addition to the economic ones: "There are national considerations, Mr. Speaker, that rise far higher than the mere accumulation of wealth, than the mere question of trade advantage, there is prestige, national status, national dominion and no great nation has ever arisen whose policy was free trade." To succeeding generations of Canadians, the protective tariff policy had become linked with Sir John's other policy achievements: the confederation of the Canadian provinces, the development of the great northwest, the building of a trans-continental railway as an essential element of Canadian sovereignty and independence.

The maintenance of that policy had become a matter of high politics – of survival or defeat of governments. A government which had advocated a free trade agreement with the United States, that of Sir Wilfrid Laurier, lost an election on the question in 1911 and a former member of that government who had lost his seat in the 1911 election,

Mackenzie King had had such a free trade treaty negotiated after World War II, and then baulked at introducing it to the electorate. It had become a truism of Canadian politics that no government would survive which advocated a free trade agreement with the U.S.

It was, therefore, a considerable act of political courage to accept the counsel in favour of a free trade agreement from the Royal Commission, to negotiate a treaty and then to stake the life of the government on its ratification. It is one thing to adopt a change of policy when a national consensus has formed on the change. But it is of a higher order of leadership to advocate a policy change that has been long contested and then fight for it on the hustings.

Going back to the deliberations of the Royal Commission, how could we be sure that national sovereignty and independence would not be put to risk by entering into such a trade agreement? I don't believe that either side of that question can be proved or disproved by the traditional formal logic. That is because the survival of a nation in circumstances such as our own depends not upon certain immutable economic factors but upon the will of Canadians themselves: we believed that after a century of successful development of our country, the will to remain Canadians was not at risk, that the will to national survival was not dependent on a tariff policy. After a century that had challenged us in war and in peace time, in prosperity and economic depression, in a geography that is about as difficult as any to be found anywhere, in a climate that is unspeakable, except that we all talk about it, we have created a Canadian political ethos that has become the admiration of the world, and the country is not dependent for its survival on the baling wire and binder twine of the customs tariff.

In the end, the last word on the question rests with the electors. And they agreed with us.

So what reflections would I have 14 years after the Royal Commission Report and 10 from the adoption of free trade?

There are many participating in the next several days who are far better qualified than I to pronounce on the economic consequences but broad statistical aggregates show a positive Canadian performance. For example, in the total Canadian exports of goods of all kinds to the world in the seven years between 1990 and 1997, the dollar value increased from $152 billion to $302 billion, or nearly doubled. And in categories of exports with high value added: machinery and equipment, exports increased from $29 billion to $68 billion; automotive products from $35 billion to $70 billion; and other consumer goods from $3 billion to $11 billion.

To be fair, there have been costs on the down side as well as benefits, both in the case of individual firms and in the case of workers. That was anticipated for general free trade just as it occurred when the specialized free trade agreement of the Auto Pact came into force. What one cannot compare is the losses to adjustment to the trade agreement against losses that might have occurred through economic stagnation. Yes, there have been losses and it was not made easier for those suffering them in the early years that the economy was weathering a North American economic recession and punishingly high interest rates.

Most of the adjustments occurred quietly and unseen by wider public scrutiny. But through the period there have been, as there were before, some highly publicized areas of dispute with the United States and with American industries. There are special interest groups on both sides of the border who would seek to deflect the course of economic change that might affect them by protective measures that are contrary to the trade agreement. That's what the elabourately negotiated dispute settlement process was about. Those problems would have existed whether there were a free trade agreement or not. I can say this as someone who has practised in the international trade law environment, Canada is advantaged when it can have these disputes decided on the basis of law rather than of power. But there will inevitably be disputes, and the structure of the American government is such that the local, parochial, the special interest has much greater leverage than it does in our country. They are not about to correct that and it is something we have to live with.

What the Canada-U.S. Free Trade Agreement did was offer Canada a process to adjust to a much more competitive world. The Royal Commissioners sensed they were at a moment of change without pretending to predict the specific events of change that were to occur. The past decade has seen dramatic changes worldwide that neither we nor anyone else in the mid-80's would have chanced at:

- the collapse of the Soviet Union, and with it the concept of the command versus the market economy; a set of political events that opened up a very large population and a host of new countries to market competition;
- a similar, if not so dramatic, turn of events in Latin America bringing in democratically elected governments and an end to dirigiste and restrictionist economic polices;
- the Information Revolution: it was apparent to the Commission that the ability to send large volumes of information over long distances almost instantly was an important source of change; none of us would have imagined the phenomenon of the Internet – one of the

most powerful institutions for by-passing national restrictions and overleaping border controls ever invented;

- the negotiation of a set of much more comprehensive trade laws at the international level: The North American Free Trade Agreement, and then the worldwide application of the World Trade Organization agreements.

In the perspective of those subsequent events, it is clear that Canada would have been at a substantial disadvantage in the expansion of worldwide commerce that has occurred if we had not undertaken that first bold "leap of faith" in our ability, as a people, to meet international competition.

DONALD S. MACDONALD was the Chairman, Royal Commission on the Economic Union and Development Prospects for Canada (1982–1985). Formerly Minister of Finance in the Trudeau government, and later Canada's High Commissioner to London, he is counsel to the law firm of McCarthy Tétrault in Toronto.

NOTES

1 Anthony Westell, "Economic Integration with the U.S.A.," *International Perspectives*, November/December 1984, 22

A Signal Moment

JAMES A. BAKER III

Part of my pleasure in being here is admittedly personal: this conference gives me an all-too-rare opportunity to renew my acquaintance with many old friends, both American and Canadian, with whom I worked to achieve the U.S.-Canada Free Trade Agreement back in 1985–88. But I am also delighted to be here because the subjects of this conference – the tenth anniversary of the FTA and the fifth anniversary of NAFTA – are both important and timely.

The FTA and later NAFTA were events of significance not just in economic terms but also, more broadly, in terms of the evolving relationship among the three countries involved. But the anniversaries of the FTA and the NAFTA are also urgent reminders of how much remains to be done in fulfilling the promise of these agreements by taking concrete steps towards the creation of a truly hemispheric free trade area. that is why I believe it vitally important that this conference look forward as much as back.

We should remember that the FTA and NAFTA, as historic as they may be, are merely parts of a broader agenda of international economic liberalization – an agenda where, I might add, much work remains to be done. Of course, the years since the FTA have been ones of extraordinary change and dramatic progress. The Agreement itself has been expanded by NAFTA to include Mexico.

The Uruguay Round of the GATT has been completed and the WTO created. The countries of North and South America have agreed in principle to a Hemispheric Free Trade Zone. And, not least, with the financial crisis that struck first in East Asia two years ago now seemingly behind us, the modern "globalized" economy appears to have weathered its first great storm.

Far from diminishing the importance of the FTA, however, these developments in fact point to its real significance. This is because, in a real sense, the Agreement marked a signal moment not just in the history of economic relations between our two countries or even among the nations of the Americas, North and South. It also represented an important step in the ongoing global trend towards liberalization of trade and investment. As many around this room are aware, the FTA also very nearly didn't happen.

There is a natural tendency, when looking back, to imbue decisive events like the Agreement with an aura of inevitable. The negotiations leading to the FTA were protracted, painful and, more than once, on the verge of complete collapse. The fact that there was an agreement at all is testimony, at a simple human level, to the personal commitment and physical stamina of negotiators on both sides.

I speak here from personal experience. I had, of course, been involved with the general course of the negotiations from the very beginning, first as White House Chief of Staff and then as Secretary of the Treasury. But my role changed dramatically in the month prior to the deadline for submission to the Congress, when President Reagan made me the point man on the agreement. My mandate was clear: if a deal were at all possible, get it! Now, I had been engaged in intensive negotiations before, both as White House Chief of Staff and Secretary of State during the Bush Administration – including some associated with concluding NAFTA. But I assure you that few compared, in complexity of the material or contentiousness of the issues, with what I confronted in late September and early October 1987.

I want to say a word or two in general terms about why we succeeded and what that success has meant both for our countries and for the world. Let me turn first to the "why" – the lessons of the FTA that might be put to use negotiating other international agreements, whether in the economic, political or strategic realms.

LESSONS OF THE FREE TRADE AGREEMENT

The first and foremost of those lessons is, I believe, the imperative of political will. As important as the work of negotiators was, the FTA was ultimately the creation of two men: Ronald Reagan and Brian Mulroney. Only they could commit the respective bureaucracies to the difficult process of negotiating a pact. Only they could provide the vision necessary to sway public opinion. And only they could make the hard decisions required to broker a final agreement.

Now, Brian Mulroney and Ronald Reagan were – and are – quite different men by age, background and personal disposition. Both shared, first, a profound belief in the importance of free trade and, second, the political courage to pursue that belief in face of significant domestic opposition. That commitment and that courage were perhaps most clearly articulated in March 1985 when, at the Quebec City Summit, President Reagan and Prime Minister Mulroney pledged themselves to freer trade and investment between their two countries. But they were also to prove critical in the difficult years of negotiation that followed. Both placed an agreement at the very top of their administrations' respective agendas.

Had they not done so, it is inconceivable that an agreement could have been reached. When it came to the FTA – as with all major foreign policy initiatives – active, sustained leadership at the top was truly indispensable. In other words, political will was key.

I might add that everything I have said about Ronald Reagan when it comes to the FTA holds true – in spades – for George Bush when it comes to NAFTA. Again, Presidents Reagan and Bush were two vastly different men in terms of personal background and management style; but, like Brian Mulroney and – let us not forget – Carlos Salinas, Ronald Reagan had the conviction and the courage to make the dream of free trade a reality.

A second lesson that we should draw from the negotiations is the importance of political pragmatism. Now, I readily admit that I speak from personal bias. I am an unabashed pragmatist. During my entire public life, in fact, I have been criticized – sometimes harshly – for my supposed preference for a deal over the ideal.

Well, I plead guilty – so long as the deal in question gets us closer to the ideal that we desire. In my experience, pragmatism – a sense, if you will, of political limits – is a prerequisite to successful negotiations. From a negotiator's point of view, that pragmatism must be twofold. The negotiator must first be aware of the political dynamic within his or her country. This dynamic is all the more complicated in a democracy, where interest groups are varied and vocal, power divided and diffuse. Such complexity is particularly acute in the United States, where, in contrast with parliamentary systems such as Canada's, party discipline is weak and authority shared by the Executive and Legislative Branches. A pragmatic sense of what will or will not "sell" politically is key.

I spent much of my time during the negotiations, for instance, gauging congressional opinion and cultivating bipartisan support from friends of free trade on Capitol Hill. But the negotiator must also be aware of the political constraints under which his or her counterparts labour. Here, I must confess, I suspect that the Canadians came better prepared than we were. There is a tendency – regrettable but real – for we Americans to take our northern neighbours for granted. We sometimes forget that Canadian politics, like our own, are complex, contentious, and prey to all the contradictory influences of an open society. But if we were perhaps a little slow at the beginning to grasp Canadian sensitivities, I believe that we had become, by the end of the negotiations, experts by necessity.

This brings me to what I consider to be the third lesson we should learn from the experience of the FTA: the importance of proactive policy-making. We would be wise to remember just how strong protectionist sentiment was in both our countries at the time the treaty was negotiated. In the United States, for instance, our large trade deficits had prompted calls for punitive measures against major trading partners and put immense political pressure on the Reagan Administration to act. This had the effect of putting us in the position of responding constantly to protectionist initiatives by the Congress – and, frankly, occasionally taking action we would otherwise have avoided in order to avert even more dangerous measures on the Hill.

The FTA – like NAFTA later – allowed us in the Administration to move beyond political passivity by changing the terms of the debate from specific trade figures and individual industries to our broader national interest in more open trade and investment. I suspect the same held true for our Canadian counterparts. And I know the importance of a proactive trade and investment policy holds true today – although, I am sorry to say, the Clinton Administration seems not yet to have grasped it. The President's decision not to seek fast track authority before the 1996 election because of pressure from the protectionist wing of his party was not just craven. It was also a truly lost opportunity. With the U.S. trade deficit likely to rise to the $300 billion range in 1999, protectionist sentiment, quiescent for a number of years, is likely to be far stronger than just a few ago, making free trade an even harder sell.

As the FTA reminds us, it is simply not enough for supporters of free trade and investment to put our fingers in the dike when it springs a leak because of protectionist pressure. Instead, we must build new dikes that open up ever more of the world economy to free trade and investment.

The best defense, in short, is a good offense – and the FTA is a dramatic and, I believe, educational case in point. Moreover – and here I plainly differ with the Clinton Administration – I believe that free trade, if patiently explained and forcefully advocated, is a winner, not a loser, in electoral terms. And I hope that the U.S. Presidential campaign of 2000 will grant Americans an opportunity for a sober debate on the subject.

CONSEQUENCES

I would now like to turn to my second general topic – what the FTA has meant for our two countries and, indeed the world.

First, of course, is the two-way increase in trade and investment that the agreement has fostered. During the period 1988–98, that trade more than doubled – much of it in the cutting edge areas of computer and information services. Now, isolating the specific impact of the FTA is admittedly problematic in economies as large and complex as those of the United States and Canada. And, like any major effort at economic liberalization, the agreement has no doubt created losers as well as winners on both sides of the border. But, on balance, the winners have clearly outnumbered losers – and the net effect of the agreement has to been to increase trade and investment. The result: higher economic growth, and with it more jobs and better wages, in both the United States and Canada.

Second, the FTA set the stage for NAFTA and the creation of a free trade around of 400 million inhabitants reaching from the Yukon to the Yucatan. In many ways the issues involved in NAFTA were more difficult than that of the FTA. For all our differences, after all, the economies of the United States and Canada were and are fundamentally similar in terms of per capita output and sectoral composition. By no stretch of the imagination could the same be said of the Mexican economy on the one and the United States and Canada on the other. That NAFTA was negotiated – and negotiated so quickly – was due in large part to the lessons learned from the negotiations leading to the FTA.

Third, the FTA and its direct descendent, NAFTA, laid the groundwork for hemispheric free trade. But we should all be deeply disappointed by the lack of progress achieved since the agreement in principle to a hemispheric agreement at the Miami Summit in 1994. Nevertheless, I still believe that a hemispheric free trade zone will be created, if only because it is so obviously in interest of all the countries involved. And I know that such a zone is only conceivable today because of the earlier success of both the FTA and NAFTA.

Fourth, the FTA demonstrated that regional arrangements, if properly crafted, need not come in conflict with broader global efforts to liberalize trade and investment. Far from undermining the GATT Uruguay Round, as some feared at the time, the FTA actually complimented it. This is an important lesson in a world where the possibility of competitive trading blocs remains a constant threat to further progress towards freer trade and investment.

Fifth, last and perhaps most importantly, the FTA, like NAFTA after it, committed the signatory countries to a course of openness and optimism. This openness to the new and this optimism about the future represent the very best in us – Canadian, American and Mexican alike. The agreement committed our countries to looking outward rather than inward, to fostering a desire to excel instead of fear our competition, to encourage productive cooperation and not destructive resentment.

The FTA and NAFTA, taken together, marked a true revolution in relations among Canada, the United States and Mexico – a revolution that allows all of us to look forward with confidence to the next century and indeed the next millennium.

JAMES A. BAKER III, previously White House Chief of Staff in the Reagan Administration, was Secretary of the Treasury at the time of the FTA negotiations (1985–89), and later Secretary of State in the Bush Administration (1989–92).

Where There's the Will ...

DEREK H. BURNEY

I am delighted to be here, along with Jim Baker, to commemorate more than ten years of free trade between Canada and the U.S. I begin by congratulating our host, Des Morton and the McGill Institute for the Study of Canada for taking this initiative and for assembling such a distinguished group of participants.

You have heard from Don Macdonald on what might be called the intellectual backbone for the initiative in Canada. There can be no doubt but that the thorough analysis and virtually unanimous recommendation by Mr. Macdonald and his associates proved to be a major catalyst for the negotiation and a bedrock of faith for the political will in Canada that drove those negotiations to conclusion.

I have been asked to speak specifically about that political will and I do so from a position of privilege and pride – as well as bias – in that I was directly involved in the final round of negotiations and monitored developments closely throughout in my capacity as the Prime Minister's Chief of Staff from March 1987 to January 1989. I had been involved even before in a major study of Canadian trade policy. As well, from my earlier position in External Affairs, I was heavily engaged in several bilateral meetings between the Prime Minister and the President including the Quebec Summit in March 1998 which helped launch the free trade initiative.

From that vantage point, I can attest, without qualification, that this initiative required enormous political will, disproportionately so on the Canadian side. It was highly controversial and politically very divisive in Canada and almost failed. There were definitely times when

I did not believe it would happen, times as well when it would have been easier to stand down. Easier, but not smarter. We had an election in Canada on free trade, because our appointed Senate refused at first to ratify the agreement. It may all seem straightforward now but it was anything but at the time.

I salute Jim Baker for his indispensable role in galvanizing the American team towards an agreement. His hallmark in the service of his government was to get things done. The FTA was one of many such achievements because, quite literally at the eleventh hour, he acted decisively to close the major gap. President Reagan had a vision for continental free trade – from the Yukon to the Yucatan – and Jim Baker helped make that vision a reality.

For our Prime Minister, it was a question of political courage as well as will and we were fortunate to have had a leader with the stomach as well as the head to prevail through what were some very rocky moments from beginning to end. I have no doubt but that the success of this initiative, and that of NAFTA which followed, will stand as the most prominent legacy of Mr. Mulroney's government. That so many of its fiercest opponents are now among its champions is perhaps the greatest compliment to him and to all who were involved with both negotiations.

As students of Canadian history we knew that the issue of free trade would be politically sensitive. After all, it had been attempted twice before. It defeated a Liberal government in 1911 and intimidated another from going beyond very private exploratory discussions in 1948. There was almost an allergy to the term. In Canada we talked of "freer trade." The Americans, for their part looked to "free and fair trade" leaving the definition of fairness suitably ambiguous. Fairness is in the eye of the beholder. A nineteenth century French satirist once observed that the sun offered unfair competition to candle makers. If windows could be boarded up, he contended, more jobs could be created making candles.

Euphemisms, labels and flights of rhetoric were among the obstacles on the path to free trade. But there were others. Trade in cultural products was and is a Canadian hot button. What we regard as culture; the Americans see as business. What Canadians see as dominant; Americans regard as popular. Take movies for instance, something President Reagan was quite emphatic about. At one point, Jim Baker told me that, "in Texas, sugar is culture!" These days, of course, it is about magazines.

Even the politics in Canada were, well, confusing. The Conservatives, after all, were the nationalists dating back to our first Prime Minister, John A. Macdonald and his National Policy of tariffs to build an industrial economy within Canada. (Although, as Des would attest,

John A. Macdonald adopted this only after his efforts to conclude "reciprocity" with the U.S. had, for the most part, been rebuffed.) Nonetheless, in this century, the Liberals had, for the most part, been trade liberalizers; the Conservatives less so. All that changed under Brian Mulroney's Conservatives, thanks in part to a Liberal named Don Macdonald. In fact, there was a new brand of conservative ideology in the western world favouring more open trade and investment along with privatization and less regulation. Conservatives had, in effect, become classical liberals. But there were other factors motivating a new look in Canada at an old concept.

Most prominent was the increasing importance of Canada's trade with the U.S. and the particular success of the Autopact. Forty years of incremental GATT negotiations had also provided an umbrella of sorts for a steady liberalization of Canada – U.S. trade, so much so that the prospect of "free trade" had become a more logical, certainly not radical, extension of the prevailing trend. Or, at least, that is what logic suggested. Besides, the best laid plans of government to divert or dilute this growing trend – including, notably, the third option calling for "counterweights" to increasing bilateralism – had not moved much beyond speeches.

More generally, the structure of the global economy had been shifting since the mid-seventies, reducing the importance of natural resources and increasing the relative supply of goods produced by unskilled labour. For Canada this posed a particular challenge. On top of that, the 1982 recession hit Canada hard. Confrontations with the U.S. on trade were the order of the day. Slow growth, scepticism and frustration produced political solutions or, in reality, managed trade solutions – new protectionism in old bottles. By the mid-eighties there was growing concern that relations with the U.S. had become more vital than ever to Canada's well being, but were in need of refurbishment. Officials were told repeatedly that we needed "to get things right" with the Americans even though the definition of what was intended was less precise than the directive. What was evident was that the trend of increasing trade with the U.S. placed a higher priority on the need for Canada to protect and preserve our access and to dampen or contain U.S. "trade remedy" actions – another euphemism meaning in effect protectionist measures against Canadian lumber, steel and agricultural exports.

Many of us in government had also concluded, after extensive dialogue with exporters and academics from coast to coast that, if Canadian industry and Canadian exporters were to be more successful globally, they needed first of all to have a stronger, more secure base for success here in North America. We knew that what was needed was a better, rules-based platform for our most crucial trade relationship, one which would provide a greater degree of certainty for Canadian exporters with all the value-added benefit that would bring in terms of investment and productivity. We also thought, naively perhaps, that it just might prompt more tangible moves to dismantle trade barriers within Canada. Unfortunately, this domestic objective, even to this day, evolves at a snail's pace. We also knew, however, that Canada needed to move beyond our branch plant system of manufacturing – under the cocoon of higher tariffs – in order to become more competitive and to stimulate the innovative and entrepreneurial skills necessary for future growth.

Meanwhile, in the mid-eighties, the multilateral talks on trade liberalization under the GATT were sputtering. Initiatives, including ones spearheaded by Canada, had failed to generate the necessary will. Multilateral discussions produced more finger-pointing than progress. It was, in a real sense, more palatable politically to conserve than to expand. The pain of liberalization was more apparent to politicians everywhere than the benefit. When further sectoral arrangements – along the lines of the Autopact – proved too difficult to negotiate bilaterally, too difficult to find balance *within* a given sector, a broader approach became more appealing.

The Canadian business community, generally speaking, rallied behind the initiative, cautiously at first but with unprecedented passion and commitment as the debate rose to a fever pitch in Canada. Significantly, there was strong support for free trade from Quebec and the provincial Liberal government of Robert Bourassa. Historically, free trade had been popular in Western Canada but less so in Quebec and Ontario. The change of heart in Quebec was pivotal because, while Mr. Mulroney's government had significant representation from all regions, its power bases were the West and Quebec. But to be successful, good ideas, even with broad support, need a political champion. That is the vital role our Prime Minister played and, in Canada, when the Prime Minister chooses to lead, the cabinet and the system fall quickly into line. Even though there were times when a vote, if taken in cabinet, would have been Lincolnesque – you know, ten to one against but the *one* carries. But, in fact, Mr. Mulroney had solid, consistent support throughout from several of his senior Ministers.

Despite the Prime Minister's firm commitment, the process of engagement at the negotiating level was excruciatingly slow. For one thing, our systems of government are very different. Our negotiating teams reflected many of those differences, as did their mandates and their methods. The FTA was an over-riding objective for the Canadian government. It dominated our government's policy agenda. In the U.S., it was one of many policy initiatives on a very crowded agenda for a Republican Administration that had difficulty gaining support from a Democratic Congress for its domestic, let alone its international priorities. Our negotiating team met regularly with Ministers and the Prime Minister, sought and received instructions at each juncture. Throughout the process, the Prime Minister and his cabinet colleagues also dealt with the intense public dimension of the debate which was constant and, at times, more raucous than influential, but which reflected the enormous sensitivity of this initiative for Canadians. After all, we can be a bit hesitant about the kind of relationship we want to have with the U.S. We may want many of the advantages from our proximity but are leery of being consumed by it. We want our relationship to be friendly, but not too friendly, cooperative but not too cooperative. We want Canada to have a distinctive role in world affairs, a distinction which, for some, is determined solely by the degree of differentiation with the U.S.A. We want to be recognized as being different but Americans keep spoiling it by saying things like "you know you are just like us." More than anything else, this ambivalence reflects the enormous power imbalance between our two countries and creates, in turn, a vastly disproportionate risk for a Canadian leader who initiates any agreement with the U.S.A.

It is often as difficult for Canadians to explain this ambivalence as it is for Americans to comprehend it. When I served in Washington, I tried to use humour to make the point: "Americans are proud of what they are – Americans; Canadians are proud of what they are not – Americans; Americans believe anything worth doing is worth overdoing; Canadians believe anything worth doing is probably worth a government grant." But the fact is that, unless it is hockey, Canadians tend to see themselves as being short-changed or handicapped in a two-way contest with Americans. They have difficulty seeing balance let alone advantage flowing from any bilateral agreements and, for reasons both historical and sociological, negotiations over trade arouse the most visceral emotions.

The free trade debate in Canada went well beyond the topic of trade and the actual provisions of the agreement. Proponents were accused of selling our sovereignty, our birthright, and our health care system (in those days, we were all proud of our health care system). Senior citizens were told they would be turned out of their old age homes which would be privatized by Americans – threats which, by the way, prompted calls of concern from both my mother and the Prime Minister's mother. (When Bob Rae later told me he had met my mother, I wondered then if he had helped initiate her call.) One of the more peculiar canards was that we had struck a secret deal guaranteeing that the Canadian dollar – then trading at 82¢ U.S. – would move to par with the U.S. dollar. If only! I have often wondered how trade negotiators would be expected to fulfil this "secret" accord. I am sure that, over at the Bank of Canada, John Crowe and Gordon Thiessen wondered too.

We had many versions of Ross Perot in Canada before Ross himself took on NAFTA. Instead of a "giant sucking sound" of jobs moving to Mexico, our water was being drained south and our border was being erased. Virtually everyone in Canada had an opinion and was determined to express it. Epithets flew fast and furious and reason or logic seldom surfaced. In the midst of the 1988 election campaign, some of the Prime Minister's senior political advisors suggested that he pledge to call a referendum on the agreement. He wisely ignored their counsel. In fact, he never flinched during the protracted, often frustrating negotiation, nor during the even more frenzied election campaign. Mr. Mulroney was explicit when he launched the negotiations. He was convinced that the objective, if attained, would benefit the national interest. He accepted without question the judgement of his negotiating team when Canada suspended the negotiations. And he accepted, with relief and satisfaction, the unanimous recommendation from his team on October 4, 1998, that we sign the agreed outline. He then defended the agreement with his cabinet and his caucus and in the ultimate public arena – a national election. That was courage with conviction – the essence of political leadership. I recall that, when Mr. Mulroney asked me to serve as his Chief of Staff, he said that he wanted someone to help him concentrate on major issues like free trade instead of "tainted tuna." And he did just that – with one firm instruction at each step. "Make sure we will be better off with this agreement than without it." Not "any" agreement or "an agreement for the sake of an agreement" but one that met his fundamental objective.

Fortunately, in 1987, there was political will on both sides and at the very top. We were determined to conclude a good agreement for our Prime Minister and for Canada. I know that Jim Baker, Clayton Yeutter and their colleagues wanted a good agreement for their President and for their country. Ultimately, their will coincided with that on the Canadian side and is what, more than anything else, prompted the success of the negotiations. We knew, for instance, that an agreement which did not temper the unilateral, if not arbitrary, nature of U.S. trade remedy actions would simply not wash in Canada. There had been expectations of total immunity which were impossible to attain. Instead, we sought a respectable compromise and, in the end, and at the very last moment, that is what we got. I happen to believe that the Dispute Settlement mechanism of the FTA was the litmus test for its success to Canada. The fact that it has worked, despite overuse and even abuse, is a testament to its effectiveness. The fact that it was emulated, in fact, in NAFTA and in spirit by the World Trade Organization is its finest tribute. Remember too that this unique mechanism was achieved without the pain for Canadian exporters of greater disciplines. Because of the importance of exports to virtually every segment of Canada's economy, our companies would have been more vulnerable than their U.S. counterparts to any common or harmonized regime of trade remedy rules. That is essentially why so many formulae – "safe harbours"; "red light/green light" – and the like failed to connect.

In a world of rapid change, rules properly adjudicated help reduce uncertainty and provide a measure of stability or, at least, greater predictability. But, if you think what was achieved in the FTA on dispute settlement was easy or meaningless, think again. As the American academic Stephen Blank noted recently "getting the U.S. to accept the principle that its own trade remedy judgements should be 'internationalized' in a binding mechanism involving experts from each country was extremely significant. It was a major gain for Canada."

I first met Jim Baker on the aprons of the IMF/World Bank meetings in the fall of 1987. Together with our Finance Minister (Mike Wilson) and our Ambassador (Allan Gotlieb), I had been instructed by the Prime Minister to convey a message of urgency to the Secretary of the Treasury. Our real objective was to try to get him involved. Formal negotiations had been going on for eighteen months at the level of officials but were making little progress on the crunch issues. I summoned my best diplomatic skills and asked the Secretary how it was that the U.S. could contemplate concluding a nuclear arms reduction agreement with the Soviet Union – as it was then – but were unwilling to test the Congress on issues essential to a genuine Free Trade Agreement with Canada. Alas, my diplomatic charm did not work ... at least not immediately. Shortly thereafter, the negotiations ran aground. There was no give by the U.S. on relief from trade remedy or dispute settlement and, for Canada, a deal exclusively on tariffs – ours being higher than those of the U.S. – was not worth the political price.

When the Americans pressed at the political level for a resumption, I was then instructed by the Prime Minister to get directly involved. I recall advising our U.S. counterparts in our first encounter that the deal we saw, i.e., tariffs only, we did not want, and the deal we wanted, we did not see. The impasse continued until the weekend in early October when the fast track deadline expired. Then and only then the major obstacles started to move and eventually, thanks to the ingenuity of Jim Baker, Clayton Yeutter and their officials – as well as Canadian tenacity – the logjam was broken. But what was agreed first was, in effect, a term sheet – the outline for an agreement. From October through December the negotiating teams grappled with the "legal text" which was, of course, the actual agreement. And it was a real negotiation – everything from content percentages for autos to the simulcasting of cable television commercials – with diversions as well into limitations on sugar containing products and unstructured suits. As well, the American team raised what seemed then to be an obscure point of constitutional law. This gave rise to the extraordinary panel or "dead judges" provision, intended, we were told, for constitutional or political cover but NEVER for real use.

Two years into implementation, however, the "dead judges" were resurrected by the U.S. not once, but twice. Fortunately however, the sanctity of dispute panel verdicts prevailed. But, eventually, back in December of 1987, we succeeded in Ottawa, as we had in Washington in October of the same year. The tone was civil – for the most part – and the intent was deliberate. Both teams had a task to complete to respect the will and commitment of our two governments at the highest level. And that is what was achieved.

The process of that negotiation and the result has been the subject of several books, memoirs and articles – some very recent and stronger on colour than fact – but memories are, for me too, highly subjective. So is history.

My memory is clear today. When I am asked whether the agreement fulfilled its objectives, I have no hesitation in responding firmly in the affirmative. The trade numbers speak for themselves – more than one billion dollars of goods each and every day – and studies show consistently that both sides are benefiting enormously in trade volume terms. As the smaller of the two, I believe Canada is the greater beneficiary. In fact, enhanced access to the U.S. has fuelled much of the growth that there has been in the Canadian economy over the past decade. Evidence also suggests that a significant part of the trade increase has been due to faster growth in sectors that were liberalized.

And there have been significant side benefits stimulated by the FTA – an open skies agreement greatly facilitating air passenger traffic between our two countries; NAFTA and the concept of even broader regional free trade arrangements for this hemisphere. The FTA was also a catalyst for the successful conclusion of the Uruguay Round and the creation of the WTO. It broke new ground on services since replicated both in NAFTA and the WTO.

Has it meant an end to trade disputes? It would be naïve to assume that would ever be the case. There is still a tendency to lapse into managed trade solutions, e.g., on lumber, beneficial to neither side. But, I do believe that the agreement has helped temper many trade disputes and the threat of unilateral action has abated. There is still too much hassle on border entry – both for people and for goods.

So, is there scope for more bilateral negotiations today? Yes, indeed, but does the political will exist to do more? I wonder. Has it meant an end to protectionism? Of course not. In fact, one inescapable feature of the unique U.S. system – and a nation with many lawyers! – is the almost infinite capacity for "protectionism by process" – border processes, standards and inspection regimes, rules of entry for personnel, etc. Alan Greenspan acknowledged recently that Americans were losing faith in the benefits of free trade. He warned firmly against efforts to pursue protectionism. The forces of protectionism are always present, and not just in the U.S., for politicians seeking soap boxes rather than policies to win votes. Political champions of free trade are hard to find. Mercantilist thinking is in the ascendancy and, combined with the growing phobia about "globalization," this can be lethal for advocates and beneficiaries of freer, let alone free trade. WTO rulings are going unheeded because the major players are unwilling to accept WTO verdicts. The WTO cannot resolve problems which are political anymore than it can inspire initiatives which are political. That takes leadership or, in short, political will.

I do not envy the task of today's trade negotiators. New disputes are more complicated and issues extending well beyond the norm of trade policy are increasingly part of the trade agenda. Obviously, progress on trade cannot run on faith alone. But I do believe that the achievement of the Canada – U.S. agreement demonstrates convincingly that the theory works provided the political will and leadership exists to make it happen. We were fortunate to have had that in 1987–88 and our success is a continuing source of pride for me and many others. It is also, I hope, a foundation of faith and confidence for those in the forefront of trade negotiations today.

DEREK H. BURNEY, Chief of Staff to the Prime Minister during the FTA negotiations (1987–89), was later Ambassador of Canada to the United States (1989–93). He is now President and CEO of CAE Inc.

PART TWO

The Making of the Deal

The Negotiation and Approval of the FTA

The difficulty of achieving a successful negotiation of the Free Trade Agreement was matched only by the difficulty of the political machinations required to have the deal passed into law, both in Canada and the United States. A hostile U.S. Congress and a heated Canadian election threatened to render null the product of years of talks between the two countries, a process that involved many people at all levels of government. Assembled for this plenary were several of the key figures involved in negotiating and selling the deal. On the Canadian side, John C. Crosbie, Simon Reisman, William A. Dymond, Michael Hart, and Stanley H. Hartt. On the American side, Clayton Yeutter, Jean Anderson, Peter McPherson, William S. Merkin, and Charles E. Roh. Their roles are fully explained below in Ian MacDonald's introductory remarks.

L. IAN MACDONALD: On October 1, 1987, Mr. Mulroney, on his way to Toronto for a day of speeches, met senior negotiators in the Billy Bishop lounge on the military side of Uplands Airport in Ottawa, and signed off on the instructions of their government for one last effort to reach an agreement with the Americans before the clock ran out on President Reagan's fast-track authority at midnight on October third. Twelve hours later, on a phone at the York Club in Toronto, where Conrad Black was hosting a dinner of the Bilderberg Group, the Prime Minister ordered his team home. There was no movement on dispute settlement, the heart of the Canadian negotiating position.

But while he was in the air travelling back to Ottawa, there was, and meeting Derek Burney and his team at 24 Sussex, he ordered them back to Washington again the following morning. And on October third, at 25 minutes before midnight, Treasury Secretary James Baker and senior Canadian and U.S. officials, announced an agreement and despatched a messenger in the President's name to the Congress. The truth of the matter is that they stopped the clock, because the Prime Minister and his Cabinet back in Ottawa, had not agreed to it, and did not, until 1 o'clock in the morning, an hour after the fast-track actually expired.

Half a dozen senior ministers met with the Prime Minister in the second floor offices at the Langevin building. They spoke with the team in Washington, and finally the Prime Minister came to his bottom line, and asked Derek Burney: "Is this better than what we've got?" And Derek's momentous reply was "Yes, Prime Minister."

Well, is it? That's one of the reasons we're here ten years on, and uniquely the people who made the history are here to talk about it. We're going to try recreate the drama of those three days in October, and the larger issues around those days, the dealmakers and the deal-breakers, as well as the selling of the deal in the fall of 1988, a year later, the most tumultuous election campaign in the second half of the twentieth century in Canada.

First allow me to present Team U.S.A.: Clayton Yeutter, United States Trade Representative during the Reagan years from 1985–88; Dr. Peter McPherson, now president of Michigan State University, but then Deputy Secretary of the Treasury; Bill Merkin, a prominent Washington trade consultant, specializing in Canadian issues, well known to Canadian audiences, but then Deputy USTR; Charles "Chip" Roh, a Washington trade lawyer, but then Assistant Deputy USTR; and his law partner, Jean Anderson, former Lead Negotiator for Trade Law.

And from Team Canada: John Crosbie, Minister of Trade from 1988–91, who had the task of selling the deal to the country in the toughest election campaign in modern times, and the first Canadian politician to propose this in the 1980s in the 1983 Canadian Conservative leadership campaign; Simon Reisman, Ambassador and Chief Negotiator for Canada; Stanley Hartt, now Chairman of Salomon Smith Barney, but then Deputy Minister of Finance; and Bill Dymond, former Senior Advisor to Mr. Reisman in the TNO. And we begin with Team U.S.A., and Ambassador Yeutter.

CLAYTON YEUTTER: I'd like to go back a little bit to the beginning and sort of put this whole exercise in context, at least as we saw it as it evolved from the U.S. side. First of all, Jim Baker and Derek Burney both mentioned that we were 10–10 votes in the Senate Finance Committee, and almost didn't get this exercise launched at all. That was a pretty critical time, and I mention that again because it gives a bit of a flavour of the political environment that existed in the U.S. at that time.

It was shortly after I came into the government from having headed the Chicago Mercantile Exchange, and I was incurring the wrath of all the members of Congress at that time who felt that the Reagan Administration was ignoring the $150 or $160 billion trade deficit that we then had, which was the largest trade deficit in the history of the nation at that time. And all of that came to a head at the time that we had this vote in the Senate, because these members of Congress and the Senate in that case wanted to send messages to the Administration.

They wanted to vote "no" on the U.S.-Canada Free Trade Agreement not because they were really opposed to us negotiating the U.S.-Canada Free Trade Agreement, but because they wanted to send a message to the White House that nobody over there was paying any attention.

So we had some "no" votes as a result of that. There were also some additional "no" votes, in fact one that almost eliminated the entire process by one of my fellow Republican Senators, whose vote related to slave labour in China, and again had nothing whatsoever to do with the U.S.-Canada Free Trade Agreement, and this was the one where we had to stop the whole process because we had counted his vote as being in favour, and that's what led to President Reagan getting on the telephone with Senator Matsunaga in Hawaii. It was the late Senator Matsunaga, who finally cast the vote that got us the 10–10 and made it possible for us to move forward.

That's a little bit of the history of getting this operation rolling. Somebody asked if anybody paid any attention until the final weeks, and the fact of the matter is that, yes, people did pay a lot of attention prior to those final weeks. Nobody put a trade agreement of this magnitude together in the last three days or in the last 30 days. Clearly you zero in on the key remaining issues in any negotiation in those final hours or days or weeks. By then, in a major negotiation, a lot has to happen ahead of time, and a lot did happen ahead of time in this one. For example, one of our major objectives in this negotiation was energy security and the whole chapter on energy security had been put together and basically put to bed well before all of these crucial final hours that everyone had been talking about. Now that's only one of many, many elements of the negotiation that really had taken place during these months of negotiations. So it wasn't that people were sitting on their hands and not paying attention.

In fact, as the trade minister at that time I sometimes thought we were paying too much attention, and devoting too much time, effort and energy to this process. At times we were getting frustrated just as our Canadian colleagues were, and I was saying "why don't we reduce our level of involvement and go do other things." And that's a part of this picture too, because although this was a big deal in both countries, it was a really big deal in Canada as you know, whereas in the U.S. we had a lot of other things on our table at the time.

For example, we had a major problem with huge bilateral deficit with Japan, and I was spending a huge amount of my time on U.S.-Japan negotiations. We probably did, during the time period of this negotiation, as many bilateral negotiations with Japan. If you had totalled them all together they would be of the magnitude of this one, and maybe even more in terms of pages or the numbers of issues resolved.

So that was a fundamental demand of the U.S. negotiating team at that time, and we were also spending a lot of time on the multilateral process as a result of the launch of the Uruguay round, pulling some of the rest of the world into this process. I felt when I became USTR that the only way we were going to dissipate some of the political heat in the U.S. was to get some exercises going that would result in the opening of market opportunities around the world for U.S. exporters, and the U.S.-Canada Free Trade Agreement fit that need. So did the Uruguay round of trade negotiations. I wanted to change the mindset of the U.S. public which had been focussing in on protectionism and keeping imports out of the United States. We needed to turn that around and get people to think about export opportunities. We were devoting a lot of time, effort and energy into this whole multilateral process as well.

One of the appeals of having the U.S.-Canada free trade negotiation was that it gave us a little leverage in the other direction as well. Because we could say to the European Union, Brazil, India and other countries that were not enthusiastic about the multilateral process, "Look guys, if you don't want to get serious about the GATT negotiation, we're going to devote all our attention bilaterally to something like the U.S.-Canada Free Trade Agreement." Clearly we were serious, that we were prepared to do that.

Aside from that, I really felt that this was something that we needed to get done. At no time did the U.S. give up on this process. At no time did we ever give up on the idea of completing the U.S.-Canada free trade negotiations. We felt that it was historic, maybe it wasn't quite as relevant in the U.S. as it was in Canada, but it was pretty darn relevant for us, too. We were persuaded that it was historic, and we wanted this to be one of the major legacies of a Reagan administration. It fit in well with everything he believed, as you well know.

I also felt strongly that it was a win-win, and it was going to result in a lot of additional economic activity both in Canada and the United States. That was disbelieved by a good many people up here in Canada, as you recall. I gave a good number of speeches during that time frame, some in Canada, many in the United States, in which I said that both countries were going to win, that Canada would win more in relative terms, we might win more in absolute terms, but we were going to see a dramatic increase in international trade in both countries. That's precisely what happened. At the end of the day, we felt that we had to be credible with what came out of this exercise, and I believe we were. And I also believe that we are able to sell it in the U.S. Congress, because we did put together a package that was marketable in the U.S. Congress just as it turned out to be marketable here, and I believed we laid our groundwork well, a lot better than our successors did on the NAFTA. I think we laid our groundwork well in preparing for the Congressional debate that proceeded thereafter. As a consequence, we feel good about what transpired, because I don't believe we ever overpromised on the U.S.-Canada Free Trade Agreement. If anything, I believe we under-promised a little bit; I believe we overdelivered, and I do believe that's one of the reasons we had a lot of credibility at the end of the process.

SIMON REISMAN: Agreements do not get made in three days. There is no question that the last three days in Washington were critical days, and, with Clayton, I want to underscore that if there weren't for several years intensive work, by hundreds of people, covering a range of matters that will defy you if I were to name them, then they couldn't possibly have gone forward with what occurred in the last few days. That's not to take any credit away from Jim Baker and Derek Burney, who had the political authority to proceed and to cut a deal on some of the really tough issues which we were not able to cope with, that we were unable to make a deal.

I'm not going to go into the detail, I will say something like this: prior to Prime Minister Brian Mulroney asking me to take on as leader of the negotiations, he was wise enough to say, "Would you prepare a short bit of paper for me on how someone should go about doing this. We want to enter into a negotiation with the Americans, but you've been around, you've led on the Autopact, you've been involved in GATT close to fifty years, how would you go about doing this?", with no notion about how anybody go about doing this. Now, I want to make only one point on that – it's a good memo, I prepared it in about three hours, I gave it to him the day after he asked for it, but I said one thing in it that is relevant to the discussion at this moment about the last three days. I said, "Prime Minister, however we try at the official level, there are going to be a number of issues of profound political importance, that can only be resolved at the political level. I didn't identify what those issues would be, but I can tell you the issues I thought they would be were not the issues that came up to stump us in the end – I want you to know a bit about that.

I had a team of over one hundred people, working on a range of issues that were formidable. Bill Dymond, Mike Hart were two of them.
Stanley Hartt was on that – he was Deputy Minister of Finance at the
time, and he was responsible for banking and insurance and financial
services, and he was good enough to let me pick a former colleague of
mine to lead off on that, but we had tremendous support from the
Ministry of Finance.

I want to tell you that Clayton Yeutter came to Ottawa, I think it was in
the month of November of 1985, to meet a few people. Don Campbell,
who I think was an Assistant Deputy Minister, he shepherded Clayton
Yeutter from place to place, to see so-and-so and so-and-so, and he finally brought him to see me. Clayton had a couple of his lieutenants
with him, including Bill Merkin. Well, I want you to know something
about Bill Merkin. Bill Merkin was in it at the start and he was in it at the
finish. Apart from myself, I think he was the only other person who was
in it before Day 1 and after the end of the process, and there's a lot he
could tell.

I want to say a word about the meeting with Clayton Yeutter. You've
seen him now, you've heard him. He's an exceedingly pleasant person,
and he knows a great deal, and he was deeply involved in this as USTR.
We were engaged in pleasantries, we didn't go into very much deep
substance as to what we should be doing in the negotiations.

Peter Murphy, who unfortunately died as a young man, he was the
chief negotiator for the United States at the table, under Clayton
Yeutter. But he was not yet appointed at that time. He was on his way
back from Geneva, and I think that was the reason he was not with
Clayton Yeutter when he came to Ottawa. I must say if we had
Peter Murphy here, a great deal would be added to these discussions.
He and I spent a lot of time in the woods, and in the fields, sometimes
one-on-one, and we played baseball, we did all kinds of things, and he
would have been a great credit to this conference, if he was here. We
all regret that he's not here with us.

To Clayton Yeutter, on that day, I don't know what got into me,
I guess it was just sort of enthusiasm and seeing Clayton so positive
about it, I said, "You know, it'll be harder to make a small deal than a
big deal, so let's go for a big deal." Now what is a big deal? A big deal is
something that will fire the imagination of Canadians, and perhaps
Americans might get interested in it too. You know, for them, it wasn't
nearly the same sort of game. I said, "What we ought to go for … what
would you think, Clayton, if we went for the following objective: a border between Canada and the United States completely free of restrictions on goods and services by the year 2000."

Pretty bold. I didn't have authority to carry that through, but
I thought with something that imaginative, and with the strong sup-

port we were getting from Brian Mulroney and his key ministers, that we would pull it off. I got encouragement from Clayton. Maybe he was too optimistic. Certainly, I was too optimistic. Perhaps I had forgotten the 10–10 vote in the Senate Finance Committee. Because I do remember, and Bill Merkin will too, that Mike Smith, who was on his way to some other job in this cold Canadian winter – no it was not a winter day, it was November – but he had a tuque on, it was cold in Ottawa, and he was sitting there and he was more worried about the cold than what we were talking about, but very quietly he said, "Have you ever heard of Congress?" I had spent many years knowing that whatever the United States executive wanted to do, and they wanted to do many things, there were times when the Congress stood in the way. And this could be one such occasion. I didn't answer his question, but I said, "You look after Congress, I will look after the provinces." I don't know why the provinces were looked upon as they are. As it turned out, it was something like that in reality.

And by the way, we tried that, we went after the U.S. on the whole ten yards on procurement, we went after them the whole business on services, we went after them on a half a dozen other things that were probably not doable but would lead to that ultimate objective of a border free of restrictions and restraints. And of course, as Secretary Baker indicated, you've got to be pragmatic about this, you have to know what's possible, you have to know the political constraints. But that doesn't mean you shouldn't have objectives.

During the entire process, we made it very clear to the U.S. side that we had to have something on the trade remedy side and in the dispute settlement side which you give Canadians greater security than they had in trade with the U.S. We had to have something on that. It didn't matter what else was in the agreement, and I would disagree with Derek Burney on this – it was more than tariffs. We had a lot of stuff, but we had to have something on that, and we did not get a respectable offer on that over the several years. And when some of us suspected that not enough was being attention was being paid by the political level in the United States, it was because we had not had anything that was substantive on those critical issues.

There was one event that occurred that Clayton may not know anything about. – there was a man by the name of Bob Strauss. Now the last time this came up I referred to him as the first USTR. He wasn't called USTR, but he was doing that job. It was when the U.S. government took the trade function out of State Department, and made a separate job out of it, and Robert Strauss who's on the political level, the highest level in the United States, I think Chairman of the Democratic National Committee. He was working for one of our bankers, a man at the Bank of Nova Scotia, a man by the name of Cedric Ritchie, and he had a big meeting going on in New York with all his clients and they wanted to hear about the trade deal. He said, "Come on down, I want you to do this." And I said, "I can't come down, we're right in the middle of negotiations." He said, "I'll send the plane around for you." He got me into deep trouble that I accepted a plane ride from a bank. But any way, I talked my way out of that.

When I got there, it turned out that the reason I was invited down was to have a session with Bob Strauss. I don't know who put him on to me, but Cedric said, "Before you make your speech in this group, I want you to have ten minutes with Robert Strauss." He was one of the Texas mafia and he knew all that was going on. And he sat me down, literally, and he proceeded to tell me that what I was seeking at the table was not available and would not become available. The notion that we could get some kind of exemption or some softening or some security in our trade, or that there could be a dispute settlement mechanism that had equal representation of the two countries with binding provisions on the countervail – he said forget it, you're not going to get that. You can't get that.

Then he got up from the table, it was in a little room, and he proceeded to the door. And I said, "Aren't you going to want a reply? Wouldn't you like to hear what I have to say about this matter?" "Well," he said, "If I have to." It was like that. And I said, "Well, I'm going to say one thing to you. If we don't get some significant and substantive concessions in that area – trade remedy, dispute settlement – there will not be a deal." And very properly, being both political and on the bureaucrat side, he said, "How can you say that? Who the hell are you to say that?"

I said, "Well, Canada works in peculiar ways. In the past, whenever I was involved in trade negotiations, from 1946 on, we spoke to nobody. I can remember on the first occasion when we went to the second session of the Parity Committee for GATT, Hector McKinnon and I, and John Deutsch, went to meet with Mackenzie King, and I was there to take some notes. I remember Mackenzie King saying – this was in 1946 – go and make a good deal for Canada. Come back and tell me about it when you are ready, and don't speak to anybody on the way." Literally. He didn't want to hear about anything himself, and certainly, the idea of talking to the press.

Well things had become quite different by 1985, and on the first occasion that I met with the provinces on something called the Continuing Committee on Trade, when the meeting was over I walked out, right through the press, and they were unhappy. A man by the name of Joe Clark, who was a colleague of our friend John Crosbie, he was Minister of Foreign Affairs. He was the chairman of a cabinet committee of which John Crosbie was a prominent and continuously attending member, who I reported to when I was negotiating. And he ticked me off, and he said, "You walk through the press, I got a lot of complaints. You shouldn't do that." I said, "Well, you know, if that's the way you want it …" He said, "You don't have to tell them everything, but talk to them."

Well as it turns out I talked to them, and I kind of enjoyed it, and I talked to them some more, and I got to the point where I was better known in the country on trade matters than almost anybody with the exception of the Prime Minister. And for one reason or another, perhaps because I was pretty outspoken and pretty tough, they felt confident.

I said to Bob Strauss, "My position in Canada as a bureaucrat is such that if I were to say to the Prime Minister, 'this is not a good deal,' and for some godforsaken reason the Prime Minister wanted to go ahead any way, and I said to the country, 'this is not a good deal,' there would not be a deal." That's what I said to him. So he sat down again, and his face dropped about a yard, and he said, "So what are we going to do?" And I said, "Well, you'll have to make some concessions in this field if you want an agreement."

Well later I had similar visit from a couple of people from the Brookings Institute, and I don't know who the hell put them on to me. But I want you to know that this was no cake walk, this was a difficult thing from beginning to end. The most unhappy day in my experience during negotiations is when I walked out and reported to the Prime Minister a suspended negotiation. Of course the PM knew about that and the key ministers knew that we were going to do that, and we had to do that. But I knew once I did that, you'd begin to lose control of what happens. If you say to the Prime Minister that you can't make a deal at the table, well, you know, in a way you are throwing in the towel. So I didn't like that, I would have liked to make a deal.

Clayton said to me one day, "If it weren't for you, we could have had a deal a year earlier." And I said to him, "Yeah, if we settled on your terms." And that's not what I was being paid to do. We had terms of our own. But, Clayton, if you had been able to euchre out that concession that we eventually got on trade settlement, I wouldn't have had to quit or walk out or turn it back to the PM. So you have a bone to pick with me, and I have a bone to pick with you.

I want to say just two more things and very briefly, and it's this: Brian Mulroney was stalwart on this from beginning to end. He said to me, "You can call me if you get into trouble, if things are difficult." I didn't call him very often, but Brian used to like to use the telephone, and he would phone and we would talk. And throughout the process, and there were a number of occasions when it looked like this was dead, particularly in the period after the election was called.

Maybe this is tales out of school, but I'm old enough now not to worry about that. I'm probably the oldest man in this group. Right around his own table, with the exception of a very few stalwart ministers, there were people who said, "Back off. Walk away from it. We'll come back to it some other day. You're going to lose the election if you proceed on this basis."

And I know that the Prime Minister said, "We should do this, it's good for Canada, and we're going to win it." So I want you to know that he deserves tremendous credit. In the end when it was settled, I think it was Jim Baker who said that it was the President of the United States, who was Ronnie Reagan, and it was Mulroney, at the political level who made this thing happen. For Canada, it was the greatest trade deal – I'm not saying everything was perfect, there are a lot of things left to do – but it was the biggest and perhaps greatest trade deal in our entire commercial history. And I think it was important for the U.S. too.

PETER MCPHERSON: I think when we step back and look at what was involved here, the U.S. wanted to open up Canada in terms of reducing tariffs and investment, generally. Canada wanted to keep the U.S. open. That was sort of the two sided motivation. How that translated into specifics though became quite difficult. The U.S. was saying we have to constrain subsidies in Canada, and the U.S. weren't particularly willing to constrain our subsidies, because we thought in most cases they didn't really affect the trade between the two countries. Canada was saying that we have to restrain countervailing duties and anti-dumping provisions, and we have to have a dispute settlement mechanism. That was very difficult for us, because our Congress was really making it very clear that they didn't want to do that.

And so, when you think about the political dynamics – there's a lot of substance, as Clayton was referring to earlier, energy and a number of other things that were worked on – but the political dynamics, what made it possible to have an agreement or not, really rested in this set of issues and solutions to these problems. That was really clear almost from the beginning. It was clear in those discussions between Simon and Peter, it was the reason that the September 23rd negotiation was broken off by Canada, and it was clear right up until, for example, 8:30 or so the night of October 3rd, when despite all that happened, the negotiation almost stopped and we didn't deliver the letter up to the Hill.

Let me talk about those various steps for just a moment. Peter Murphy felt – the U.S. side felt – that in those lengthy discussions that he really couldn't say no to Canada, on the key things that Canada wanted on anti-dumping etc., because in effect the negotiations would stop.

On the other hand, he couldn't really move towards doing those because it would have closed it down in Congress. So I think while it is easy to look back and be critical or concerned about negotiation tactics, Peter Murphy was in a very tight box. During that period of time when there was sort of fencing on the table on this issue, there was a lot of other very substantive work going on.

The next point I would like to make is when Canada broke off negotiations over this set of issues. I would say, and I don't know if Americans have broadly said this, I don't think we would have had an agreement if Canada hadn't broken off the negotiations. I think if anything, Simon, I would say that you broke them off a little too late. Maybe a couple of weeks earlier wouldn't have been bad, because in fact you left us very little time to get it done before the October 3rd deadline, and breaking off the negotiations really galvanized and brought up to the very head at the highest levels the key issues within the U.S. government. Clearly they were already there in Canada, but it brought it up in the U.S. government with Jim Baker, who was in a unique position, having been chief of staff to the President, Chair of the Inter-Regency Economic Group, etc.

But also it got Congress to reconsider their position. I think for the most part the Congress said, well, Canada's tariffs are too high, they need our market, let them come to us. I think the fact that maybe there wasn't going to be an agreement really began to dawn on people on the Hill because of the breakoff of negotiations. Not the first day, by the way – it took a few days. If Canada had come back the next day it wouldn't have had the same impact, in my judgement.

But then we of course had to solve these problems. It is Jean Anderson who is the real expert in all this. In the end what the mechanism does on law then into effect substitute the U.S. Judiciary under certain circumstances with a panel, that applies U.S. law. It's very complex and I don't need to deal with it here, but in effect it voided the most severe questions that our Congress had, and, at the same time, I think showed some restraint.

Then at 8 o'clock or so, 9 o'clock that night, October 3rd, we almost had another crisis, over whether or not the Congress could adopt new law. In my mind there was almost no more serious point, because I believe Canada felt extraordinarily strongly about how we are going to handle this. Ambassador Gotlieb, who had been stalwart throughout this process came up – he being an international lawyer – with some wording and concepts that essentially got us through this. In any case, it was a very clever way to work through this.

Central to this whole process was the difficulty to deal with this set of issues, and we never dealt with them totally, but we dealt with them in a way that was politically acceptable to both countries. I will make two last comments:

One, it seems to me that it isn't widely enough talked about that a lot of egos were submerged during this whole process. When it moved up to a different level in the U.S. government with Jim Baker taking the lead, almost historically positioned to do this, Clayton Yeutter who was then the USTR, continued to play an enormous role, and a deeply substantive role, but not as visible publically. Clayton is to be congratulated for what he did, and his staff, and the USTR generally as the institution had a different public profile.

In the same way, Simon, who was always a contentious character with us Americans, but was so key in all this. In fact, if he had not taken the position under his Prime Minister and under Derek Burney, and supported what had happened in a very constructive way, we would not have had an agreement. I don't think our countries have broadly recognized the role, because as we all know individuals don't always work together even for the most important of objectives like that.

My last point is that President Reagan felt deeply about free trade. As Jim Baker said today, President Reagan was talking about it in his campaign back in 1979. So it was no surprise that he was right there. We all knew where he was. That leadership is greatly appreciated. It is true, however, that in your country, you had a Prime Minister who really put on the line his whole political future, changed the policy really.

I mean, it was a historical event, and when we in the United States – we don't know about all the politics and the struggles the way we no doubt should here – but we think that your Prime Minister here as making a historical position that we think forty or fifty years from now people will look back and think, that was really something.

CLAYTON YEUTTER: If I may I would like to add about a 20 second supplement to that. Peter's comments were very gracious with respect to how we handled things at the last. What really happened there was that we felt that this was the kind of situation where you had to throw out the organizational charts and use the structure that would get things done. And it had to be done at the presidential and prime ministerial level. We couldn't fool around any longer lower than that. You had to get it up to the very top, get these very difficult issues resolved, and put them behind us. That's why we just fundamentally restructured and did it, as Peter said, with a lot of team work on our side, and I think, a lot of teamwork on the Canadian side as well. And all the egos did get submerged and it brought about the final result in a very satisfactory way.

But the other thing I really wanted to mention in this regard is that Peter brought up a very good point when he said that the breakdown of the negotiations finally awakened the Congress. And it takes a lot to awaken the U.S. Congress. Because they have so many things on their agendas that they don't really pay too much attention unless there is a crisis at hand. Fundamentally the walkout created a crisis, and they had to say, "Hey, what's going on here! Are we going to torpedo things?" Until then, I don't think there was any chance whatsoever that we could have done any tweaking of the anti-dumping and countervailing duty laws. That was just out of the question, and it was only at that point that people finally said, well maybe we have to find some room to manoeuvre. That gave us some flexibility to have a little creativity.

But because this is a primarily Canadian audience I wanted to mention that because in my view what that awakening process reflected was the great affection Americans have for Canadians. Underlying all of this was the fact that Americans like Canadians. That's probably an understatement. At the end, I think everyone in the U.S.was really galvanized to not let this thing go down because of the U.S.-Canadian relationship and the very closeness that existed all this time. I think that was a very fundamental factor at the tail end.

JOHN C. CROSBIE: I am not going to discuss the negotiations leading up to the conclusion of an agreement, because I wasn't the minister at that time, as some of you who read the papers may know. Since I have some knowledge of Pat Carney, I want to make it quite plain that I wasn't the Minister of International Trade at that time. But on March 31st, 1988, the Prime Minister had a cabinet shuffle – it's very common in our system. And it was Jeremy Thorpe who said this: "Greater love hath no man than this, that he lay down his friends for his life." This is what these cabinet shuffles are designed to do. Now Hubert Humphrey once said, "I've never made a speech which was too long. I've loved them all." That's my problem as well, so I'm conscious of the time here.

Anybody who is going to try to promote a free trade agreement must remember what Macauley said in 1824. He said "free trade, one of the greatest blessings which a government can confer on a people, is in almost every country unpopular." That is the first thing to understand. Free trade is unpopular. And it's unpopular because everybody who has some protection and has an immediate interest in it is automatically against free trade, while the great collectivity who free trade is going to help know nothing about it, they are not excited about it, they aren't going to come out and sacrifice anything for it, they don't know what the hell it is all about. So the people who are on the side of arguing in favour of a free trade arrangement are on the difficult side of the equation.

My own position was this – Thomas Paine said this in his book on *The Rights of Man*: "the prosperity of any commercial nation is regulated by the prosperity of the rest. If they are poor, she cannot be rich; and her condition, be it what it may, is an index of the height of the commercial trade in other nations." In other words, we can only all become wealthier if we trade freely with one another. If all our neighbours are poor and inconsequential, then how can we be rich because we'll have nobody to trade with?

So I was very keenly in favour of free trade, and was delighted when the Prime Minister announced that we were going to attempt to reach a free trade agreement with the United States.I was on the committee that the Trade Minister and Simon reported to, and I was delighted when Simon was appointed, because I had knowledge of Simon. And I knew what a bulldog he was, and what his fantastic abilities were, and he had negotiated the 1965 Auto Pact. He was the ideal man for the job.

The agreement has now been reached, and I think Clayton said that in the United States they had to get it through Congress, which is what their job was. In Canada, we had to get it through the people. Our problem wasn't getting it through the Congress, getting it through the House of Commons. We had a majority. And of course, we could get it through the House of Commons. We didn't have a majority in the Senate. We could not force it through the Senate, which meant we were going to have to go through the people. So we had to get it through the people. And that's an even harder job that getting it through the Congress.

Now, what happened when the agreement was announced? It was denounced by the leader of the Liberal Party at that time as a "sellout." That's the support we got from the national Liberal Party. Ed Broadbent, leading the NDP party, "within a quarter century, we could be absorbed totally, lock, stock and barrel, if this is not stopped.". Have you ever heard such piffle and such nonsense? But this was the official position of the NDP party, this is what they spent months trying to put across. That if we signed a trade agreement with the United States, within a quarter century we were going to be absorbed lock, stock and barrel by the Americans. That shows a lot of faith in Canada, that we're so supine, that we're so spineless, we're such jellyfish that if we sign a trade agreement with another country we're going to become completely absorbed by them. I'd like to see an American that could absorb me!

The Liberal Party of Canada has completely reversed itself, as we all know, and are enthusiastically supporting the FTA and the NAFTA, and as well they are supporting free trade with every other country of the world who will pay them any attention. The next country to get their attention will likely be Albania when that's all settled down there. The NDP persist in ignoring the real world and ignoring the fact that their union membership in Ontario in the auto industry, has gained immensely from the 1965 Canada/U.S. Auto Pact bringing free trade to the automobile industry. They ignored that.

Why? Because the labour movement today, and socialist parties have gotten so much from the status quo that they cannot stand to see any change in it. These are the the most reactionary, conservative bodies in society today. The union movement, and parties which depend on the union movement for support, they are against any change in the status quo. And who were the revolutionaries? God help us, it was the business community, who wanted to see change. It was a complete reversal – Karl Marx would have dropped his drawers had he witnessed it.

The opposition party and the labour movement, assisted by many in the media who love promoting the negative – that was your vice-president down there of remote memory who said "the nattering nabobs of negativism," are represented in the media, because it's easier to report the negative than anything positive. So the claim that we were giving away Canadian sovereignty, God help us, surrendering our independence, creating a branch plant mentality ... We had to deal with lies, distortions and misrepresentations of what the impact of the trade deal is going to be on Canada.

And you have to got to understand this: a simple lie or exaggeration or allegation is far easier for the common, ordinary person to follow than the complicated response that we who were defending the deal had to make. Because if you are going to explain the truth, it's complicated. The truth is not simple. It's a very complicated thing, particularly in these situations. So what did we face as the Liberal Senate, under the instructions of Mr. Turner, refused to pass the legislation authorizing this agreement? So we were forced to go into an election.

What were the themes of the opposition parties in the election? Its provisions were distorted and misrepresented. I mean, I witnessed this myself, I had my opponent in my district, going with a loud speaker going to old age homes, telling them that it was the end of old age security, of old age pensions, they were in dire peril, if this fantastically treacherous free trade deal with the United States went through. That was the tactics used.

The fears of people who are dependent upon government are easy to arouse and they are very difficult to assuage, because the public tends to believe predictions of dire effects no matter how far-fetched they are. The arguments were crass and false, we were going to lose Medicare, we couldn't continue programs to assist regional development or to overcome regional disparity, our cultural institutions would be unprotected and our books, magazines, radio and TV, music, movies and stage productions would completely be dominated by the U.S. and American conglomerates. According to Bob White, the whole auto industry would go south. The only part of the auto industry that has gone south is his members going down to Florida for holidays.

The other major argument was that we were going to lose all our water, we were going to have our water cut off. Canada's got about a third of the world's resources of water and people were led to believe that the Americans would be able to siphon off our water. We'd have to sell it to the Americans. Well, we should sell it to somebody – what good is it doing us to have all that water and the rest of the world needing water. But any way you can't be reasonable or rational, so don't put that in the record.

So this is the kind of things that were being said, so I was asked by the Prime Minister to lead the affirmative campaign, to try to sell the free trade deal. I didn't think an attitude and approach of quiet reasonableness was going to be heard in the midst of the hysterical opposition that the Liberals and the NDP and the organized labour movement was putting up. The choice wasn't between free trade and the status quo, it was between free trade and growing U.S.protectionism. That's we had to get across. We tried the third option, under Mr. Trudeau, tried to divert our trade so we didn't become too dependent on the United States, and we couldn't do it, because the pull of having that huge market next to us, and they are all down there pretty well speaking English, and they can understand us and we can understand them, which makes us increasingly suspicious of course of them. It's a lot easier than selling to a country where you have to use a different language.

We were completely dependent on international trade for our prosperity, and we lack the brute political power of the U.S. or the European community, so how do protect ourselves? We know we haven't got much power. We can only protect ourselves if we use our heads. If we can fool them into entering into a free trade agreement. If we can fool them into agreeing somehow to blunt this shocking weapon they have with countervail and other problems that we have. What we need is a fair and rules-based open international trading system, which is why the point was so important that Simon had to walk out.

We had a free trade agreement once in my home province of Newfoundland, in 1890, between Newfoundland and the United States. We're way ahead of anything that is here on the mainland here. It was entered into by Sir Robert Bond and Secretary of State Blaine. And who stopped it? The Canadian government. They complained to the British, the Imperial authorities, that this was going to be damaging to Canada, and they wouldn't ratify our free trade agreement. So I was a free trader from a way back, and delighted that we were going to attempt this.

Now I say I didn't think that taking a mild, reasonable, rational route was going to get me anywhere, I spoke two days after being appointed to a group in Ottawa. I pointed out that the "CBC-type snivellers" in Toronto were spreading alarm about the loss of our cultural identity, and I advised the audience to be aware of the self-anointed fakirs and philosophers of hog town where that kind of alarmist reasoning came from. The professional anti-Americans – envious, morally smug – that's who spreads this nonsense about our culture. We don't have to love the Americans but we have to live with them. That's the simple sense of it all. I denounced those I described as the "cultural literati" and the "encyclopedia peddlers" who opposed the FTA.

The opponents of the FTA didn't think Canadians can hack it. They didn't think that we could compete. These are subsidy seekers, the security-blanket supplicants. Well, I haven't got time to get into more of that, unfortunately.

Just to deal with the premiers – there were five of them that supported the agreement from the beginning, including Mr. Bourassa, very important. Two later joined them, Peckford from Newfoundland and Buchanan of Nova Scotia. But Mr. Peterson of Ontario, Pawley of Manitoba and Ghiz of P.E.I. opposed the pact. Now we didn't have to have their support, fortunately, to enter into the agreement. But we needed some help from them to implement it. And I wanted to say a kind word about Mr. Peterson here, because while he vigorously argued against entering into the agreement, he calmly accepted the reality of it, and didn't fuss too much when we proceeded on any way, even with respect to liquor, beer and wine.

The biggest problem we had was the storm about what jobs would be lost. Every day, you'd pick up the paper, another employer or labour movement or opposition was announcing that X business was closing, X manufacturing plant was closing, because of the FTA, and so many jobs were going to be lost. This was very hard to deal with, so we had to scour the papers ourselves to see where a new business was being announced or where a business was going to expand. It didn't matter or not if it had anything to do with the free trade agreement. Actually, we'd claim that it was because of the free trade agreement.

After these negotiators did their job, and they did a super job, and we were lucky that we had rational Americans acting for the President on trade, and serious attention was being paid attention to the cause, we were successful in getting this agreement adopted, which ten years later is a brilliant success, and which everybody else apparently thinks is a brilliant success, because they are now all in favour of it.

I'm going to end with this little thought here. My late mentor, Premier J.R. Smallwood of Newfoundland, once said "So long as the light holds out to burn, the vilest sinner may return." Welcome back Jean Chretien.

IAN MACDONALD: Now we've finished with the prepared statements, so we want to give the other members of this enlarged panel a moment to make brief comments. I know that Bill Merkin wants to say a word about Peter Murphy.

WILLIAM MERKIN: Thanks, and I appreciate Simon saying a few words too. A number of us at the table here on the U.S.side that the good fortune of working with and getting to know Peter Murphy over the years. He was an extraordinary individual, an experienced, first rate trade negotiator despite what some people write in their memoirs. I think it's well known that Simon and Peter were of different ilk, different negotiating styles, and that led to a lot of entertaining sessions for us. But I think that any conference that looks at the results of the free trade agreement needs to recognize Peter's contribution to this. He's no longer with us to trumpet his own accomplishments, and I just felt as having been his deputy all those years, that I just wanted to say a few words about Peter.

CHARLES E. ROH: While I would certainly echo Merk's remarks and I would also like to give a lot of credit to the living, all the people here, whatever their differences along the way were all devoted to getting a free trade agreement. I also have to live up to my reputation. I'm not in the U.S. government any more, but I have friends who are there, and I want all the Canadian government officials to know you don't necessarily have to walk out of a deal with the U.S. to get the thing finished. That was the dynamic of this particular deal. We actually got a NAFTA without any walkouts at all.

The last thing is, I would like to close with a quote from Peter Murphy, which is one I've used many times when I've been involved in deals and were at that sort of point where everything seems a mess and there's no way out. I vividly remember Peter coming out to address the rather disheartened U.S. delegation and say to all of us – and this will sound very familiar to Canadians who know Peter's speaking style – "Well, I think we're moving forward, but I'm not sure in what direction."

CLAYTON YEUTTER: About what John had to say ... I can recall, John, as this marketability process began the United Auto Workers of Canada announced their opposition, and if I remember the numbers correctly, they estimated 300,000 automobile industry jobs would be lost to the United States as a result of this agreement. And that very same day, the United Autoworkers in the United States announced their opposition and they estimated 300,000 automobile industry jobs would be lost to Canada.

IAN MACDONALD: Question for both sides – why was dispute settlement the dealmaker and the dealbreaker?

SIMON REISMAN: As I think was indicated by Clayton, the notion of an exemption for Canada on the countervail and antidumping was not offered. And when we came to examine the U.S. countervail and antidump law as it then stood, it wasn't very different from ours, and it wasn't all that different from what they had internationally. The problem was how they interpreted it, and what they did with it, and how responsive they were to the protectionists, and how arbitrary the handling of that legislation was. Now if we would get a good dispute settlement mechanism in place, it would make up for some of the problems that we had with the trade remedy legislation. And it was critical, critical from the opening day because what's the point of entering into an agreement when as soon as you are successful, some protectionist – and in the U.S. you'll get lots – are going to be able to prevail on the Administration, through the Congress and get things done that interfere with our trade. We were not going to make any such deal, and it was vital that we get something on those fronts.

IAN MACDONALD: Why was it so tough with the Congress?

JEAN ANDERSON: If you mean why the Chapter 19 dispute settlement system was tough with the Congress, I mean, the whole issue was tough with the Congress, but the interesting issue in getting this passed as a part of the implementing legislation for the agreement was the question whether is was constitutional in the U.S. system to have a system whereby private individuals where other nationalities, not judges, were playing the role of judges, taking the role of judges, to review national, legal cases, if you will. And we did a lot of work – I remember the night that the proposal to do this kind of dispute settlement system had crystalized, and actually Chip Roh and I, it was about midnight, were sitting in USTR, and we looked at each other and we said, "Oh my God, is this constitutional?" That was the beginning of figuring it out. And it is constitutional, I have no doubt in my mind about that. There have been a couple of really frivolous cases filed, challenging it. But it is.

IAN MACDONALD: So there is a big difference between an agreement in principle and a legal text.

JEAN ANDERSON: Oh, yes. That too.

WILLIAM DYMOND: Could I just add to what Simon said on the economics? We knew going into this that taking away our tariff would expose Canadian industry to massive competition in the United States. And we knew that huge investments would be required to rationalize ourselves out of a fragmented, small-scale manufacturing base. How could we defend that if the benefits got from the United States were not some way insulated, protected, defensible, against the application of what we call contingent protection? I remember Simon making the point so many times to say that a zero tariff in the United States isn't worth anything if, from one day to the next, it can be replaced with a 10–15% antidumping or countervailing duty. That's why if we couldn't get the immunity, we needed a dispute settlement system in order to insure investors that we had a mechanism in place.

CLAYTON YEUTTER: Politically this was a really tough issue on both sides. We knew that would probably be the last issue in this negotiation. And we knew that somehow we were going to ultimately reach an accommodation on this issue if we were going to have a U.S.-Canada Free Trade Agreement. But that didn't make it any easier. And I say that speaking as someone who doesn't like antidumping laws; I would just like to see them disappear from the face of the earth. But the fact is that Congress likes antidumping laws, and not only do they really don't want to tweak them in the way that Canada was asking here, their proclivity would have been to go the other way, and make them more stringent rather than less stringent.

IAN MACDONALD: Was it part of your strategy all along that the thing would be kicked upstairs at the end with the President and the Prime Minister?

CLAYTON YEUTTER: I am not surprised that we had to go to that level. It's rare in any trade negotiations that that occurs, because hopefully you'll work things out at the trade minister level. But this was different, this was historic. You know, the only other free trade agreement we ever negotiated was with Israel, which was a very small one that we had done a year or so before, so it wasn't all surprising that it got kicked all the way up.

IAN MACDONALD: Let me ask Stanley Hartt a question. There's a story that on the night of October 3rd, Mr. Mulroney wanted to speak to President Reagan, who was at Camp David, and that the Americans were not very anxious for that to happen. Can you speak to that?

STANLEY H. HARTT: I'm a great admirer of President Reagan so I don't want to impugn the given reason for why it was that Prime Minister Mulroney was discouraged from speaking to him, which was that he was watching a movie. I suspect that what had happened by that time was that Secretary Baker was seized with these very difficult issues that we've been discussing, how to find a very narrow way through this difficult minefield of dispute settlement. He was groping towards a solution, and I don't think that he thought it was a very useful idea to have the Prime Minister and the President start to negotiate it in a state of the President's briefing on the subject. I mean it was Baker, who very shortly thereafter, stormed into his own anteroom, where we were headquartered, and made the settling offer on dispute resolution, which was of course that the binational panels would render binding decisions on disputes under the agreement, that we would have a regime where we would continue to try to negotiate a new remedy regime, over five, later extended to seven years, which we did, and it just petered out.

Finally, that changes could be made to existing national laws but to do so you would have to specify that you intended to apply to the other party, and that the change itself was reviewable at to whether it conformed to the spirit of the agreement and the GATT. So that's where you were, and the Prime Minister is going to phone the President, anything could have happened. I think it was smart of Baker to keep the group which were discussing it.

PETER MCPHERSON: The problem that night was over the new law, the changes, and the Canadians didn't want to have new law to come into existence, and we had a terrible problem telling Congress that they couldn't have new law. That's where I commented earlier that I thought Allan Gotlieb had some very interesting ideas, and so forth ... And I can see you shaking your heads there ... But in any case, I believe that we were in the middle of that, and Baker felt strongly that we just needed to struggle.

CLAYTON YEUTTER: I just want to say in terms of handling any negotiation, you never go to the top person, in this case the President of the United States, until you are ready. We weren't ready to do that. You have to have an appeal mechanism in here, and once you get all the way to the top, there is no further appeal, and you either get a deal or you break down. You can't afford to run that risk.

SIMON REISMAN: My recollections about Presidents and Prime Ministers and conversations between them relates to a somewhat different time and a somewhat different issue. I think it was the day after I walked out with my team, and I think on the American side they wanted to establish that this was bone fide, I mean, who the hell is this guy to walk out. So word came through the U.S. Ambassador to Canada, to the President's either Chief of Staff or I don't know Derek whether it was you or someone else in the Prime Minister's office, but the President wanted to speak to the Prime Minister. And the Prime Minister was wise, and he wanted to consult his people, before making any kind of a reply to this.

The advice he got – Derek talked to us, and we gave him our views and other ministers did – there's no point in the Prime Minister talking to the President if he has nothing to put on the table. In other words, confirming that the decision to walk away was a government decision, not the decision of a bureaucrat. It was well thought out and it was done, and unless they've got something to put on the table, there's no point to that conversation taking place. And it never took place. I think the answer went back that there was nothing to talk about.

But what happened is that it confirmed that this was real. And then things began to happen. It was after that that solutions were sought of an extraordinary kind, of an imaginative kind.

And Peter, you were asking earlier, about who sort of found the answer to that last conundrum, what do you do in respect to changes that Congress may wish you to make. My recollection – and it could be wrong – is that Jim Baker said to you, the Canadians will break off on this, they've advised the Prime Minister. The Prime Minister spoke to each member of the delegation after talking to Derek. And Derek went back to Baker and said, "It's off. Can't do it. Can't take it." Then Baker to you, Baker said to you and probably to Clayton, "We've got to go back to the drawing board and find an answer." Now you may have consulted Jean, or Charles or your battery of very efficient legal people. All I said earlier is that it wasn't Allan Gotlieb.

IAN MACDONALD: Let me ask one question then. President Reagan called this deal a win-win at the time. Has it been?

CLAYTON YEUTTER: It really has. The trade numbers clearly indicate that, and you'll have some more discussion of that tomorrow. So I think that there is no question about that. I've seen some articles in the last couple of days that indicate some question about whether the productivity advances that were anticipated in Canada actually occurred, and there is some disappointment on that level. In my view, that's misdirected, because although the productivity increases in Canada have not been – and this is basically manufacturing – have not been as great as they have been in the U.S. in the last ten years, they've still been reasonably impressive in my view.

What they reflect is the fact that we've done even better in the U.S., but that's been primarily to a massive restructuring of the American economy and a huge adoption of computer technology and other information technology, a little faster and more extensively than in Canada. I think the gains of productivity and efficiency have occurred. In fact, I picked up an article yesterday that quoted somebody here in Canada as saying that we know have a regional economy going north-south with the U.S., and that is precisely what we figured would happen. In fact, I had companies in the U.S. telling me if we're going to get massive improvements in efficiency and productivity in our operations because we're going to start going north-south instead of east-west, and obviously that has occurred, and to the benefit of everybody.

The Shamrock Summit, March 17, 1985: President Reagan flies into Quebec City aboard Air Force One. Prime Minister Mulroney lays on a red carpet welcome that includes an honour guard of red-coated Mounties – a touch undoubtedly appreciated by the former Hollywood actor. On the bilateral agenda: Free trade. (CP Picture Archives)

Ron and Brian, as they called each other, shake hands on it as the Canada and U.S. delegations meet at the Chateau Frontenac, site of the Shamrock Summit. Reagan and Mulroney agreed to engage on two issues – acid rain and free trade. (Prime Minister's Office)

Leap of Faith: On September 5, 1985, Donald S. Macdonald, chairman of the Royal Commission on Canada's Economic Prospects, tables his three-volume report recommending Canada enter a free trade agreement with the United States. Within the month, Mulroney asks Reagan to begin the negotiations that lead to the Free Trade Agreement.
(Montreal *Gazette*, Pierre Obendrauf)

Staunch allies: Mulroney and Robert Bourassa, on his return to office as Premier of Quebec in December, 1985. From the beginning, Bourassa was a solid supporter of free trade. Quebec's support, and Alberta's, proved indispensable for Mulroney in selling the Free Trade Agreement in the 1988 election. (Montreal *Gazette*, John Mahoney)

"I believe you have sold us out": The defining moment of the 1988 election – the leaders' debate on October 25, where Liberal Leader John Turner accused Mulroney of selling out Canada in the free trade deal with the U.S. The electric exchange resulted in a Liberal surge and a Conservative meltdown in the polls. But in the end, on November 21, Mulroney's Tories were returned with a second majority government and a mandate to implement the FTA. (CP Picture Archives)

On the campaign trail: The 1988 Canadian election became a referendum on free trade, and the campaign was the most tumultuous in the second half of the twentieth century. On the last weekend before the November 21 vote, Mulroney campaigned in Quebec, whose support, along with the West, was crucial to selling the deal to voters. (Len Sidaway, *Montreal Gazette*)

It's a deal. Trade ministers Jaime Serra Puche, Carla Hills and Michael Wilson sign the NAFTA agreement in San Antonio, Texas, in October 1992, as President Carlos Salinas, President Bush and Prime Minister Mulroney look on. (Prime Minister's Office)

PART THREE

The Record

The Canada-U.S. FTA: Real Results Versus Unreal Expectations

RICHARD G. LIPSEY

This year the Canada-U.S. FTA observed its tenth anniversary. The first tariff cuts took place ten years ago and the current year saw the end of its 10-year transition period. Its terms are now fully implemented. Measured against the predictions of disaster by some of its most severe critics, the FTA must be seen as a massive success. Measured against the prediction made by many of its more enthusiastic supporters that it would be a universal panacea for all of Canada's ills, it must be seen as a failure. Measured against reasonable expectations, it is a significant success.

A first step towards a reasoned assessment comes with the realisation that the FTA was not a wholly new initiative. Instead, it represented a continuation of a long-standing policy of trade liberalisation pursued by all Canadian governments since the 1930s.

The first steps in Canada's slow march towards trade liberalisation occurred in the late 1930s when Canada and the U.S. signed two reciprocal trade liberalising treaties. The first was in response to a U.S. initiative. Alarmed by the rising tide of protectionism, the Roosevelt administration negotiated several trade liberalising treaties with individual countries. Tariffs reductions were negotiated bilaterally and then extended to other countries on almost favoured nation basis. The second treaty was negotiated in 1937 at Canadian initiative. These treaties made significant cuts in both countries' very high tariffs.

Reproduced from *World Economic Affairs*, fall, 1999.

In 1948, a free trade agreement with the United States was discussed at some length but the private discussions were broken off without any public debate when the Prime Minister, W.L. Mackenzie King, turned against the proposal. In the same year, Canada became a founding member of the General Agreement on Tariffs and Trade (the GATT), committing the country to a policy of progressive trade liberalisation. Over the next 40 years, the GATT rolled back tariffs among developed countries from the high levels that ruled in 1945 to the much lower levels that ruled in the mid 1980s – these averaged less than 5% in the United States and about 10% in Canada. *The C.D. Howe Institute estimated that by 1985 Canada had removed approximately 80% of the trade barriers that it had in place in 1934!*

The Canadian economy underwent major structural adjustments to these tariff cuts, particularly as a result of the Kennedy and Tokyo rounds. In almost every industrial classification old jobs were lost and new ones created, while Canadian imports and exports both rose dramatically. These big changes took place without major public debate and without significant outcry over any perceived massive economic dislocation. On the evidence, by 1980, Canadian industry had grown up and was able to compete in the world league without heavy tariff protection.

GROWING PROBLEMS IN THE WORLD TRADE REGIME

By the early 1980s, the world multilateral trading system was under growing stress. The GATT Secretariat wrote of the "Increasing difficulty, not only in furthering trade liberalisation, but also in safeguarding previously negotiated levels of market access." World-trade-law experts Gerard and Victoria Curzon were even more outspoken: "[The GATT] is now incapable of halting daily violations of its most innocuous rules, let alone defend its basic principles. Evidence of breakdown is everywhere ... [A]n undeclared trade war is in progress."

Most importantly from Canada's point of view, protectionist sentiment was rising in the U.S., which had been the moral leader in the post-war trade liberalisation movement. There were several causes of this U.S. turnaround but I mention just two. The first were the very large U.S. budget deficits in the early years of the Regan administration. The so-called twin deficit link shows that a domestic budget deficit leads to a deficit on the current account in the balance of payments. The budget deficit raises interest rates as funds are sought to finance the growing public debt. The high interest rates attract foreign capital and when foreign investors buy U.S. dollars they bid up its value on the foreign exchange market. The result is a deficit on current account because U.S. imports grow and U.S. exports languish. This mechanism, which takes a good hour to explain properly to graduate students well versed in economic analysis, is little understood outside the economics profession. It was thus far easier for legislators to look at the trade deficit in isolation blaming it on a failure of U.S. exporters and unfair competition from foreign firms selling into the U.S. market.

Their view was exacerbated by a series of spectacular failures of U.S. firms to compete with their Japanese rivals in such products as automobiles, TVs and micro chips. It is a matter of debate how much these competitive failures contributed to the trade deficit but they were visible and dramatic and they fed the widespread belief that the U.S. was losing its ability to compete. It seems almost quaint today but in 1985, when the U.S. automobile industry was hard pressed and had been saved only by extraordinary restrictions on imports of Japanese cars, the Japanese competitive menace and the corresponding U.S. competitive failure seemed all too real to U.S. policy makers.

GATT commitments prevented an increase in tariffs and, as a result, an evolving array of U.S. non-tariff barriers (NTBs) was developed. Two of the most worrisome were countervailing and antidumping duties. Countervail is meant to create a level playing field by imposing a duty equal to any subsidy given by foreign governments to firms selling into the U.S.. This sounds well and good on paper except for two major drawbacks. First, the administration of these "safeguards" was often arbitrary and stacked against foreign firms. Second, U.S. subsidies were not taken into account, and as a result foreign firms selling into the U.S. market sometimes faced countervailing duties against the subsidies they received although their U.S. competitors received larger subsidies from U.S. sources.

Anti-dumping duties are meant to offset predatory pricing by foreign firms who sell at a loss in order to wipe out domestic competition. As they have evolved over the years, however, they now can be levied against any firms selling below its "full allocated cost," costs of production plus full overheads. Since competition often leads firms to sell at a profit over direct costs of production but at a price which does not cover some notional allocation of overheads, most firms are vulnerable to countervail much of the time.

Another major U.S. change was to take the initiation of investigations leading to countervail and antidumping out of the hands of the administration and into the hands of private firms. Instead of being an instrument of national geopolitical policy, these measures became instruments of competitive policy wielded by U.S. firms who could initiate an investigation more or less on command. Not surprisingly, Canadian policy makers were alarmed.

CANADIAN RESPONSE

Vitally concerned with the growing crisis in the world trading system, many Canadian observers surveyed Canadian policy options. The arguments for Canada seeking an FTA with the U.S. were both defensive and offensive. The defensive reason was that the best defense against rising U.S. protectionism was to act bilaterally to eliminate all tariffs and to contain the use of non-tariff barriers. Supporters pointed to the well-established principle of international law that: *Small countries have more to gain from imposing the rule of law than do large countries who can expect to be the winners in an unregulated game involving naked power.*

The offensive arguments for an FTA were that the Canadian economy had matured and was ready to compete openly in world competition. The infant industry stage had been passed when Canadian firms successfully weathered the removal of 80% of their tariff protection, and it was time to remove the last 20% – at least on trade with our major trading partner, the U.S. This would allow successful Canadian industries further access to the U.S. market which would generate employment to replace the employment lost when less successful industries declined. After all, Canadian industries had already quietly adjusted to several rounds of multilateral tariff cuts, so there was no reason to think that they could not adjust to the final round in which tariffs were eliminated on most trade.

More broadly, an FTA was seen as part of a policy package of liberalising the whole Canadian economy, exposing it more fully to market forces. Among other things, crown corporations were privatized, subsidies were reduced, unemployment insurance was reformed, and the manufacturers' sales tax was replaced by the GST. All of these were in line with the world-wide movement to concentrate government into its areas of core competence. The private sector was seen as the best creator of wealth while the government was the provider of environmental protection and a universal safety net.

Seen in these ways, the FTA was a major step towards completion of the government's 40-year-old trade liberalisation policy and a part of its new market-orientation policy. Had the tariff reductions been a part of a new a GATT round and extended to all countries, the cuts would probably have proceeded unnoticed, as had all previous GATT-negotiated reductions.

UNREASONABLE EXPECTATIONS

But the fact that the new round of tariff reductions was to be restricted to the U.S. caused the proposal to become a centre of public debate. Both opponents and supporters were led to make increasingly extreme predictions which created quite unreasonable expectations – expectations of disaster among many opponents and expectations of unrealistically high pay-offs among some supporters.

Wildly extreme fears were quickly aroused by the opposition's rhetoric: Canadian industry would be wiped out by U.S. competition; Canadian firms would flee to the U.S.; U.S. firms would take over Canada; employment would fall drastically; Canadians would lose control over their resources; we would be forced against our will to sell water and oil to the U.S., to adopt U.S. management of our hospitals and, according to Canadian author Margaret Attwood's testimony to a Senate committee, to adopt U.S. gun laws. According to Liberal leader John Turner and publisher-critic Mel Hurtig, the very existence of the country was at stake. Here is a sample of Hurtig's prose, drawn from his book *The Betrayal of Canada*: "The single most important overall impact of the Free Trade Agreement is already clear – a big decline in the standard of living of Canadians. And the future will be much worse. The less obvious result is as certain as the fact that you are now reading these words – the destruction and disappearance of our country."

Many of the opponents knew nothing of the history of Canadian trade policy and assumed that the FTA was a new initiative. Few saw any need to explain why the disasters they predicted from removing most of the last 20 percent of Canadian protection had not ensued when Canada removed the first 80 percent between 1935 and 1985.

Hurtig's kind of nonsense is refuted by the fact that, 10 years after the FTA, the country is still here and prospering, rated by international judges as one of the best places in the world in which to live. We have our problems but they are largely domestic, related to Quebec, taxes, and, until recently, budget deficits. But these problems are not caused by any inability to compete with the Americans, or any FTA-unleashed loss of Canadian sovereignty and identity.

I put the point this way in a convocation address at Carleton University in 1988. After analysing the major differences between social, cultural and political attitudes of Americans and Canadians, I went on to conclude that the decision as to whether or not to have an FTA with the U.S. should be based on: "The real economic and political issues that are at stake, not on the mistaken belief that the Canadian identity, of which we are justly proud, is so skin-deep that it will not survive eating one more McDonald's hamburger, watching one more installment of "Dallas" or doing five percent more trade with the Americans. Do your country, and your national identity, the honour it deserves by understanding that it *is* more than skin-deep ... and that whatever sensible or misguided policies we follow in the future, our identity as

Canadians will be around for quite some time." For their part, proponents, many of whom were trade policy experts, were clearer from the outset about the more limited gains that were offered by free trade with the U.S. and of the adjustment costs. But in the great heat of the debate, many proponents promised too much. On the political level, Prime Minister Mulroney promised "Jobs jobs and more jobs" in spite of the fact that trade liberalisation is about replacing low quality jobs with higher quality ones, not about creating more jobs in total. Others promised a rapid convergence to U.S. productivity levels and to U.S. living standards.

REASONABLE RESULTS

None of the dire predictions of the opponents came to pass. As with all previous Canadian tariff cuts, the adjustments, although painful for a few years, were followed by more employment (not caused by the FTA), more investment (to some extent caused by the FTA), no U.S. confiscation of Canadian water and petroleum (because such action was not covered by the treaty) and no unplanned loss of sovereignty (exactly as was to be expected). For example, in the first two years of the FTA total Canadian employment rose by 200,000, only to fall in the third year as the world sunk into the most serious recession since the Great Depression of the 1930s. Not surprisingly, the opponents blamed the loss of employment during the recession on the FTA instead of on a world-wide recession, and a highly restrictive Canadian monetary policy that resulted in both an unusually high spread between Canadian and U.S. interest rates and a severely overvalued Canadian dollar.

Nor were the extreme predictions of some supporters borne out. In particular, Canadian productivity, wages and living standards did not appear to converge on the higher U.S. levels. The failure of these extreme predictions has created among some observers the mistaken impression that the agreement was a failure.

Yet, measured against the reasonable expectations that proponents expressed in their more sober publications (including three books and numerous pamphlets of my own) and not their platform rhetoric, the FTA has been a substantial success.

Here is a short list of some of its major accomplishments:

• Canadian exports have expanded greatly from around 25 percent of Canadian total output (our GDP) to close to 40 percent, proving that Canadian industry was ready to compete on equal terms both with the Americans and the rest of the world.

- Canada had an export-led recovery from the deep world-wide recession of the early 1990s. The U.S. economy recovered when domestic demand recovered; Canada recovered when exports to the U.S. rose dramatically.
- Significant adjustment occurred as inefficient areas of production contracted and efficient areas expanded.
- According to Canadian economist Daniel Trefler, the FTA lowered prices to consumers by between one and two percent. Again a significant accomplishment that refuted predictions of disaster, but well below many unreasonable expectations of massive consumer gains.
- Canada got a dispute settlement mechanism that by and large has worked well. Dozens of disputes have been settled by international panels which, except in a very few cases, have not split along national lines. The rule of law has helped to keep all of these disputes from escalating into trade wars and has made Canada a secure base for firms wishing to serve the North American market. (Two disputes that do threaten trade wars, softwood lumber and "culture" are both outside of the Agreement – softwood lumber because it was subject to a special agreement reached just before the FTA came into force and "culture" because it was excluded under the terms of the Agreement.)
- Canada has been protected against the upsurge of U.S. protectionist sentiment. It is hard to calculate how much this is worth but the security of access to the U.S. market is worth quite a bit to firms located in Canada. Also, many attempted trade restrictions have been thwarted by the dispute settlement mechanism, while an unknown number that would have been tried had the mechanism not been in place have never seen the light of day.
- An increasing amount of foreign direct investment entered Canada over the first years of the FTA, indicating a willingness of foreign firms to locate in Canada to serve the whole North American market if costs and other economic calculations justified that decision.
- Canadian direct investment in the U.S. did not rise greatly, indicating a similar willingness of Canadian firms to serve the North American market from Canada if costs and other economic calculations justified that decision.

Finally, it should be noted that the productivity comparisons are still open to debate. Canadian trade specialist Daniel Trefler, writing in a forthcoming article in *The Canadian Journal of Economics*, argues that most existing comparisons have used non-comparable data. Canadian figures refer to real GDP in manufacturing per hour worked while U.S. figures refer to net value added, which excludes such purchased inputs as energy and raw materials. He also argues that the growing trend towards part time work in Canada, not matched in the U.S., biases comparisons of productivity per worker. When he measures output comparably, labour inputs as hours instead of numbers of workers, and controls for other influences, he finds large gains in Canadian productivity statistically associated with tariff reductions. He estimates that for all industries the FTA raised productivity between 0.4% and 0.8% per year over an 8 year period. For the industries that had highest pre-FTA tariffs, and hence were most impacted by the FTA, he estimates an effect of between 1.6% and 2.9% per year over the same period. As Trefler observes these are "enormous numbers."

In my opinion, they are too big to be taken at face value. For example, we do not know how much of the measured increase resulted from the closing of the least efficient operations (which raises the average productivity of the whole group) and how much from a genuine increase in efficiency of those who survived. But at the very least, Trefler's work shows that the last word has not yet been said on the productivity effects of the FTA. The best existing estimates now suggest that the productivity effects were positive and significant. Productivity pessimists will have to think again!

CONCLUSION

The FTA was a far less dramatic policy initiative than its critics assumed. In trade policy, it continued, and nearly completed, the process of reducing trade barriers that began in the 1930s. In broader economic policy, it was part of a new package of reforms that increased the degree of openness of the Canadian economy to market forces. On both counts, it was a marked success–as well as making Canadian access to the U.S. market more secure than ever before.

It was a failure only in that it failed to fulfil both the dire predictions of disaster promoted by its many opponents and the more extreme claims made by some of its supporters. Looking back on the massive debates that surrounded the FTA, we can only be thankful that the similar Canadian policies of trade liberalisation from 1935 to 1985 never came into the spotlight of public debate. One such divisive debate per lifetime is surely enough! We can be thankful that the debate is behind us and that we can now direct our attention at the very real issues that seriously affect Canadians, such as the international effects of Canadian political uncertainty, and our high taxes relative to those in the U.S.

RICHARD G. LIPSEY is Emeritus Professor of Economics, Simon Fraser University and Fellow, the Canadian Institute for Advanced Research.

From Leaps of Faith to Lapses of Logic

ANDREW N. JACKSON

The tenth anniversary of Canada-U.S. Free Trade Agreement (FTA) was marked by an ironic tension within mainstream media commentary. On the one hand, pundits generally hailed the success of "free trade," and poured scorn on the critics of the past. It was taken as more or less obvious that exports had grown hugely, and that their surge had fuelled growth and new opportunities. Yet, at almost precisely the same time, the same pundits were gripped by mounting anxiety over the "productivity gap" between Canada and the U.S.. The fact that the FTA could be counted a success despite a large and growing gap between Canadian and U.S. economic performance over the past decade must count as a triumph of ideology over logic.

From 1989 through 1998, Canada's real economic growth rate averaged 1.8 percent compared to 2.5 percent in the U.S.. Though much of this gap is attributable to the more severe Canadian downturn of the early 1990s, the U.S. continued to outperform Canada in 1997 and 1998, well into Canada's economic recovery. The difference in the two countries' real growth rates has meant a growing gap in terms of national income per capita.

Under free trade, moreover, the Canadian unemployment rate rose from 7.5 percent to more than 11 percent, and it finally fell below eight percent only last year. Meanwhile, after a much smaller increase in the early 1990s, the U.S. unemployment rate is currently running at well under five percent, a 30-year low. The difference in job creation performance is even greater when account is taken of the fact that in recent years new Canadian jobs, particularly jobs for women, have come mainly in the form of self-employment or part-time jobs. The absolute number of full-time paid jobs did not return to its 1989 level until last year.

The dominant view among economists is that these overall Canada-U.S. differences are mainly the result of different macroeconomic policies. The much deeper Canadian recession of 1990–1991 was caused by tighter monetary policy, while our recovery, when it did come, was made sluggish by major cuts in public spending. It's true that the Bank of Canada's "zero inflation" policies of the late 1980s were much more severe than those of the U.S. Federal Reserve, and that the consequent overvaluation of the exchange rate between 1989 and 1992 had a devastating impact on our manufacturing sector – just as the FTA came into force. The lethal combination of recession and high interest rates led to the rapid growth of public debt, and set the stage for much more stringent fiscal policies than were pursued by the U.S. in the 1990s.

But while macroeconomic policy has had a much greater impact than the FTA, deeper Canada-U.S. economic integration has played an independent role in depressing the living standards of working people. International competition has increased the downward pressure on wages and social standards, and there is little evidence that the FTA and NAFTA have solved the underlying structural problems of the Canadian economy.

The central case for Canada-U.S. free trade was that it would close the long-standing productivity gap between Canadian and U.S. manufacturing, and thus set the stage for more rapid economic growth. On top of a one-time increase in incomes through tariff elimination, free trade was expected to lead to greater efficiency in manufacturing as both Canadian companies and U.S. multinationals operating in Canada achieved economies of scale by producing longer runs of more specialized products for a larger continental market. Both the Economic Council of Canada and the Department of Finance forecast a (relatively modest) gain in real GDP of 2.5 percent over 10 years, mainly because they assumed there would be a significant productivity increase. In effect, this was a quantification of the famous "leap of faith" called for by the Macdonald Commission.

The case for the FTA was not that exports would grow faster than imports – the crude mercantilist position of many media pundits – but that increases in two-way trade would boost productivity through greater specialization and the workings of comparative advantage. Adjustment to freer trade was seen as a small problem because it was assumed that both capital and labour would flow reasonably smoothly to new areas of opportunity.

For their part, critics of free trade argued that greater liberalization of trade (and of investment flows under NAFTA) would increase the bargaining power of mobile capital in its relations with workers and governments, and that threats to move investment, production and jobs to the U.S. would force "downward harmonization" of wages in relation to productivity, and of any social standards that added to business costs. The critics argued that corporate efficiency gains would not be shared with workers and society as a whole, and that economic integration with the U.S. would promote greater inequality and the erosion of a more humane form of capitalism.

Both sides in the debate largely accepted that Canadian manufacturing was less efficient and less innovative than its U.S. counterpart. Free-traders said that dismantling tariff and non-tariff barriers to trade and investment flows and "letting the market work" would help solve the problem, while critics argued that Canada needed to keep and exercise policy tools such as foreign investment review, the strategic use of government procurement, resource-processing requirements, sectoral trade deals, industrial subsidies and so on, most of which were undercut by the FTA and NAFTA. The critics also warned that adjustment problems would be very severe, and that plant closures and reduced investment would bring de-industrialization.

The impact of the FTA and NAFTA on two-way trade has proved to be much greater than either side expected. Both exports and imports have grown very rapidly, from about 25 percent to more than 40 percent of nominal Canadian GDP, and increased Canada-U.S. trade accounts for all of the change. The rapid increase in two-way trade was unprecedented, much larger than in the 1970s or 1980s, and, as Daniel Schwanen has shown in his studies for the C.D. Howe Institute, was greatest in the sectors that experienced the greatest liberalization. Perhaps the most striking indicator of the extent of the change is that the U.S. is now a larger market for Canadian manufactured goods than Canada is. The post-FTA reality is one of very close continental integration through cross-border production networks. Trade deals clearly can have much bigger impacts than even economists predict. Of course, bigger-than-expected trade flows should have brought bigger-than-expected productivity gains, but they didn't.

It is often argued that sophisticated, "knowledge-intensive" Canadian exports, such as telecommunications equipment, have grown quickly under free trade. But the data can be misleading. Because there are substantial cross-border flows of intermediate goods, large increases in shipments from Canada do not always imply large increases in Canadian value-added. To take a key example, the auto sector contributes 20 percent of Canadian manufacturing shipments,

Table 1
Hourly Labour Productivity Growth in Manufacturing

	Canada	*U.S.*
Annual Average 1981–88	2.3	3.1
Annual Average 1989–96	1.8	2.8
1997	2.8	4.5

Source: U.S. Bureau of Labour Statistics.

but only 13 percent of manufacturing value-added. The difference arises from the fact that much of the value of auto exports consists of imported components. In terms of value-added – which reflects productive activity undertaken in Canada rather than the shuffling back and forth of components across the border – there has been very limited structural change in the Canadian manufacturing sector. Between 1988 and 1997, the share of electrical and electronic goods (which includes most "high-tech" manufacturing) fell from 8.1 percent of total manufacturing output to 7.9 percent, and by far the largest change has been the increased weight of the automotive sector, which has grown from 10 percent to 13 percent. There has been a modest decline in the importance of labour-intensive manufacturing (leather, footwear, textiles, and clothing) from 5.7 percent to 4.9 percent, and a modest increase in mechanical machinery and equipment. The share of finished goods has remained unchanged, however.

Overall, as carefully documented in the 1998 OECD Economic Survey of Canada, there has been no noticeable increase in the pace of transition to a "knowledge-based economy" over the past decade, and the Canadian capital goods sector remains much smaller than in other OECD countries. After free trade, as before it, Canada is a heavy net importer of advanced machinery and equipment, and under-invests in research and development and work force skills.

The FTA was supposed to close the productivity gap with the U.S. in manufacturing, but in fact the gap has widened (see Table 1). Moreover, as during the expansion of the 1980s expansion, Canadian cost competitiveness in manufacturing has been maintained only by the continuing fall in the dollar. As Table 2 shows, Canadian unit labour costs – which fall with productivity gains and rise as wages rise – have been much more buoyant during the recent recovery than U.S. costs. The same was true of the 1980s recovery. Our problem, as noted below, has not been faster wage growth than in the U.S., but slower productivity growth.

Table 2
Cumulative % Change in Unit Labour Costs in Manufacturing

	U.S.	*Canada ($ Canadian)*	*Canada ($ U.S.)*
1982–87	-5.4	+3.7	-3.4
1992–97	-7.6	-0.7	-13.4

Source: U.S. Bureau of Labour Statistics.

Had it not been for the dollar's continuing sag, the 1990s would have seen much slower export growth, and much faster import growth. Our healthy trade balance owes almost everything to the dollar, and almost nothing to fundamentally improved competitiveness in terms of either costs or increased industrial sophistication.

Because productivity tends to grow fastest when economies are running up against capacity, stronger growth in the U.S. likely played a role in the widening Canada-U.S. productivity gap. But in view of the greatly increased two-way trade in manufactured goods, and Canadian manufacturing's consequently greater reliance on the more buoyant U.S. economy, the growing productivity gap is something of a puzzle. A large part of the explanation appears to be structural. Canadian manufacturing is much more heavily tilted to resource-based manufacturing and the automotive sector, and our capital goods sector is much smaller. In fact, Canada has done at least as well as the U.S. in most sectors, but, as recent analysis by Statistics Canada and the Centre for the Study of Living Standards has shown, overall manufacturing performance has been dragged down by the capital goods sector (see the article by the CSLS's executive director, Andrew Sharpe, in the May issue of *Policy Options*). The longstanding structural weakness of Canadian manufacturing remains very much with us, contrary to the expectation that closer integration would lead to convergence.

A number of Bay Street economists have recently tried to pin the blame for poor productivity performance under free trade on their favourite villain, high taxes. In fact, there is little evidence that high taxes lead to low productivity growth, which is not surprising, since high taxes tend to be associated with high levels of productivity-enhancing public investment in education, skills, research, transportation and communications infrastructure, and the like. As Table 3 shows, recent U.S. productivity performance has been no better than in many high tax countries, and the highest-tax country among those shown, Sweden, led productivity growth in the 1990s.

Table 3
Productivity and Taxes

	Increase in Hourly Labour Productivity in Manufacturing, 1992–96 (%)*	*Taxes as % of GOP (1996)***
Sweden	25.4	62.1
Netherlands	22.6	47.3
U.S.	20.2	31.9
Germany	17.0	45.1
France	17.0	50.7
Japan	14.3	31.9
Italy	13.3	47.9
Canada	8.6	43.5
U.K.	6.1	39.0

Notes:

*   Monthly Labour Review, U.S. Dept. of Labour – October 1998.

**   OECD Economic Outlook, December 1998, Annex Table 29.

Liberalization of investment under the FTA and NAFTA and the replacement of the Foreign Investment Review Agency by Investment Canada were expected to lead to increased foreign investment in Canada. The FTA was supposed to spawn new investment and the expansion of Canadian branch plants of U.S. transnationals, rather than disinvestment and the substitution of U.S. exports for Canadian production. However, as Table 4 shows, in the 1990s money has been flowing out of Canada, not into it. In terms of foreign direct investment (FDI), Canadian investment outside Canada has grown about twice as fast as FDI in Canada, with the net outflow totalling $55 billion. While Canadian companies have invested in countries other than the U.S., between 1990 and 1996 Canadian FDI in the U.S. grew from 71 percent to 76 percent of the value of U.S. FDI in Canada. Remarkably, the total stock of Canadian foreign direct investment is now larger than the total stock of FDI in Canada. Canadian investments in portfolio stocks (representing an equity interest of under 10 percent) have also resulted in a large net outflow, amounting to $48 billion in the 1990s.

Although there is no close link between financial flows and real investment, the total investment outflow of more than $100 billion in the 1990s was, by definition, not available to finance real investment in Canada. (Some of it may have contributed to Canadian exports, as

Table 4
Canada's International Investment Position ($Billions)

Canadian Assets	FDI	Portfolio Stocks
1990	98.4	30
1997	239.8	108.9
Canadian Liabilities		
1990	130.9	20.7
1997	217.1	51.6

Source: Statistics Canada, Cat. 67–202 XPB and the *Daily*, March 30, 1999.

Canadian companies abroad shipped inputs from their home offices, but the tie between Canadian FDI and Canadian exports is not strong.) The $100-billion financial outflow may help explain why real private non-residential fixed investment in this country has lagged the U.S. in the 1990s, growing by an average of just 4.1 percent annually, compared to 8.3 percent in the U.S. By contrast, in the 1980s real private investment grew faster in Canada than in the U.S., increasing by an average 3.5 percent per year between 1982 and 1989, compared to 2.6 percent in the U.S. A recent study by Industry Canada has confirmed that the FTA encouraged a net outflow of foreign investment from Canada in all sectors.

Overall, then, liberalization of investment has been associated with retrenchment rather than expansion of U.S.-owned operations in Canada. At the same time, far from flowing to areas of new opportunity, as predicted by the FTA's proponents, Canadian capital has been pouring out of the country. It is worth noting that most economic models of free trade exclude the possibility of capital outflows by assumption, even though, as even the most casual reader of the financial press must know, outflows are clearly a possibility, given greatly liberalized global capital markets.

Though pre-FTA fears of Canadian de-industrialization may now appear to have been exaggerated, the scale of destruction of manufacturing jobs and community economies in between 1989 and 1991 should not be minimized. The high dollar and the FTA destroyed one in five manufacturing jobs in a matter of two or three years, and underpinned a serious national recession. Ontario and Quebec were hardest hit, of course. A careful study by Daniel Trefler of the University of Toronto found that job losses in manufacturing between 1988 and 1996 were significantly compounded by the FTA, and that restructuring driven by tariff cuts may have directly accounted for as many as one in three of the lost manufacturing jobs. Tariff reduction clearly played a major role in job losses in hitherto protected sectors, such as clothing, and workers lost these jobs at a time when few others were to be found. The deep recession of the early 1990s was mainly the result of macroeconomic policy, but the fact that adjustment to the FTA was so heavily concentrated in a recession greatly worsened the human and social impacts of trade-driven changes.

With the dollar's fall from its very overvalued levels of the late 1980s, manufacturing production and employment have both grown strongly, and export growth has led to job creation in manufacturing and in the rest of the economy. But the absolute number of manufacturing jobs has still not quite recovered to the late 1980s level, and manufacturing output has slipped from 19 percent of GDP to 17 percent. It is true that manufacturing has been shrinking for many years as a share of employment and, more slowly, as a share of production, so its further decline may not constitute "de-industrialization as a result of free trade." But the point remains that the widely-hailed "export boom" has produced very few new direct jobs.

Nor has it led to widespread prosperity. In both the 1980s and 1990s, wages have increased less in relation to productivity in manufacturing than in the business sector as a whole. Between 1991 and 1997 unit labour costs in manufacturing fell 0.1 percent a year, compared to a 1.0 percent average annual increase in the business sector. This pattern, which was also observed in the 1980s, presumably has something to do with the fact that competitive pressures are generally much more intense in the traded goods sector than in the business sector as a whole.

As Table 5 shows, in both Canada and the U.S. real hourly wages in manufacturing have barely increased during the 1990s recovery, despite significant increases in hourly labour productivity. The disconnect has been even greater in the U.S., given the Americans' stronger productivity growth. The most likely explanation for wages' failure to keep pace with productivity growth is that the rate of unionization is lower in the U.S. The absence of wage growth, despite rising productivity, has meant that production worker wages have fallen as a share of value-added in Canadian manufacturing (from 31 percent in 1988 to 27 percent in 1995).

To be sure, some of the difference between productivity growth and wage growth has been shared with society as whole through lower prices, but there has also clearly been an increase in the return to capital. By 1996, large Canadian corporations had regained the real rates of return achieved at the peak of the 1980s expansion, even though the economy was still operating at well below capacity. Rates of return

Table 5
Hourly Productivity and Wages in Manufacturing in the 1990s Recovery (1992–97) (%)

	Canada	U.S.
Cumulative Increase in Output per Hour	9.6	25.6
Cumulative Increase in Real Hourly Wage	1.1	1.5

Source: U.S. Bureau of Labour Statistics.

in winning export sectors like auto and electrical machinery and (until the recent slump in prices) the resource sector have been as high or higher than in the late 1980s. High rates of return have, of course, resulted in large gains for shareholders and corporate executives. (The fact that corporate profits as a share of GDP remain slightly below the late 1980s level is mainly explained by low rates of return in still depressed parts of the domestic economy, such as retail trade and construction.)

The disconnect between productivity growth and wage growth is just as evident at the detailed sectoral level. The studies by Trefler and Schwanen mentioned above found no link between higher productivity in "winning" sectors and wage growth. Recent data show, for example, that while value added per employee in the motor vehicle industry rose by an annual average of 15.1 percent between 1990 and 1996, annual wages and salaries rose only 5.4 percent a year on average. (Detailed data are available from the Strategis data base at www.ic.gc.ca.) Moreover, the increase in annual earnings largely reflects longer hours, rather than higher hourly wages, and there is substantial evidence that workplace stress has increased greatly in the 1990s due to the increased pace and intensity of work and a shift to unsocial hours, such as night work.

Unlike their trade-theorist colleagues, labour economists and academics who study industrial relations have long recognized that when markets are fiercely contested there are intense pressures in collective bargaining to increase the firm's competitiveness by lowering wages in relation to productivity, and by intensifying work. Few firms operate according to the maxim offered by Tom D'Aquino during the NAFTA debate that "wages are only a small part of the competitive equation, and far from the most important." Under the FTA, there has not been a convergence between Canadian and U.S. unionization rates, not even in manufacturing. Even so, there has been constant downward pressure on wages and working conditions because of the increased intensity of competition.

Free trade theory holds that efficiency gains will be shared. But the reality for those Canadian workers most directly effected by free trade has been that real wages have been flat or even falling, while work has become more intense. Many workers lost their jobs because of trade-driven restructuring. The promised adjustment programs did not appear, and the most fundamental adjustment program of all – Unemployment Insurance (UI) – has been repeatedly cut over the past decade. Canada's UI program is now approximately as "generous" as the U.S.'s, and only about one in three unemployed workers currently qualifies for benefits. To the extent that policy-makers saw UI cuts as being necessary to "discipline" the wage demands of Canadian workers, this process of "downward harmonization" to the U.S. standard was clearly linked to free trade.

Free trade has also prompted an even wider process of harmonization to the U.S. model, though this is still on-going and strongly contested. Business and politicians of the right certainly argue ad nauseam that Canada can no longer maintain higher corporate tax rates or more progressive personal income taxes than the U.S., and that collective bargaining legislation, employment standards, environmental regulations and so on must take "competitive realities" into account. In response, labour and the left argue, with good reason, that high labour and social standards and high levels of public investment promote a more productive economy as well as a more decent society. But that does not alter the fact that the "international competitiveness" argument is constantly deployed to reverse past progress, and that the increased power of business to pick up and move is used as a lever. Even more direct leverage for downward harmonization comes from explicit challenges to social and environmental regulation using NAFTA's Chapter 11 provisions for investor-state challenges.

In sum, there is little convincing evidence of a "positive restructuring" of the Canadian economy under free trade. Fears of de-industrialization may have been exaggerated, but the structural gap between Canadian and U.S. manufacturing has grown rather than narrowed, while any efficiency gains attributable to free trade have not been widely shared. Quite the contrary, there has been significant downward pressure on wages and social standards. The "leap of faith" of 1988 has not been vindicated.

To put these conclusions into a wider context: The 1997 Trade and Development Report of the UN Agency UNCTAD argued that global trade and investment liberalization had resulted in greatly increased inequality both between and within countries. There is no demonstrably strong link between liberalization and economic convergence across countries, and there is a strong association between liberalization and social inequality within countries.

These essentially critical conclusions do not mean that liberalization of trade and longer-term investment flows should be rejected. Rather, they underscore the continuing importance of public policy in shaping comparative advantage, instead of "leaving it all to the market," as well as the need to create a social context around economic liberalization, as the European Community has been doing.

Though close economic integration between Canada and the U.S. is here to stay, the terms and conditions of NAFTA and the wider policy environment are certainly subject to change. A sober evaluation of actual performance under the FTA should rekindle a lively debate over the potential role of active industrial and regional development policies. We may not want to bring back all the tools of the 1970s and 1980s, but there is a strong case for public investment and intervention to offset the large and continuing structural weaknesses of Canadian industry. And, as trade and investment liberalization continues, there is an urgent need to incorporate protection for labour rights and for the right of governments to regulate in the public interest in areas like the environment and public health and safety. Liberalization need not result in downward harmonization. But it will, if conscious action is not taken to counter market-driven trends.

ANDREW JACKSON is a senior economist at the Canadian Labour Congress.

Free Trade in North America: Some Observations

PAUL WONNACOTT

In my view, John McCallum's background paper comes out about right. To date, the U.S.-Canadian FTA deserves two cheers. It has worked well, although some of the expected long-run results have yet to occur.

While trade flows have increased in roughly the way that might have been anticipated following the FTA,[1] overall Canadian productivity apparently has not – at least not yet. This is very important. The point of freer trade is not simply to increase trade, but to improve living standards. Trade can contribute to higher incomes in two ways – by changing the composition of production between sectors according to comparative advantage, and by increasing productivity within sectors. In the run-up to the free trade negotiations, productivity improvements were seen as the key to large Canadian gains.

For supporters of free trade, the difficult puzzle is that a number of studies indicate that the U.S.-Canadian labour productivity gap in manufacturing has increased since the free-trade agreement – although at a very much slower rate than in the previous decade. Because productivity is so important, I want to comment on it, even though my observations will partly overlap those of John McCallum.

One answer to the productivity puzzle may lie in difficulties in the data, which are considered in detail by Daniel Trefler. He concludes that there are, in fact, major data problems in comparing trends in U.S. and Canadian productivity; the basic U.S. and Canadian productivity data, which have been at the center of the debate, are, in his words, "*completely* incomparable" (5, italics his). When calculated correctly, Canadian labour productivity in manufacturing grew o.6% more per year than in the United States in the 1989–95 period – a narrowing of the productivity gap that he attributes entirely to the FTA (Trefler 1999, 1).

A second study that throws light on the productivity puzzle is that of Donald Daly, who focuses on differences between large and small plants. For large plants – those with over 500 employees – Daly finds that Canadian productivity has improved more rapidly than overall U.S. manufacturing productivity – a result "in line with the studies showing larger gains from freer trade" (12). The Canadian productivity lag lies in the smaller plants. While this conclusion is somewhat reassuring to those who expected large Canadian gains from free trade, it is also somewhat disconcerting, given the contributions which smaller firms can make to economic dynamism and employment.

A third approach to untangling the productivity puzzle is to look at sectoral trends in productivity. In a paper delivered at the 1999 Canadian Economics Association meeting, Daniel Schwanen presented evidence that Canadian productivity would have increased by 0.4% more per annum since the late 1980s if Canada had had the same sectoral composition as the United States.

One of the most important sectors, of course, is the automobile industry. Because of the AutoPact of 1965, the U.S.-Canadian productivity gap had been substantially closed by the end of the 1970s, and recent Canadian improvements in productivity in this industry have been similar to those in the United States. However, productivity increases in automobiles have lagged behind industry in general. Because autos are more important as a percentage of Canadian than U.S. manufacturing production, the result has been a drag on overall Canadian productivity compared to U.S. productivity.

The sectoral issue is reinforced by the fact that Canada has lagged in ultra high-tech industries where U.S. productivity growth has not only been spectacular, but seems to be accelerating. Canada has probably been hurt in the competition for high-tech industries by the migration of the computer-related industries toward the South and West, most notably to California and Washington states. This seems to me to be rather close to a pure economic accident. Geography was not the cause of the collapse of Wang Laboratories, nor of the relative decline of the computer companies based in New York, Minnesota, or Michigan. At the starting gate, the MIT and Stanford areas were essentially equal; geography counted little. But, even though the industry was footloose at the beginning, it is less so now; there are strong benefits in going where the action is. And now the action is, most importantly, in the San Jose-San Francisco area.

Even though I would classify the migration of the computer industry as primarily an historical accident, there has also been a broader, more general shift of the center of gravity of the U.S. economy to the south and west, away from the Chicago-Boston-Baltimore triangle which is so close to the major Canadian manufacturing regions. [For example, upstate New York population and labour force were lower in 1998 than in 1990 (Deitz and De Mott, 1999.)] In other words, the center of Canada's population is now further away from the core of the North American economy than it was several decades ago. This may be a continuing negative factor for the Canadian economy.

Although rising living standards are built on rising productivity, the tie between productivity and real wages is not tight in an open economy. Productivity gains may go either to the producing country (in terms of higher incomes) or to the importing country (in terms of lower prices), or a combination of the two. While the composition of Canadian output – relatively large in autos but small in high tech – has acted as a drag on Canadian productivity, its effect on relative Canadian real incomes has been much less clear. Automobiles – and particularly automobile assembly – are a high wage sector, providing good incomes for many Canadians with moderate skills. Although there are lots of millionaires in Seattle, most of the gains in the high-tech industries have gone to buyers, in the form of precipitously falling prices. Incidentally, high tech is one place where protection simply doesn't work. A country may get along with a protected automobile industry that is ten years out of date, but producing computers that are ten years out of date is a waste of time.

In terms of the important issue of assured market access, one of the notable NAFTA contributions came in the wake of the 1994–95 Mexican crisis. Mexico responded with devaluation and tight monetary and fiscal policies, rather than the trade and capital controls so often used by developing countries in trouble. Although the crisis of 1994–95 was extremely painful to Mexico, it was conspicuously shorter than the prolonged crisis of the 1980s. By 1996,the Mexican economy was growing again – by more than 5%. NAFTA probably contributed to the speed of the recovery, although the Mexican economy also benefited from the reforms of the 1980s. There is just one negative note in this favourable picture: NAFTA may have increased the pre-crisis complacency of Mexican officials, by reinforcing expectations of a continuing capital flow.

Finally, I note that one of the fears of the critics of a free-trade agreement has conspicuously failed to come true. Canada didn't hitch its economy to a falling star. Since 1982, the performance of the U.S. economy has been very strong. Let us – in all three countries – hope that this strength continues.

PAUL WONNACOTT is the Alan R. Holmes Professor of Economics, Middlebury College in Middlebury, Vermont, and a former member of the President's Council of Economic Advisers.

NOTES

I have benefitted from discussions with Donald Daly, Jeffrey Schott, Daniel Schwanen, and Ronald Wonnacott.

1 Although Trefler (1999, 2) concludes that "the recent explosion of Canadian trade ... was not primarily driven by specifically FTA tariff cuts." He notes (28) that "Most of Canada's increased trade was in industries that had no tariffs in 1988." Clearly, the long, strong expansion of the U.S. economy in the 1990s was a major cause of the increase in U.S. imports from Canada, Mexico, and elsewhere.

BIBLIOGRAPHY

Bergsten, C. Fred, and Jeffrey Schott. "A Preliminary Evaluation of NAFTA." Testimony before the Subcommittee on Trade, Ways and Means Committee, U.S. House of Representatives, Sept. 11, 1997.

Daly, Donald J. "Small Businesses in the Canada-U.S. Manufacturing Productivity Gap." Toronto: Schulich School of Business, York University, xeroxed, rev., March 1999.

—, B.A. Keys, and E.J. Spence. *Scale and Specialization in Canadian Manufacturing.* Economic Council of Canada, 1968.

Deitz, Richard, and Mike De Mott. "Is Upstate New York Showing Signs of a Turnaround?" Federal Reserve Bank of New York, *Current Issues*, May 1999.

Fuss, Melvyn A., and Leonard Waverman. *Costs and Productivity in Automobile Production.* Cambridge: Cambridge University Press, 1992.

McCallum, John. "Two Cheers for the FTA." *Econoscope.* Royal Bank of Canada, June, 1999.

Schott, Jeffrey. "NAFTA: An Interim Report." In Shahid Javed Burki, Guillermo Perry and Sara Calvo, eds. *Trade in the Americas: Toward Open Regionalism.* Washington: World Bank, 1998, pp. 109–124.

Schwanen, Daniel. "Trading Up." Toronto: C.D. *Howe Commentary* #88, March 1997.

Trefler, Daniel. "The Long and Short of the Canada-U.S. Free Trade Agreement." University of Toronto, Institute for Policy Analysis, xeroxed, rev., Feb. 1999.

Wonnacott, Ronald J., and Paul Wonnacott. *Free Trade between the United States and Canada: The Potential Economic Effects.* Cambridge: Harvard University Press, 1967.

NAFTA and the Manufacturing Industry in Mexico: A Preliminary Balance

FERNANDO CLAVIJO*

INTRODUCTION

During the last twenty years, the Mexican economy has been involved in a broad process of structural reforms in almost all the economic realms. Among these reforms, the importance of NAFTA, as the culmination of the previous liberalization efforts, is unquestionable.

Before NAFTA was put into force, important and intense discussions towards the effects that the agreement would have on the Mexican economy took place. The positions towards the convenience of the agreement were extremely opposite. However, five years after, not much has been written about the evolution of the Mexican economy under a free trade agreement with North America, not only because the issue seems to be politically difficult, but also because its evaluation is methodologically complicated.

The assessment of NAFTA effects on the economy implies a broad analysis of all sectors of the economy: agriculture, services and industry. However, for the case of Mexico it is still too early to detect changes in both agriculture and services. For the former, some tariffs – although decreasing over time – were maintained, in particular, for important crops as corn and wheat. And, for the latter, some protection was kept, at least in terms of market shares (similar to the case of Canada).

* The author wishes to acknowledge the collaboration of Jana Boltvinik.

In this sense the assessment of NAFTA's effects should focus on the industrial sector and, in particular, on the manufacturing industry, the sector more exposed to competition and where the major gains were expected.

Trade and financial liberalization and NAFTA are driving important changes in the Mexican manufacturing sector. Industry was pushed to make significant efforts in terms of efficiency and competitiveness. This is reflected in a greater industrial concentration through the reduction of production facilities. However, some of these closings – not surprisingly – are the natural outcome of some weak industries facing a more competitive environment. Furthermore, NAFTA and the overall economic reforms have generated important changes in the composition of the industry. For example, a greater utilization of high technologies and scale intensive production processes can be noted.

Although these trends appear to be relatively clear, five years of NAFTA is still a very short period to generate powerful conclusions. It is also difficult to isolate NAFTA from 20 years of economic reforms and other current circumstances such as the Mexican strong exchange rate realignment (1994–95) and the extraordinary expansion cycle of the United States during the NAFTA years, among others.

In this context, this paper is organized as follows. In the next section, some general considerations towards a broad evaluation of NAFTA are briefly discussed. Later, in section 2, an analysis of the recent evolution of the manufacturing evolution is presented. This analysis is complemented by a broader examination of the structural changes of this industry, which can be assessed, for example, by classifying the manufacturing industry in accordance to the OECD criteria. These criteria are derived from a production function that classifies manufacturing activities according to the use of production factors, namely; technological levels and wages for different skills. Finally, some concluding remarks summarize the pace of these changes and the remaining challenges.

1. SOME CONSIDERATIONS TOWARDS THE EVALUATION OF NAFTA

In the more than five years of its implementation, NAFTA has had various opportunities to demonstrate its expected benefits on the Mexican economy. The main benefits are:

Sustained growth of non-oil exports: Between 1994 and 1998, non-oil exports, excluding in-bond industry, have increased (at constant prices) at an average rate of 21.5 percent. Manufacturing exports stand out with an average growth rate of 22.7 percent during the same period. During 1995, due to the contraction of domestic demand and the recovery of exchange rate competitiveness, an important number of Mexican enterprises reoriented their production to the external market. This was definitely facilitated by the channels previously established by NAFTA. In fact, during 1995 and 1996 the export sector was the main and virtually the only growth driver.

Access to the U.S. market: As a result of both the opening of the economy and the sustained growth of the nineties, Mexico has become the U.S.'s second-largest trading partner, after Canada. Thanks to NAFTA, Mexican products have not been displaced by the competitive devaluation of Asian countries currencies? Given Mexico's level of competitiveness, this has been possible mainly because of special treatment of NAFTA.

Greater stability: Given the current situation of the world economy (1998–99), greater economic and financial integration with the United States has contributed substantially to sustain Mexico's economic growth, while in most Latin American economies strong economic recessions are taking place. In this sense, NAFTA has placed the Mexican economy in a superior position relative to other emerging economies.

Although these benefits can be definitively associated with NAFTA, its is impossible to isolate the growth of exports from the important exchange rate adjustment of 1995 (just one year after NAFTA was put into force). In this sense, an assessment of NAFTA effects on their own requires a contrafactual analysis. That is, the estimation of export response must be made with a constant real exchange rate that did not exist in practice.

Notwithstanding the important role of the exchange rate adjustment in Mexico, the fact that imports and exports in the U.S. and Canada exploded at the same time indicates that this is not just an exchange rate history (Chart 1).

On the other hand, since the United States receives almost 80 percent of Mexican exports and the transmission mechanisms have been reinforced by NAFTA, the benefits of this agreement have been magnified by the extraordinary expansion cycle of the U.S. economy. The real test will take place when the U.S. economic expansion stops or reverts to its previous levels. Although the Maquila regime, which accounts for almost 50 percent of total merchandise exports, was not significantly modified by the agreement, the relation between both cycles can be observed by considering these exports (Chart 2).

Given the excellent performance of the U.S. economy during the last eight years, Mexico has not yet experienced the "other side of the coin" of this greater dependence. It can be expected that when the U.S. economic growth reverts or decelerates, the negative effects for Mexico will be much more accentuated and dangerous than in the past.

With an economy almost 20 times greater than Mexico's and much more productive, any contraction in the rate of growth of U.S. domestic demand may provoke a strong flow of goods and services to the Mexican market. At the same time, a contraction or at least deceleration of Mexican exports to the U.S. can be expected. A similar situation was observed during 1992–93, when the U.S. recession was transmitted to Mexico via imports, even without NAFTA.

Under these circumstances, an analysis of NAFTA during the last five years should exhibit better results than analysis of long run trends or steady state. That is, considering a stable growth path of the U.S. economy (not only the expansionary part of the cycle), equilibrium of the exchange rate in Mexico, and the maturation of structural reforms in the Mexican economy, the benefits from NAFTA will be softened.

2. NAFTA AND THE MANUFACTURING INDUSTRY

Current situation of the manufacturing industry:

During the first five years of NAFTA, the evolution of the manufacturing industry, excluding in-bond industry, has been relatively favourable (Table 1). The value of production (at constant 1994 prices) has grown at an average annual rate of 5 percent. This growth trend was stronger during 1995 and 1996, when the exchange rate adjustment along with the internal demand contraction encouraged manufacturing exports. In contrast, during 1997 and 1998, when the real exchange rate suffered an important appreciation, production value decelerated significantly.

Employment, although recovering since the important drop of 1995, occupation did not surpasse 1994 levels until 1998. This trend is clearer for workers (blue-collar) than for employees (white-collar), since in 1998 the latter were at almost the same levels as in 1994. In this sense, the composition of employment has remained constant at 30 percent employees and 70 percent workers.

The behavior of the main indicators is extremely heterogeneous among the division and sub-divisions of the industry. Mexican manufacturing is highly concentrated in three divisions, which account for the 76.4 percent of total production value: foods, beverages and tobacco (23 percent); machinery and equipment (35.6 percent); and chemicals (17.8 percent). Among these divisions the differences are

Table 1
Manufacturing industry. Main indicators*
(annual percentage changes, 1994=100)

	1995	1996	1997	1998	Ave. 95–98
Production value	8.8	8.0	0.5	2.6	5.0
Occupation	− 8.9	3.6	5.6	3.6	1.0
Workers	− 9.5	4.8	6.4	3.7	1.4
Employees	− 7.4	1.0	3.7	3.4	0.2
Remuneration	−20.5	−6.1	4.9	5.7	−4.0
Wages	−23.9	−3.5	8.5	6.7	−3.1
Salaries	−19.4	−5.4	3.6	6.5	−3.7
Medium product	19.4	4	−4.8	−1.0	4.4
No. of establishments	− 4.0	−1.2	−2.6	−7.7	−3.9

Source: ESANE Consultores with data from the Monthly Industrial Survey (INEGI).
Note *Excluding in-bond industry.

meaningful: while machinery and equipment is the more competitive manufacturing activity (more than 70 percent of total manufacturing exports are in this division), foods, beverages and tobacco is not as competitive and its production is mainly oriented to the domestic market. Furthermore, production of machinery and some chemicals is characterized by sophisticated processes and consequently requires a more skilled labour force.

In this context, in order to determine whether the manufacturing industry has experienced the structural changes expected from NAFTA and the overall economic reforms (particularly in terms of benefits to higher technologies and sophisticated production processes), the OECD classification of this industry is more adequate. (The OECD criteria group the different activities in terms of production factors, technology and wages.)

Main Trends of Mexican Manufacturing under the OECD classification:

Before presenting the analysis, the criteria of the OECD classification of the manufacturing industry are briefly described:

Technology: Industries are grouped on the basis of their R&D intensity in the OECD area as a whole, defined as the ratio of business-enterprise R&D to production. The following groups emerge:

Table 2
Production share by type of industry (percentage)

	Total		Without automobile industry	
	1994	*1998*	*1994*	*1998*
TECHNOLOGY				
High	9.7	13.0	11.6	16.5
Medium	36.4	39.8	23.6	23.9
Low	53.9	47.2	36.4	39.8
ORIENTATION				
Resource-intensive	37.6	31.5	45.1	39.8
Labour-intensive	9.5	8.2	11.4	10.3
Specialized supplier	6.9	6.9	7.8	8.8
Scale-intensive	41.5	45.5	29.7	31.1
Science based	4.8	7.9	5.8	10.0
WAGES				
High	38.4	32.5	46.2	41.1
Medium	29.7	29.2	35.7	36.9
Low	31.9	38.3	18.1	22.0

Source: ESANE Consultores with data from the Monthly Industrial Survey (INEGI).

i) *High-technology:* aerospace, computers and office equipment, communications equipment and semiconductors, electric machinery, pharmaceuticals and scientific instruments. ii) *Medium-technology:* chemicals (excluding drugs), rubber and plastic products, non-ferrous metals, non-electrical machinery, motor vehicles, other transport equipment and other manufacturing. iii) *Low-technology:* food, beverages and tobacco; textiles, apparel and leather, wood products, paper and printing, petroleum refining, non-metallic mineral products, iron and steel, metal products and shipbuilding.
Orientation: This classification is based on the primary factors believed to affect competitiveness. Industries are classified into:

i) *Resource-intensive (access to natural resources):* food, beverages and tobacco; wood products, petroleum refining, non-metallic mineral products and non-ferrous metals. ii) *Labour-intensive (labour costs):* textiles, apparel and leather; fabrication of metal products; other manufacturing. iii) *Specialized supplier (differentiated products):* non-electrical machinery; electrical machinery; communications equipment and semiconductors. iv) *Scale-intensive (length of production runs):* paper and printing; chemiclas excluding drugs; rubber and plastics; iron and steel; shipbuilding; motor vehicles; other transport. v) *Science-based (rapid application of scientific advance):* aerospace; computers; pharmaceuticals; scientific instruments.

Wages: This classification is based on average labour compensation across nine countries (Australia, Canada, Finland, Germany, Japan, Norway, Sweden, U.S. and U.K.) for 1985. The groupings appear to be quite stable compared to other time periods and for additional countries:

i) *High-wage (industries in which the wage is more than 15 percent above the median):* chemicals excluding drugs; aerospace; pharmaceuticals; petroleum refining; computers and office equipment; motor vehicles. ii) *Medium-wage (industries within 15 percent of the median):* paper and printing; rubber and plastics; non-metallic mineral products; iron and steel; non-ferrous metals; metal products; shipbuilding; non-electrical machinery; scientific instruments; communications equipment and semiconductors. iii) *Low-wage (industries with wages at least 15 percent below the median):* food, beverages and tobacco; textiles, apparel and leather; wood products; electrical machinery; other transport; other manufacturing.

Classifying the manufacturing industry by the criteria described above makes it possible to assess the structural changes that trade liberalization and NAFTA have induced. Those changes can be summarized as follows.

Whereas in 1994 production was highly concentrated in industries with low technology, scale intensive and paying low wages; by 1998, even though the Mexican industry was still low technology based and scale intensive, the percentage of high technology and science-based areas have increased substantially. Furthermore, for 1998 production jumped from low to high wages (Table 2).

It is worth mentioning that the important part played by the automobile industry (20.8 percent out of the total) explains the concentration of Mexican manufacturing production in scale intensive processes. If this industry is not considered, manufacturing production appears highly concentrated in resource intensive enterprises. Furthermore, the qualitative change from low to high wages is also explained by the weight of the automobile industry in total manufacturing production. Unfortunately this industry only employs 9.5 percent of the total employed in manufacturing.

Growth of production, employment and average wages has been surprising in those industries with high and medium technologies and production processes intensive in scale and requiring specialized suppliers, as well as those with high wages. For example, during the last five years the value of production in industries with high and medium

Table 3
NAFTA's winner industries: Production, remunerations and establishments
(average annual change in percentages, 1994–98)

	Production	Wages	No. of establishments*
Cars, parts and accessories	11.1	- 2.7	- 0.5
Pharmaceuticals	8.2	2.0	- 0.8
Chemicals	6.0	- 3.1	- 2.8
Synthetic fibers	12.5	- 1.3	0.0
Other chemical products	1.8	- 4.0	- 3.1
Office machines and computers	38.4	6.9	-17.4
Scientific, professional eq.	21.8	8.2	- 3.5
Total	10.9	- 1.8	- 3.0

Source: ESANE Consultores with data from the Monthly Industrial Survey (INEGI).
* Average annual change in percentages (1995–97)

Table 4
NAFTA's winner industries. Shares of manufacturing

	Production		Employment	
	1994	1998	1994	1998
Cars, parts and accessories	16.8	20.8	8.8	9.5
Pharmaceuticals	3.3	3.7	2.8	3.0
Chemicals	4.2	4.5	2.4	2.2
Synthetic fibers	1.2	1.3	1.1	1.2
Other chemical products	5.1	4.5	4.0	3.6
Office machines and computers	1.3	3.9	0.6	1.2
Scientific, professional eq.	0.2	0.3	0.3	0.5
Total	32.1	39.0	20.0	21.2

Source: ESANE Consultores with data from the Monthly Industrial Survey (INEGI).

Table 5
NAFTA's Loser Industries – Production, Remunerations and Establishments
(average annual percentage change, 1994–98)

	Production	Wages	No. of establishments*
Food, beverages and tobacco	0.3	- 4.5	- 0.3
Textiles, apparel and leather	- 0.5	- 6.8	- 2.0
Wood, cork and furniture	- 2.4	- 9.3	- 3.5
Total	0.0	- 5.3	- 1.0

Source: ESANE Consultores with data from the Monthly Industrial Survey (INEGI).
* Average annual change in percentages (1995–97)

technologies has grown at an average rate of 13.1 and 7.4 percent, respectively. As a consequence, employment in high-tech industries has grown at a higher rate than total employment (5.2 percent vs. 1 percent), although it represents only 11.6 percent of total employment in manufacturing.

In contrast, in industries with low technologies total employment is still lower than in 1994 while in medium-tech industries it grew only at an average annual rate of 1.8 percent. Furthermore, only in the high-tech industries has the number of white-collar employees surpassed pre-crisis levels.

Under the orientation classification, for example, industries with scale intensive and science-based production processes have also grown significantly. For the former, between 1994 and 1998 the value of production increased at an annual average rate of 7.6 percent, and for the latter at 19 percent.

Finally, under the wages classification, higher growth is registered in high wage industries while in medium and low wages industries the value of production has been growing at an lower rate than total manufacturing. Industries with these characteristics are automobile, chemical products and pharmaceuticals, and computers and scientific equipment. These sectors are clearly the winners (Table 3).

In the long run, this trend should result in a more skilled aggregated labour force. However, since employment is still highly concentrated in the looser industries, in the short term the adjustment has been painful.

The traditional manufacturing sectors, as foods and textiles, with less sophisticated production functions (low technology, low wages

Table 6
NAFTA's Loser Industries – Shares of manufacturing

	Production		Employment	
	1994	*1998*	*1994*	*1998*
Food, beverages and tobacco	28.0	23.0	25.4	24.6
Textiles, apparel and leather	5.7	4.5	13.3	13.1
Wood, cork and furniture	0.9	0.6	2.1	2.0
Total	34.6	28.1	40.8	39.7

Source: ESANE Consultores with data from the Monthly Industrial Survey (INEGI).

and labour and resource intensive) have been negatively affected by the economic reforms and NAFTA and, unfortunately, it is in these sectors that most of the employment continues to be concentrated. These sectors are clearly the losers in the short term (Tables 5 and 6).

3. CONCLUDING REMARKS

Most of the expected changes from almost twenty years of reforms are clearly going on the right direction. However, in comparison with other cases (namely Spain and Portugal when they joined the European Union) it seems that those changes are going at a slower pace. The primary manufacturing industries are still very important in the composition of the industry (in terms of both production and employment) so that in the aggregate the figures do not reflect the successes of the winners. For example, in order to avoid a sharp increase of unemployment in the manufacturing sector, the winner industries must increase their employment share by a rate at least double the rate that the looser industries are reducing theirs. In this context, an effective industrial policy should support not only the leaders in technological changes but also the primary activities in which the labour force is lagging.

The following caveats must be made about Canada's experience before a comparison can be attempted: Industrial integration between Canada and the United States was greater before the FTA than integration between Mexico and the U.S. before NAFTA. Some studies indicate that most of the industrial transformation took place during the early 1980s (when medium technology industries boomed), while the rhythm of structural change in the late 1980s and early 1990s slowed substantially. In this sense, initial industrial conditions were different for Canada and Mexico.

Although these findings can be useful to generate preliminary conclusions about the transformation of the manufacturing industry as a result of economic reform and NAFTA, we must keep in mind that five years are not enough. At the moment we can analyze only some trends while a profound structural analysis requires longer time. Recognizing this should encourage further and richer studies of the Mexican economy transformation under NAFTA.

FERNANDO CLAVIJO, an economist and trade consultant with ESANE Consultores in Mexico City, was senior economic advisor to the Mexican government during the NAFTA negotiations.

Sectoral Perspectives: Results and Opportunities

Sectoral Results and Opportunities: An Introduction

FRANCIS FOX

My role here is to facilitate the presentations and discussions of a sectoral perspective on the results and opportunities under Free Trade. The sectors represented on this panel – telecommunications, telecom manufacturing, energy, transportation and aerospace, and the automotive sector – are crucial to the Canadian economy and vital to its growth in the next century.

They're particularly important here in the Greater Montreal Region, which accounts for about 75% of Quebec's exports. This province's merchandise exports to the U.S. grew, as the Royal Bank impact study demonstrates, from just over 10% to just under 25% of Quebec's output in the last decade. Altogether, with trade in goods and services, exports now account for 37% of Quebec's economy, up from 20% just 10 years ago. As John McCallum notes in his paper, it would "the coincidence of the century" if this growth had nothing to do with free trade.

It's no mystery where the growth is – in telecommunications equipment–in firms such as Nortel Networks, Ericsson and Motorola, which make wireline and wireless telephones for companies such as mine. When AT&T brought out the first cell phones in 1985, it predicted 1 million customers worldwide by the year 2000. Make that 400 million. And as Red Wilson likes to say, half the people in the world haven't even made their first phone call.

And the Internet, for which Nortel makes backbone fibre here in St. Laurent, will have 300 million end users at the end of this decade for a medium which had no commercial applications at the beginning of it. Internet commerce alone is forecast to be a $2 trillion business worldwide in 2002. When you think that America On Line has a market cap exceeding that of General Motors, that tells you something about where we are going.

As Jean Monty has pointed out, more has been spent on telecom equipment in this decade than in the century and a quarter since the invention of the telephone. And about 45% of the industry in Canada is based in the Montreal region.

The deregulation of international long distance markets has unfettered some $1 trillion of potential trade in services and Teleglobe is right in there, with something like 40% of its volume in global overseas traffic, as compared with only 3% six years ago.

In aerospace, some 56% of the industry is Montreal-based, and 72% of their sales in 1997 were exported. The industry leader, Bombardier, has a 42% global share of sales of regional jets, a plane so successful its brand name is becoming generic in the industry. CAE has 75% of the world's simulator sales.

These are all high-end, R&D intensive industries, which are our future. But it is not to forget some of the more traditional industries, such as clothing, which have done surprisingly well under free trade, certainly better than expectations and better than the Americans would like.

The Ontario-based automotive industry, represented in Quebec by GM and Kenwood trucks among others, has certainly put up big numbers in the last decade, as the Auto Pact was continued in both the FTA and NAFTA. Led by the auto sector, Ontario's merchandise exports to the U.S. have doubled to 40% of provincial GDP under free trade, On a stand alone basis, Ontario is America's second largest trading partner after Canada, and Quebec is number six.

Beyond the sectoral perspective, I think the core question for business and labour alike is how free trade has changed the mindset of Canadian business, and how it has changed the way Canadians do business?

FRANCIS FOX, Chairman of Montreal International, is Chairman of Rogers-AT&T for Eastern Canada, and was Minister of International Trade in the Turner government (1984).

A Matter of National Interest

LAURENT BEAUDOIN

Our company, Bombardier, was among a small group of Canadian businesses that worked to promote free trade with the U.S. in the early days before any trade agreement was signed. Our efforts in promoting free trade were mostly a matter of national interest. For our company, there were no major barriers at the time, selling our products in the United States, because our snowmobiles were included in the auto pact and no duties were imposed.

However, in the mass transit business, if we wanted to sell our products to transit authorities, we had to comply with the Buy America Act which imposed a 60% U.S. content rule. Despite the rule, we were able to win major contracts. But we had to open an assembly plant to meet the U.S. content. To this day, the Buy America Act rules have remained while duties on Canadian mass transit equipment have gradually been eliminated.

In aerospace, the market was already very open and it was a global one. The commercial aircraft market was still dominated by U.S. manufacturers, Boeing and McDonnell Douglas. At that time, Canada was a small player with Pratt & Whitney's engines, de Havilland's turpoprops and our Challenger aircraft. The issue for our aerospace industry was more one of establishing a level-playing field with other countries in a business which was directly or indirectly heavily supported by national governments.

I think our industry has demonstrated since then, that in opened markets, we can compete successfully all over the world. Sales growth for Canada's aerospace industry over the last five year period has surpassed that of other leading aerospace industries in the world. Today, Canadian aerospace ranks number five in the world and employs directly some 67,000 Canadians. But 10 years ago, for a growing company like ours, free trade was essential, mainly to continue to have open access to the U.S. market. It was then, as it is now, the richest and most attractive market in the world and it is where we were already making more than 50% of our sales.

We had to defend our interests because there was a lot of "protectionist talk" going on in the U.S. in the mid-1980s. Most of it was aimed at the Japanese as a result of the market share they were gaining in automobiles, electronics, and so on. But "foreign is foreign" and any sanctions or penalties that could have been imposed such as the proposed 10% surtax penalty on foreign goods, could have spelled disaster for Canada. We needed a guaranteed access to the U.S. market for the long term and that was achieved through the dispute settlement process that was put in place in the FTA. However, the impact of the agreement, put into effect in January 1989, was not immediately felt and our exports did not increase during the first few years. That was because the Canadian dollar which was worth 83¢ U.S. at the beginning of 1989 was up to 88¢ by June 1991 and that 5-cents made all the difference in the world, considering that even 83¢ was too high. Fortunately, market forces finally prevailed and the dollar started dropping to a more realistic level. And the more it dropped, the better things got for everyone in Canada – employers and workers alike and only then, the benefits of the FTA started to materialize. We also backed the North American Free Trade Agreement to include Mexico, a country in development but dynamic and ready to take its place in the North American economy.

I believe that Free Trade also helps our company in other ways. With trade barriers coming down, it has given us access to the best suppliers in the world, thus greatly improving our competitiveness. We are also firm supporters of the World Trade Organization as a body to enforce trade laws and to settle disputes among its member countries.

We look forward to the continuing evolution of free trade and we enthusiastically support the Free Trade Area of the Americas initiative, which will ultimately create the world's largest free trade zone, with a population of some 800 million and a combined GDP of over $10 trillion. We believe now – as we did even before the FTA was signed – that Free Trade is in the best interest of Canada and all Canadians, as trade between Canada and the U.S. is stronger than ever and has a positive impact on the economies of both countries. And we believe the best is yet to come.

LAURENT BEAUDOIN is Chairman of the Board of Bombardier Inc.

A New Mindset

L. JACQUES MÉNARD

As I know all of us agree, if there is one thing that FTA, and later on NAFTA, has done it is to materially change the mindset of both governments and companies. That of course applies to the way energy policy has and is evolving here in Canada as well as the way in which power generators such as Hydro-Québec will operate their business going forward; I mean this in terms of capital expenditure decisions, the way we interrelate with our neighbouring markets and so traditional competitors as well as the way we will interface as an industry with our customers.

In the 1990s, NAFTA was among a host of causes that accelerated the move toward industry deregulation, along with rapidly changing technologies and numerous other factors, like deregulation of gas in the mid 80's, that have driven utilities' diversification strategies in the 1990's. In the U.S. it is the Federal Power Act of 1992 that initiated the deregulation. It is also in the 1990s that the Canadian National Energy Board Act was modified in order to comply with NAFTA.

In 1996, the Federal Energy Regulatory Commission (FERC) issued orders 888 and 889 for implementing open access to the transmission network and recovering stranded costs. Canadian provinces began to move toward wholesale competition with Alberta kicking things off in 1996 and Québec following the year after. Ontario, of course, is well underway to restructuring Ontario Hydro. In the U.S., many state public utility commissions are studying or in many cases implementing retail competition. California took the lead in January of last year.

With the emergence of new technologies, competitive pressures, new legislative and regulatory mandates, an electricity futures market and new players such as power marketers and independent system operators, are emerging and are playing their respective roles in reshaping the industry. Faced with the challenges of global competition and the need to reduce costs, large-volume industrial customers have become the strongest proponents of market reform as was the case in the telecommunications and gas industry, for instance. As with gas, those customers would like the opportunity to make direct purchases of the cheapest power available at any given time and not be required to purchase directly from the traditional monopoly utilities.

Trade in electricity between U.S. and Canada have constantly increased for the last decades. This has been true of us at Hydro-Québec, particularly in the recent past. For example, our volume of electricity sales outside Québec has increased 22.4% (to 18.6 TWH) and 37% in dollar terms (to $814 MM) in 1998 over 1997. We have also been much more active in purchasing power in the short term spot market when the price is right, of course, with purchases of $175 MM last year alone.

There has been tremendous growth in the number of U.S. companies entering the international energy market, both in purchasing distribution assets and in generation (Enron, Coastal, Duke). There is also a stunning acceleration in the wholesale market with billions of dollars in assets being rebundled, much of it by foreign players. Even though trade liberalisation is not the primary cause of changes currently underway in the electricity industry, the NAFTA regime has contributed to the push for open access and restructuring in North American electricity markets. It also contributed to the improving efficiency and environmental standards in power generation throughout North America.

The NAFTA regime is relevant to the electricity market in two other key ways: first, it has reinforced the market pressures for a competitive North American electricity market; second, it has and will continue to expand on the institutional frameworks within which the economic integration of the Canadian, U.S. and Mexican electricity markets may take place.

NAFTA's impact on the electricity sector in North America is arguably more important in the area of creating a more favourable environment for trade and investment flows across borders. Chapter 6 of NAFTA aims to reduce the capacity of government regulators to involve themselves in cross-border energy sales by removing barriers to free trade in energy and preventing the creation of new ones. In addition to incorporating the FTA provisions related to export taxes and restrictions on trade, NAFTA subjects energy regulatory measures in all three countries to national treatment. This discipline will very likely be important in resolving trade disputes. I could get into more technical detail here and refer to other regulatory safeguards embodied in NAFTA, but I'll set that aside for our purposes here.

In conclusion the NAFTA and the new industry environment which it influenced in the electricity sector will, in my view, basically have five consequences:

- It will reduce the cost of electricity and abate regional disparities across North America and in so doing make us more economically competitive vis-à-vis other economic blocs;
- The power generation industry will, in the process, become much more competitive and efficient thereby creating value for our shareholders be they public or private;
- The trend towards deregulation will accelerate the convergence of various energy sources in the electricity business, particularly companies emerging out of the oil and gas business as well as other new energy source providers;
- The new industry dynamics will continue to stimulate R&D so as to enhance capacity and efficiency rates of transmission and power generation assets. More than ever, the economic incentives to do so will be compelling. This will particularly be true of interconnection technologies which will be so critical to facilitating cross-border power exchanges going forward;
- Finally, the new environment will have gone a long way towards reducing regulatory uncertainty across North America markets by streamlining the rules and technical standards under which the industry will be competing. The net result of all these changes will be to accelerate yet more the process of economic integration in the NAFTA and permit industry (manufacturing and other heavy users of electricity) to expand and locate new plant and equipment on a basis of much sounder economic and business rationale.

L. JACQUES MÉNARD is Chairman of Hydro-Québec and Deputy Chairman of Nesbitt Burns.

A Sea Change

CHARLES SIROIS

The FTA was the catalyst of important economic change for our country. In Canada, where were we in 1986? Teleglobe had just been privatized. It was a monopoly. The Canada-U.S. Free Trade Agreement was a new avenue for Canada, which had traditionally used the multilateral forum of the GATT to negotiate its trade with the United States. In the U.S., in the telecommunications sector, the government had broken up the monopoly, of AT&T but most countries still had monopolies.

What difference did the FTA make for telecoms? The FTA was the first international, binding agreement to include provisions on services, and was a "ground-breaker" in this regard. While basic telecom services were not included in the agreement there were provisions securing access for customers to basic service networks and freeing up value-added services. This effort started the ball rolling.

Overall, the FTA brought about a "sea change" in the attitude of Canadian businesses and Canadians consumers who made a commitment to open markets, at least in most areas. Studies by the C.D. Howe and others have shown that this liberalization has been positive for Canada in terms of employment and productivity. The Investment picture has not perhaps been as positive and we should try and assess why this is so. For example, some commentators believe that the tax situation in Canada has made this country a less desirable location for investment.

The GATT negotiations of the Uruguay Round proceeded in tandem with the FTA but were only successfully concluded for basic telecoms in 1997. In 1997, 69 WTO members committed to the Agreement on

Basic Telecommunications. In the context of the WTO, Teleglobe saw the wisdom of asking for the end of its monopoly, provided it could get access to important markets abroad (such as the U.S.). Canada was able to contribute positively to a successful negotiation of telecoms thereby bringing this sector into the international trade regime and changing the traditional view of telecoms, based on bilateral relationships between state agencies and monopolies which had grown up under the ITU.

LOOKING AHEAD

The WTO launched a millennium round at the Ministerial meetings to be held at the end of 1999 in Seattle. There is much work to be done to continue the liberalization of services in general and telecommunications in particular. Teleglobe has gained from open market and has now grown to a company of $12 billion from the company of $500 million in 1992, the year I assumed management control. Free trade has had a major role to play in allowing Teleglobe to grow and to serve its customers who rely on international telecom to do their business.

Teleglobe has achieved a dramatic repositioning. In 1992, nearly all revenues were from Canadian customers. In 1999, non-Canadian customers accounted for 88% of revenues. E-Commerce and additional telecom infrastructure liberalization will bring additional benefits to Teleglobe's shareholders and customers. One can only imagine the additional demand for international service and Teleglobe feels sure that the growth will be very strong. That is why Teleglobe has announced a U.S.$5 billion investment in infrastructure to serve the projected needs of the marketplace. Teleglobe is working actively with the Canadian government to support the launch of the coming Telecommunications Round. The momentum and impetus for this support for free trade and telecom liberalization have their origin in the FTA and the commitment Canada made at that time to open markets. We must make the effort to convince other countries of the benefits of liberalization. We must make the trading system truly universal and include in the WTO such major economies as China, Russia, Saudi Arabia and Ukraine. We must make sure that the rules of trade themselves keep pace with the changes taking place. We must create an environment where Internet and e-commerce can grow. There is much yet still to be done.

CHARLES SIROIS is Chairman and CEO of Telesystem Ltd.

A New Frontier of Trade Policy

LYNTON R. WILSON

What I will call the "infocom" sector – essentially computers and telecommunications, including both services and equipment – is one of the world's most rapidly growing sectors, in Canada accounting for more than five percent of GDP (close to $45 billion and 450,000 jobs). Roughly 50 percent of Canadian infocom output is exported, principally on the computer and telecom *equipment* side. Infocom *services* – primarily voice and data telephony, wireless and cable TV – is about a $20 billion business in Canada, with a much smaller proportionate trade component. The panel of economists was concerned about the poor performance of Canada's high tech sector relative to the U.S. since the FTA. I do not have data which compare Canadian and U.S. performance during that period, but Kevin Lynch, Deputy Minister of Industry Canada, recently sent me some data concerning *real* growth in the Canadian information and communication technology industries sector compared with the Canadian economy as a whole over the period 1990-1998 – 69.5% for the ICT sector compared with 17.8% for the overall economy.

There has been essentially free trade in equipment for many years, whereas the services side was everywhere, traditionally subject to heavy regulation and administrative discretion. The infocom equipment industry has of course become a *global* industry. For example, Nortel Networks sells in virtually every country on earth and manufactures in many. The significant trade issues for companies like Nortel and Newbridge are no longer to be found in official agreements but rather relate to *fair access* to contracts issued by foreign parties, especially those with links to governments.

The infocom services business is a completely different story, with very different issues. In fact, as Charles has just said, so called "basic telecom services," including cable TV, were *excluded* from the FTA and NAFTA, but were finally addressed by the WTO in the agreement reached in February 1997. On the services side, the main issue has been *right of establishment* – i.e. the right to own facilities and offer domestic services in foreign countries. Much less important – to date at least – has been the question of exporting basic infocom services across borders. Given that right of establishment is such an important issue in any service business, one should not be surprised that the rules governing foreign ownership of infocom service providers have been the central trade issue in our sector. Canada was criticized, particularly by the U.S., during the last WTOfor retaining some ownership restrictions on telecom carriers – i.e. foreigners are not allowed to own more than 20% of a *facilities-based* carrier in Canada, say, a Bell Canada, plus up to one-third of a telecom holding company like BCE. But Canada applies no restrictions whatsoever on resellers of telecom services, and these have been important players, particularly since long distance service was opened to facilities-based competition in 1992.

Moreover, as everyone knows, the major U.S. long distance players have had no trouble establishing significant positions in our telecom industry – companies such as AT&T Canada and Sprint Canada. Despite some ownership limitations, these companies have been able to use the brand names of their U.S. affiliates and thus benefit from the cross-border spillover of televised advertising. The bottom line is that the telecom market in Canada – by virtue of our highly liberalized competitive rules – is among the most hotly contested in the world. Canada now has full competition permitted for both long distance and local service whereas most countries are still getting untracked from the monopoly era and, even in the U.S., there is still no competition between the major local firms and the major long distance companies. The benefit of the intense competition in Canada is that our telecom customers enjoy not only state-of-the-art telecom infrastructure, but among the lowest service rates in the world, with prices for most services now below those in the U.S. (on an exchange adjusted basis). One interesting benchmark is that an OECD study last year determined that Canadians also enjoy the world's lowest Internet access prices.

Meanwhile, most of the old restrictions that may have inhibited cross-border telecom traffic into and out of Canada have now disappeared. For example, we essentially have a common North American market for telecom traffic in that there are no longer any restrictions on routing calls between any two points in Canada via a route that travels through the U.S. – and vice versa. Another example – Bell's new national broadband company, Bell Nexxia – has a continental stretch of fibre going through the U.S. with terminating points in a number of major American cities.

The main issue for Canada coming out of the WTO 1997 agreement is less in the wording of its undertakings than in the way the undertakings are being *implemented* by the authorities in some of the signatory countries, including the U.S.. There is enough agency discretion – both at the level of the telecom regulators and the security agencies in many countries, including the U.S. – that rights *on paper* do not always translate into rights *in practice*. For example, more than a year has passed since a Canadian mobile satellite company, TMI, filed a license application with the FCC. Yet TMI still has no license despite its apparent right to one under the terms of the WTO telecom agreement. The issues that have ostensibly delayed TMI's authorization are the use of spectrum and national security. Both issues are readily addressable, but have been successfully deployed by U.S. competitors. Similarly, Telesat applied more than a year ago for authority to provide service in the U.S., as allowed by the 1997 WTO agreement, and that application is still pending.

So, while there are still policy issues to be negotiated and settled in upcoming WTO rounds (e.g. to permit foreign DTH/DBS satellites to carry TV programming), these are likely, in my view, to be less significant in practice than the need to ensure that the *existing* undertakings by our trade partners – including the U.S. – are honored in the *observance* and not in the breach.

A final, but important point – looking forward, the trade agenda for infocom services will increasingly be dominated by issues related to the Internet. The Internet is fundamentally a global, borderless medium – a medium that is defining the future of the infocom revolution. In particular, the Internet is enabling global *electronic commerce*. This will raise a host of perplexing issues related, for example, to the *locus* of economic transactions, the related issue of taxation, as well as the appropriate rules to safeguard intellectual property, personal privacy, the propagation of obscene material and so forth. For the time being, I believe that the trade policy community would be well-advised to let the Internet and e-commerce evolve largely of their own accord. Indeed, there probably isn't any practical alternative, since the field is moving so fast and the issues are still so little understood. But eventually, there will have to be an international framework for e-commerce and other issues flowing from the Internet. This will be a daunting, new frontier for trade policy and trade arrangements in infocom services.

L.R. WILSON is Chairman of BCE Inc., Canada's leading telecommunications company.

The Case of the Softwood Lumber Industry

BOB RAE

The most objective study of the real impact of free trade is by Professor Dan Trefler at the University of Toronto. His paper, prepared in 1998, assesses the impact of the Canada-U.S. Free Trade Agreement (FTA) on Canadian manufacturing over the period 1989–1995. The estimated effects of the tariff cuts are as follows:

First, by 1995 the tariff cuts had reduced employment by 10 percent, reduced output by 7 percent, and reduced the number of establishments by 12 percent. These numbers capture the large adjustment costs associated with reallocating resources out of protected, inefficient, low-end manufacturing. The fact that manufacturing employment and output have largely rebounded since 1995 suggests that some and perhaps most of the reallocation has been to high-end manufacturing.

Second, by 1995, the tariff cuts had raised manufacturing labour productivity by a compounded rate of 0.6 percent per year. The business press mistakenly reports that a labour productivity gap appeared between Canada and the U.S. during 1988–1995. Correctly calculated, Canadian labour productivity actually grew faster than the U.S. labour productivity by 0.6 percent per year over this period. Coincidentally, this is exactly the amount of the FTA productivity kick. Further, the tariff cuts lowered industry prices by 1 to 2 percent. Higher productivity in low-end manufacturers, resource reallocation to high-end manufacturers, and lower prices to consumers are the key gains from the FTA.

Third, the tariff cuts had no significant impact on average annual earnings, hourly wages, or weekly hours.

Fourth, the tariff cuts explain almost all of the increased trade in heavily protected industries. However, most of Canada's increased trade was in industries that have no tariffs in 1988 (ie. autos).

The effect of the FTA tariff cuts is smaller than one would imagine given the heat generated by the debate. This heat is generated by the conflict between those who bore the short run adjustment costs (displaced workers and stakeholders of closed establishments) and those who are garnering the long run efficiency gains (consumers and stakeholders of efficient establishments).

It is a useful rule of thumb in politics not to look back forever. NAFTA will not be rolled back. We have to invest more in training and education to assist those whose lives are hurt in the world of free trade.

We also have to do more to advance the interests of those who still cannot benefit from this more open world. The most glaring example today is Canada's forestry industry. The forest products industry in Canada is large. It directly employs in excess of a quarter of a million people in mainly smaller communities all across Canada. It indirectly supports another three quarters of a million people across the country. It is also the leading contributor to Canada's balance of trade. The forest products industry accounts for exports of approximately $40 billion and a sectoral trade surplus of roughly $34 billion.

Importantly, our forests are renewable and sustainable, generating a potentially stable source of employment and economic benefit for many generations to come. The industry is also in a process of transition. It is evolving from domination by heavy mechanical manufacturing and the mythic logger with his chainsaw, to an industry dominated by technology, science, advanced resource management systems, and tightly managed supply chains.

This brings me to trade policy, which is a critical public policy issue that will very much contribute to shaping our industry as we enter the twenty-first century. The Canadian marketplace is small by world standards, and it's dispersed over an enormous span of geography. Economic success and improved standards of living for Canadians have always and will always require access to major international markets for the goods and services we produce as well as those we consume.

As a trading economy, we rely on free, open and stable access to markets. To be globally competitive today, industries have to manage a complete supply chain, from the sourcing of our basic inputs, through to just-in-time management of retailer inventories, and often right out into after-sale service.

By the same logic, unpredictable, hard-to-manage, and costly disruptions to the supply chain are damaging to industry's future, and to the future of those who depend on it. That is precisely the situation we face today under the Canada-United States Softwood Lumber Agreement. The industry that has been the number one contributor to our balance of trade is now constantly subject to threats, countervail trade actions, and a general atmosphere of protectionist harassment. Under the agreement, production, shipment and inventories must be managed to annual and quarterly quotas with consequences for both stability of supply and price. Worse still, the quota restrictions under the Softwood Lumber Agreement do not apply to all producing regions of Canada, nor do they apply to lumber exports from other countries into the U.S. market.

As a result, we are seeing a dramatic reshaping of the geographic patterns of production among Canadian regions and between Canada and overseas producers. With the Softwood Lumber Agreement we have taken a potentially vibrant contributor to our economic future and tied it up with administered quotas and associated protectionist paraphernalia.

More shameful, this comes at a time when Canada, the United States and Mexico purport to have North American free trade. We need constantly to be reminded that Canada is a small market beside a very large market. It is inevitable that our economy will be more vulnerable to trade disputes than the large market partner. This creates an exposure for Canadian industry today, and it will hurt our economy even more as future new investments seek immunity from trade policy disruption by gravitating to the large U.S. market and, by implication, away from Canada.

Our trade agreements must be more clear, stronger, and less subject to unilateral, internal, political manipulation than is the case today. There should be much less scope for protectionist trade actions by all parties, but most particularly the United States, where such actions against small trading partners are carried out with virtual impunity. As long as trade agreements leave substantial latitude for interpretation, protectionist-minded legislators will find that that will fill the vacuum and Canada will pay the price.

In those cases where a dispute does occur, we must have dispute resolution mechanisms that are responsive, ie. quick, fair, powerful and definitive. Resolution of disputes under the softwood lumber agreement today is a crapshoot that is largely unpredictable. You may win, but you still lose because of long delays, high costs of dispute resolution, and the likelihood that rules will simply be changed to secure the interests of the large market partner in any event.

Canada faces an enormous challenge if we are to avoid long-term absorption of strategic business investment into the large U.S. market. The protectionist forces are strong and getting stronger in America today.

For Canada, I see no alternative but to tackle trade policy as a matter of national urgency and priority. A half-hearted approach will surely yield half-hearted results and leave us on a slippery slope.

Since the signing of our Softwood Lumber Agreement back in 1996, which expires in 2001, the United States administration has been under constant prodding by a powerful U.S. lumber industry lobby to increase restrictions on export of Canadian softwood lumber products not included in the Softwood Lumber Agreement at this time. Following those extensive lobbying efforts by this sector of the United States lumber industry, which is called U.S. Coalition for Fair Lumber Imports, the U.S. administration has acted. U.S. Customs was ordered by the U.S. trade representative to redefine certain softwood lumber products that were not limited by the Softwood Lumber Agreement so as to include them as restricted Canadian exports as of now. They began with pre-drilled studs. They've now moved to rougher head lumber.

I am sure you have read in the papers over the last year about that ongoing case. Notwithstanding that the WTO had previously given the U.S. government private opinions that these were not restricted by the agreement, an opinion that the United States government did not disclose throughout our whole court proceedings, throughout the whole revocation process, still pre-drilled studs became restricted imports by the U.S Customs unilateral redefinition of that product.

The U.S. customs has now reclassified two products – unilaterally, and in a protectionist manner – and the softwood lumber dispute has widened. U.S. protectionism is alive and well. The loss of these exports is measured in the order of $2 billion, which will have a profound effect on the Canadian lumber resource and remanufacturing sectors, the jobs they create, and the income taxes they pay to Canada.

The free trade agreements were seen by some – both proponents and opponents – as the "end of history." Not true. The battle continues.

BOB RAE, Premier of Ontario from 1990–1995, is a partner in the law firm Goodman Phillips and Vineberg. He serves as an adviser to the Free Trade Lumber Council.

A Reality Check

JIM STANFORD

It is often said that a central banker is someone who comes in and takes away the punch-bowl just as the party is getting fun. I kind of feel that way about this conference. Much as I hate to interrupt the mutual congratulation and back-patting which seems to be the primary purpose of this gathering, I do nevertheless feel that I must inject a bit of reality into our evaluation of a decade of free trade. I will try to do so from the perspective of someone active in the auto industry – since I was asked to speak particularly about this sector – but also from the perspective of working people in general.

It is simply incredible to me that the boosters of free trade have chosen this particular point in history to celebrate their alleged achievements. Because this is a point in time when the virtues of globalization, and the prospects for further liberalization, are more in doubt than at any time in the postwar era. Consider the following economic events and debates that have occurred within the past year.

Here in Canada we have become suddenly focused on the productivity issue – and for good reason, since productivity growth is a central component of rising living standards. Productivity is an incredibly complicated issue, of course. But one fact that has become abundantly clear in this debate is that Canada has enjoyed no productivity boom as a result of free trade, and the complete trade-oriented restructuring of so many sectors of our economy. This is nothing less than a stunning refutation of the central claims and promises that were made ten years ago. Recall the central economic argument in favour of the FTA: it would generate a significant increase in our productivity. Whole computer models of free trade were based around that single point.

And the central *social* argument for free trade was that higher productivity would translate automatically into higher wages. Neither of these claims has been true, of course. Productivity growth, at best, has continued at the slow pace of the 1980s, if not slower. And real wages have lagged behind even that productivity growth which has occurred.

How about dispute-settlement? This was supposed to be the greatest innovation of the FTA, and would protect us from arbitrary U.S. policies. Yet the recently concluded travesty of the battle over Canada's magazine policy showed dramatically that old-style power politics dominate trade policy as much as ever. What is "rational" or "liberal" about a U.S. threat to punish our steel industry because they don't like our cultural policies? That whole embarrassing charade was nothing more than a schoolyard scrap between two silly boys–and, as usual, the biggest bully won. The fantastic claim that free trade would usher in a new era of stable, rational trade law is now a cruel joke.

In the financial realm, too, the dreams of globalization have turned particularly nightmarish. The notion that self-interested private investors should simply be set free to do their own thing, and that we will all benefit from their actions, now seems laughably naive. We have experienced the most spectacular failure of private finance in 60 years. At least one-third of the world is still in a finance-induced recession. Some argue that since Wall Street is as bullish as ever, the crisis is therefore over. Think about what's happening in debt-ravaged Russia today, and the possible consequences of that worsening situation for the whole world, and you won't be quite so sanguine that this crisis is over. Ideas that until recently would have been dismissed as leftist claptrap are now receiving endorsement from prominent economists and main-street citizens alike: controls on capital mobility, aggressive measures by government and central banks to stimulate demand, and other measures to deliberately restrain the destructive actions of private finance.

Politically, too, free trade is in more trouble than at any other time since Bretton Woods. The rise and fall of the MAI provides a hard lesson to the chattering classes that policy measures which are simply foisted upon a skeptical public are doomed to failure – no matter how many so-called experts may have endorsed them. The rise of an inward-looking protectionism in the U.S., and to a lesser extent in Europe, is the ironic but direct result of free trade policy-making in the past decade: the way it was foisted on an unwilling public, the way it refused to respect labour and social interests, the way it so tilted the economic and policy-making playing fields so much in favour of private business. This is the legacy of unrestrained neoliberalism. And it contrasts jarringly with the promises of rationality and progress, the so-called "end of history," that was supposed to accompany the global triumph of free-market thinking.

And Canada, perversely, was a leader in the whole process: sacrificing our own reputation as a society which recognized the limits of markets, and replacing it with a naive and extreme faith in the virtues of unregulated competition. Indeed, the FTA and the NAFTA took principles of free trade to new and ridiculous lengths. We allowed companies to sue governments for lost hypothetical profits. We limited the ability of communities to expand their own public services. We prohibited many measures aimed at conserving and protecting our environmental and energy resources. These had nothing to do with the efficiencies of free trade. These had everything to do with making the world safe for private business and private investors–permanently. The FTA and NAFTA set dangerous precedents in expanding the institutional and legal power of business in the international economy. And sadly the WTO and other organizations have followed our lead.

No wonder there is now such a grass-roots backlash. Never in post-war history has there been such a gap between the promises of the economists and the reality faced by the rest of us–those who work in the real world, not the world of computer models and supply and demand lines that always cross. The self-interested businesses, investors, and lawyers who run the trade liberalization game will bring the MAI back, of course, along with other liberalization initiatives. But they are facing a more cynical, bitter, and educated opposition than ever.

I am not arguing that free trade has been the worst disaster to ever hit Canada. Or that free trade is the ultimate source of everything that's wrong in Canada today – as is sometimes implied by over-zealous critics of NAFTA. The really negative developments in Canadian economic and social policy over the past decade – high interest rates, huge cutbacks to public spending, and now tax cuts targeted at high-income earners – these things have had very little if anything to do with NAFTA or free trade. In fact, if anything, I have argued in the labour movement and the progressive community that we need in some ways to put NAFTA behind us. It has clearly hurt Canada, the NAFTA needs to be improved, but it's here now, and it makes no economic sense to try to undo it.

But the self-congratulation of the pundits and policy wonks is even more misplaced than the simple-minded opposition to everything "global" that many average Canadians express. We have all heard about how our exports to the U.S. have increased under free trade. But most of that would have occurred, anyway, as any honest economist should admit: pulled in by a growing U.S. economy and by a general increase in global integration that has been driven more by technology and information than by policy. Total U.S. exports have grown by as much as Canada's total exports during the past decade, even though most U.S. exports are destined for non-NAFTA markets and hence were unaffected by the trade deals.

Canada's auto industry has been perhaps the greatest "winner" during the decade of "free trade." Yet its success has had nothing to do with free trade, and in fact has been obtained *despite* free trade. The auto sector accounts for fully one-quarter of the growth in Canada's exports between 1988 and 1998. And it accounts for more than *100 percent* of the improvement in Canada's trade balance during this same time. In other words, without the auto industry, Canada's merchandise trade balance would have deteriorated under free trade, not improved. By 1988, of course, our auto industry was already mostly integrated with the U.S. under the Auto Pact. The Auto Pact was signed more than two decades before the FTA, but with a great deal more real-world foresight and intelligence. Unlike the FTA and the NAFTA, the Auto Pact provided guarantees of domestic content that went along with the elimination of tariffs. Without those guarantees, we would probably not have an auto assembly industry today. With those guarantees, we have what is perhaps the most developed and sophisticated auto industry in the world, relative to the size of our economy and population. And a decade of incredible investment in the auto industry during the 1990s has cemented our advantages in terms of productivity, quality, and cost. The principle of managed integration which underlies the Auto Pact is a model of how to capture the productivity and efficiency gains of trade.

The FTA was expanded to include Mexico in 1994. Regarding Mexico, the trade statistics confirm the continuing evolution of an almost completely one-sided economic relationship. Canada exports almost nothing to Mexico: just $1.3 billion last year, or just 0.4 percent of our total merchandise exports. Those exports to Mexico have increased by all of $187 million since 1995. New exports to Mexico account for 0.3 percent of the growth in Canadian merchandise exports since the NAFTA was implemented. In fact, Canadian exports to Mexico have actually *declined* in relative terms (as a share of our total exports and as a share of our GDP) under the NAFTA. As far as Canada's exports are concerned, Mexico could drop off the face of the earth and we wouldn't notice the difference. Bringing Mexico into the NAFTA was not about building a two-way trade relationship between Mexico and Canada. Rather, the NAFTA was mostly about facilitating foreign investment in low-wage export-oriented manufacturing in Mexico.

This is verified by our growing imports from Mexico. They reached $7.6 billion in 1998, up by close to 50 percent since the NAFTA was implemented. We import about $6 in products from Mexico for every dollar we export there. Imports from Mexico have grown by $12 since 1995 for every new dollar of export sales to Mexico that Canada has generated during the same time. And our $6 billion trade deficit with Mexico, up by 50 percent since 1995, translates into a loss of as many as 100,000 jobs in Canada. The lopsided nature of our trade relationship with Mexico is especially visible in the data on trade in automotive products (including both finished vehicles and parts). Canada exported just $242 million worth of auto products to Mexico in 1998 – up by a laughable $11 million during the first three years of the vaunted NAFTA. Meanwhile, auto-related imports from Mexico have grown by 45 times as much during the same time, totaling $3.5 billion by 1998. The resulting imbalance (of some $3.2 billion last year) is Canada's second largest auto-related trade deficit.

The prospect of the NAFTA significantly increasing Canada's export sales to Mexico was remote to begin with, but it was crushed entirely as a result of the harsh macroeconomic conditions experienced there. High interest rates and continuing government cutbacks, implemented in response to the ongoing currency crisis which Mexico has experienced since the NAFTA was implemented, have hammered the domestic economy there. Average Mexicans have no money to buy things that Canadians make. And, indeed, it seems to be the deliberate policy of the Mexican government and the international lending institutions to keep it that way. Until that changes, our trade relationship with Mexico will continue to be almost completely one-sided.

And this general lesson applies to our overall economic outlook, too. In this context, I think that both the proponents and the critics of free trade have probably given it too much attention in their views of what has been happening to the economy as a whole. If we can restore a focus on job-creation, economic security, and rising living standards for average working people, then it might be possible for free trade to make a real contribution to our economic progress. Until then, the promises of productivity and efficiency will remain a cruel joke for most of us. After all, the economic models that are used to estimate the effects of free trade all assume full employment, and they also assume that wages rise automatically with productivity. Why don't we make a point of trying to bring about that happy state of affairs, instead of merely assuming that is exists? By restoring full employment through lower interest rates and an expansion of public programs, and by facilitating higher incomes through better labour and social policies, we might create a situation in which we both realize and share the potential economic benefits of globalization – just as we done in Canada in the auto industry. Someone who is laid off because of restructuring could then actually find something productive to do with their time and energy – rather than taking early retirement or selling Amway from their basement. Only in that circumstance will free trade ever bring about some of the real benefits that so far have existed only in the minds of the economists.

JIM STANFORD is an economist with the Canadian Auto Workers.

PART FIVE

Free Trade and Social Policy

Globalization and the Social Dimension

GÉRALD LAROSE

I want to address globalization and the Quebec experience as perceived by Quebec workers and the less affluent members of society. I especially want to look at the impact of economic integration with the rest of North America, not only because it's the theme of this conference but because of the opening of the Quebec economy to the rest of the world in the last decade, particularly the phenomenal growth of trade with our neighbours to the South.

External trade, with the rest of Canada and internationally, now represents 57% of Quebec's output, compared with 45% in 1989. But international trade alone accounts for all of this growth, and trade with the rest of Canada has declined at a rate of 1% a year since 1989. The United States alone accounts for 81% of Quebec exports, and the U.S. has replaced the rest of Canada as Quebec's largest trading partner.

The growth of the share of our trade with the U.S. is doubtless explained in large part by the implementation of the Canada-U.S. Free Trade Agreement on January 1, 1989. This accord was completed by the NAFTA, which came into effect five years later, on January 1, 1994.

Anyone who lived in Canada at the beginning of the 1990s knows the economy went through a shock effect in this period. The shock was essentially not provoked by the FTA but by the simultaneous application of a draconian monetary policy, which proved fatal for many businesses and drove the Quebec unemployment rate from 9.3% in 1989 to 13.2% in 1993. In effect, producers of Canadian goods and services were confronted at the same time with the dismantling of all protective tariffs, and some non-tariff barriers, and interest rates that were as much as seven points higher than their American competitors, with a dollar that was overvalued, making Canadian products more expensive in the U.S. market. The Canadian dollar exchange rate was 89 cents U.S. at the end of 1991, as compared with 72 cents five years later and 68 cents today.

It's no surprise, then, to note that Canada's trade surplus with the U.S. melted away during the first five years of the FTA, from 1989 to 1993. No one spoke then, as many do today, about the "great success" of free trade for Canada. The meltdown of the trade surplus was reversed beginning in 1993, at the same time as the value of the Canadian dollar was allowed to fall, a fall which has only recently stopped and which represents an overall devaluation of 27% between the end of 1993 and the end of 1998.

It's all very well to recognize that Canada has recorded record trade surpluses with our number one partner in the last five years, but it would be more exact to see this as the result of successive monetary devaluations than as the success of the FTA. I think that very few economists would pretend that we can develop a productive and competitive economy by relying on currency devaluations.

On the other hand, free trade has not provoked in Canada the rise in productivity that was promised by many of its promoters. It's more through the impoverishment of Canadian society, where per capita revenue has fallen behind several industrialized countries, that our political and economic leaders have maintained Canada's competitive position.

To be sure, this decline was not experienced throughout society as a whole. But it must be recognized that these two free trade agreements, the FTA and the NAFTA, two accords where the aspect of social policy is entirely absent, served as an instrument for forcing certain classes of society to absorb losses of their income. Moreover, some businesses seized on the pretext of the trade opportunities to threaten, and in some cases, to move, to the southern United States, a region where the union presence is weak, or even to Mexico if the union didn't become more moderate. Many salaried employees had to accept wage freezes or even reductions in salary in these circumstances, especially where workers didn't have a union to protect them. It's not surprising, then, that real salaries have declined in Canada over the last 10 years.

Clearly, the massive cutbacks in public spending have also effected the standard of living of the less affluent. Take the Unemployment Insurance program, now called Employment Insurance. Nearly 90% of unemployed Canadians could count on receiving benefits at the beginning of the 1990s. According to the latest statistics, the coverage rate has fallen to 36%, following three so-called reforms, which have eliminated benefits, particularly among youth, women and seasonal workers. Some would say that it's because of deficits that the federal government was obliged to reduce its unemployment insurance benefits. But this argument has no validity in the case of unemployment insurance. Not only is the system self-financing but it has accumulated a surplus of $20 billion as a result of reducing the number of beneficiaries.

On the other hand, the federal government does not seem deaf to the arguments, and insistent lobbying, of the business community to the effect that the presence of an employment insurance regime that is too generous renders us less competitive in the face of our American competitors.

And, as if by coincidence, the employment insurance scheme we have today in Canada very much resembles the American system, as much as on the rate and the duration of benefits as on the conditions of access.

The Canadian experience with free trade, over the last 10 years, demonstrates that the opening of the doors to market forces constitutes no guarantee that a country can meet the challenges of globalization. The rapid growth of productivity, even as businesses have invested in niches where Canada has competitive advantage, has simply not materialized. Fortunately, more and more people in Quebec recognize the need of public investments in human resource formation as well as the need to create a climate favourable to innovation. After three years of draconian cuts in the health sector, the pressure from all milieu was such that the government, in its last budget, began re-investing in the health care network. And consider that Quebec's employers, usually the first to applaud cuts in public spending, called on the eve of last fall's Quebec election for the government to increase its funding of universities.

The Canadian experience of trade liberalization also demonstrates the impact of unconstrained liberalization on the distribution of incomes: while the overall GDP continued to grow, the incomes of most citizens declined in real terms, and poverty increased. The opening of markets, without considering the social dimension, also risks increasing the disparities between developed and developing countries, to the point of provoking an increase in social tensions. The example of Mexico, the third partner in the NAFTA, demonstrates this case. One year after its coming into force, Mexico experienced a massive loss of foreign capital which it was unable to contain because of provisions in the NAFTA on capital mobility. Even though the economy later recovered a certain amount of growth, real salaries remained reduced by about 40%, and there was a significant increase in unemployment and underemployment, while the number of multimillionaires in

Mexico increased dramatically. This wealth among a privileged few, as much as a growing and generalized state of misery, led to an explosion in the crime rate.

It's essential to consider the social dimension of globalization if we wish to avoid the integration of economies resulting in a decline of a living conditions for the majority, but equally if we wish to avoid populations refusing to even consider new accords for further trade liberalization. We only have to consider the fate of the Multilateral Agreement on Investment, theme of the Conférence de Montréal in 1998. The OECD countries wound up abandoning the negotiations for the agreement, such was the level of opposition within the OECD to an accord which set aside the social dimension completely, and which gave too many powers to multinational corporations which more properly belonged to sovereign states.

To avoid all kinds of difficulties, it's imperative to include certain common rules in any new agreements on economic integration, such as the negotiations to create a new Free Trade Agreement of the Americas by 2005. I'll give you one example from the labour field. Since the beginning of the 1990s, the International Federation of Trade Unions, which includes most of the world's representative unions, including the CSN in Quebec, has proposed that any new agreement include a clause on the rights of workers. Such a clause would oblige signatory countries to respect the criteria of the International Labour Organization, articles whose fundamental character was recognized by the ILO conference in June 1998: the banning of forced labour, the banning of child labour, the outlawing of discrimination in the workplace, the freedom to join a union and the right to collective bargaining.

What's needed isn't so much the establishment of common norms, such as at the level of the minimum wage, as the obligation to respect certain fundamental rights that will protect workers against the worst forms of exploitation and enable them to organize so as to improve their standard of living.

Certain steps, very timid ones, have been taken to recognize the necessity of applying certain protections in the labour field in North America. In 1993, the three signatory countries of the NAFTA concluded a side agreement, the North American Labour Accord, which sets out 11 principles on working conditions and permits the filing of complaints before international tribunals when a country doesn't respect national laws governing these principles.

Unhappily, this agreement is very weak in its ability to apply sanctions in the cases of repeat offenders, and doesn't lay out common rules to be respected by all three countries. However, it does represent a recognition by the three countries of the link between trade and working conditions, and attempts to give certain recourse to victims of violations of national rights in this area.

The four Mercusor countries – Argentina, Brazil, Paraguay and Uruguay – have gone much further than the NAFTA countries in elaborating rights to be respected in the labour domain in the Mercusor Social and Labour Declaration, signed by the heads of the four governments in December 1998. Moreover, the Declaration is overseen and applied by a tripartite commission, composed of labour representatives, employers and governments of the four countries. The concrete effect of this declaration, only recently adopted and very sketchily outlined as to sanctions, remains very much to be seen.

I mention these examples, not because they constitute precise models to be followed, but because they demonstrate that already, on our North American continent, our countries have begun to consider and take into account the social dimension of economic integration, and in a modest way, begun to put in place mechanisms which address these issues. These mechanisms didn't just fall out of the sky, nor were they put in place because governments had the wisdom to recognize the necessity of taking the social dimension into account in trade agreements. They adopted these measures pursuant to campaigns to sensitize and mobilize public opinion, campaigns organized by labour unions, the environmental movement and other organizations of civil society in the various countries.

A relatively recent phenomenon is the co-ordination throughout the Americas of campaigns to fight injustice, the increased marginalization of workers, and environmental destruction. The trade union movement has put a hemispheric structure in place with the Inter American Organization of Workers (IAOW), which includes the majority of representative trade unions on this continent, such as the CSN. The IAOW is working towards the inclusion of a clause on workers' rights in the FTAA. A much larger coalition of forces first saw the light of day in 1998, a coalition of civil society – environmental organizations, women, aboriginal peoples, farm workers, human rights groups – have joined forces with the IAOW to create a Continental Social Alliance. Several large existing coalitions, including the Quebec Network on Continental Integration, have already joined forces with the Continental Social Alliance.

The Alliance is putting in place a detailed platform calling for the inclusion, in any FTAA agreement, of certain universal rights, including basic social protections. The respect of these dispositions would be a requirement for adherence to the agreement. There is a panoply of measures that might be included, but a preliminary list is detailed in a working document that came out of a forum held in Santiago in April

1998 under the auspices of the Continental Social Alliance. It touches on subjects as varied as agriculture, human rights, environment, immigration, investment, intellectual property, rules of origin, the role of the state, financial services and labour. The document, entitled Alternatives for the Americas, is available in the four languages used throughout the hemisphere.

What the different dispositions proposed have in common, regardless of the domain in question, is the setting out of certain rights or fundamental principles that have universal character, and certain measures whose application could be modulated in light of the realities of each country. One essential element, to be sure, would be the financing of base programs, especially in the poorer countries, notably adjustment programs as a result of job losses in some sectors that would be opened to international trade, or to provide for the financing of certain social programs.

I want to emphasize that there's nothing radical about this, as the treaties of the European Union provide for the common financing of two types of measures which are provided for payments owed based on a level of income in each country. One possibility for financing, that Alternatives for the Americas invites the FTAA countries to look at, is putting in place a small tax on international financial transactions in the Americas, better known as the Tobin Tax.

I've discussed at some length the responsibilities of governments to put in place integration agreements that will respect the rights of all citizens. But I want to equally stress that all elements of society have a responsibility to assure the respect of fundamental rights and the putting in place of measures that will create a more just and harmonious society. I'm thinking notably of businesses, which have major responsibilities for the definition and respect of new rules at the international level, whether in labour, the environment or social protection. Not to mention their responsibilities as employers, business must make sure there's no discrimination in the workplace and that workers who so desire can join unions without interference. Business should also support co-operation among employees who work for the same company in different countries, an objective that the European Union has endorsed in requiring the creation of European business committees in businesses with more than two thousand employees.

The vision of building an integrated economic zone in the Americas presents an enormous but fascinating challenge. It would bring together some of the richest and most powerful countries in the world with some of the poorest. We can learn from the errors and weaknesses in some treaties like the NAFTA, the Mercusor and the European Union and build an economic and social space that assures universal respect for rights, assures durable development and a fairer distribution of the benefits of economic growth. But this project of the Americas will become a reality only insofar as all components of society, in each of the 35 countries, will have a role in it.

GÉRALD LAROSE is the former president of the Conseil des Syndicats Nationaux (CSN), the Confederation of National Trade Unions (CNTU).

Economic Arguments versus Ideological Ones

GUY STANLEY

Understanding what's happening to social programs in Canada and elsewhere requires that we make some distinctions between economic arguments and political or ideological ones. To my mind, the left's critique of the FTA/NAFTA agreements and of globalization rests crucially upon muddling these distinctions.

The FTA and its successor, NAFTA, are instruments of trade policy, not social policy. That is, they make most things coming into both countries cheaper (by lowering tariffs) and thereby make it possible for firms to organize more efficiently. This does have an impact on social policy but only in the important sense that any policy to strengthen the economy improves social policy if it is successful. To illustrate that point, the Fraser Institute recently released a study showing that in terms of purchasing power, the U.S. now spends more on social programs than Canada.

Sticking with the trade policy perspective a moment longer, even before the trade liberalization of the late 1980s, Canada's average tariff with the U.S. was around 7 percent, and the U.S. with us was 3 percent: these are not major barriers in historical terms. The argument that the state could expand social programs free of constraints before tariffs disappeared and found its hands tied afterwards can scarcely be taken seriously. Indeed, federal social transfer payments have remained fairly steady in current dollars at the same time unemployment has dropped and nominal interest rates declined. More people employed means fewer people on government income maintenance than there otherwise would be. Lower interest rates amounts to hundreds of dollars a year in the pockets of homeowners, car buyers etc. Free trade has helped achieve this by providing enhanced Canadian access to the U.S. market.

The more important point raised by the left critique of free trade is actually a critique of globalization. The left claims that open markets and the free movement of capital impose a social agenda on governments. By cutting tariffs and reducing restrictions on investment flows, so this argument goes, governments unleash competitive pressures that create a race to the bottom in terms of income maintenance programs and business regulation.

This argument is wrong in economic terms. Canada had relatively few investment restrictions when social programs benefits were increasing (during the 1970s and early 1980s) and it has relatively more now (compared with our major trading partners). If greater barriers helped preserve the design of social programs, then our social programs would not be changing shape and design, yet they are. In fact, the trade agreements are written to preserve countries' capacity to make choices. That's what the national treatment principle accomplishes. The only choice we can no longer make is to discriminate against foreign-owned firms. Governments accept this restriction because in today's capital markets, such policies make little sense. In areas where Canada has tried to maintain such policies, as in air transport and telecommunications, reality is forcing authorities to rewrite the definitions almost daily. Keeping two airlines alive in Canada required added foreign investment. Nortel Networks' status as a Canadian company needs regular re-visiting as it expands its operations world-wide and its shareholder base with it. But all companies active in Canada must abide by Canadian rules and meet the public policy requirements Canadians choose. In that sense, trade liberalization imposes nothing and respects the social choices Canada enacts.

The left also argues that Canada is converging on the "U.S. model". Historians might remind us that when U.S. policies promoted the New Deal or the Great Society, the left was generally in favour of such convergence. Now that the U.S. has re-discovered popular capitalism, the left objects. In fact it is also the case that the "U.S. model" upon which Canada is supposedly converging remains as always, extremely varied. Some states are more generous than others. And costs of doing business vary considerably from region to region.

Instructively, U.S. federal welfare support to individuals also varies according to living costs in the states. The level of allowable support for families in temporary need ranges between 124% of the poverty level to 175% percent of the poverty level for a family of four depending on region. These differences in payment levels are as great or greater than Canada/U.S. exchange rate differences. These varying levels show that even within the U.S., living expenses vary enormously: If social policies are converging, it must therefore be caused by something other than factor price equalization in open markets. I suggest that reason is political choice, not pressures from open markets.

As for the OECD, government spending on goods and service (including social policy transfers) varies between 30% and 60% with Canada still around 10% greater than the U.S. in current prices. As has been the case for years, both countries remain in the lower range of OECD government spending. Convergence on U.S. patterns, if it is occurring, is occurring for reasons other than economic determinism, such as more public support.

There is an economic constraint on social spending-productivity. If national productivity starts falling, then the burden of social programs will go up unless the programs are modified. Another strain on social spending is demographics, especially the so-called dependency ratio of non-workers supported by workers. When dependency ratios are climbing and productivity growth too weak to offset it, then social program design has to change. That is the case in Canada. But the key question asked by both right and left is, How should they be changed? The centre-right has focussed on revamping programs to help people get off state support as soon as possible. Most voters seem to support those choices, in both Canada and the U.S. These are political choices in the face of pressures that have more to do with demographics and, in Canada's case, worries about productivity, than about pressures from trade liberalization. Indeed, as the trade figures show, the economic gains from trade liberalization have helped strengthen Canada's fiscal balance sufficiently that Canadians can reopen the political debate on social programs.

Whatever its shortcomings as an economic argument, the left's critique of globalization is the basis for another suggestion or demand. They want trade agreements to be seen as a social project at the global level and consequently also want a social charter to be inserted in international trade treaties, just as in the Maastricht treaty of European Union. This demand should be seen for what it is (and globalization is not) – an explicit attempt to impose a set of social choices on countries. Such efforts are political and belong in political agreements, not economic ones. A better, less constraining, formula is that contained in the NAFTA side agreements. These provide the right of private action to call attention to and impose penalties on countries that fail to enforce their own laws. This imposes no agenda, but does help ensure that countries live up to their own highest standards.

GUY STANLEY is a Senior Associate at the Centre d'études en administration internationale (CETAI), École des Hautes Études Commerciales, Montreal.

PART SIX

Free Trade and Dispute Settlement

FTA and NAFTA Dispute Settlement in Canadian Trade Policy

JONATHAN T. FRIED

I have been asked to share with you some thoughts on the role dispute settlement plays in our pursuit of broader trade policy goals under the FTA/NAFTA framework. It is fair to begin this examination with a confirmation of some basics. Permit me to offer three propositions that we Canadian trade negotiators, as the main "clients" of the intergovernmental dispute settlement system of the WTO and the NAFTA, accept.

First: The Dispute Settlement provisions of the FTA, and the improvements made in the NAFTA, were a major achievement for Canada
The dispute settlement regime set out in Chapter 18 of the FTA, as modified by Chapter 20 of the NAFTA, provides an effective means for settling disputes between governments. The rules are largely based on the GATT/WTO framework, but provide more automaticity in the establishment of panels and adoption of panel reports than under the previous GATT system, and ensure objectivity in the selection of panelists. The system thus reinforces the rule of law and, as such, contributes to strengthening a rules-based framework for trade in North America. Five panel reports under the FTA, and the highly-publicized panel that rejected a U.S. challenge to Canada's dairy and poultry tariffs under NAFTA, have served to depoliticize disputes; all decisions have been fully respected, and implemented where required, by the governments concerned.

Chapter 19 provides for binational panel review and dispute settlement regarding antidumping and countervailing duty matters. Both the FTA and NAFTA place binational panels in the position of domestic courts to exercise judicial review over domestic determinations of dumping, subsidization, and injury in AD and CVD cases, and establish an Extraordinary Challenge Committee for dealing with allegations in circumstances where a panel decision may have affected the integrity of the panel review system. This system has been invoked in nearly 100 cases, and has successfully ensured well-reasoned decisions delivered more quickly and at less cost to private parties than domestic courts. And it no doubt continues to have a constructive deterrent effect on administrators of trade laws, who now know that their decisions are subject to close international scrutiny. Accordingly, while contingency protection has not been banished from North America, the FTA and its NAFTA progeny have injected much greater certainty and predictability into cross-border trade.

Second: The most significant impact of an effective dispute settlement system may well be its contribution to dispute avoidance

The FTA and NAFTA record the governments' commitment to using less adversarial, non-litigious means for resolving differences where possible. While less well-publicized, the record is as impressive here as in respect for panel procedures. For example, Canada and the United States settled a dispute about plywood standards for housing by referring the question to independent labouratories in the two countries.

More generally, the agreements promote what one might call, using GATT terminology, "transparency,", or put even more simply, procedural due process. The NAFTA not only requires each country to implement the obligations of the Agreement, but also to administer the rules of the Agreement in their domestic legal systems in a "consistent, impartial and reasonable manner."

Third: Scorecards of wins and losses are inevitable, but our overriding interest is in preserving and promoting a rules-based system

A coherent, rules-based system for free trade in North America, multilaterally anchored in the WTO, provides a stable framework and certainty for business. It ensures that traders and investors enjoy non-discriminatory access to foreign markets. Through consultations and dispute settlement, a system based on rules, norms and procedures helps to constrain the unilateral exercise of economic leverage. Accordingly, a rules-based system levels the trade playing field for Canada as a middle power.

If we basically agree on the merits of this rules-based system, should we be seeking to earn more "frequent fighter" points? Where does dispute settlement fit in our trade strategy? Again, three propositions:

a) *Litigation is not taken lightly: diplomacy does matter.* As in any legal system and as I suggested earlier, rules also provide deterrence. Codified rules do assist governments in the public policy process to pursue their objectives in a WTO and FTA/NAFTA-consistent manner. The various working groups, committees and informal fora available to us under these agreements do facilitate constructive dialogue, and thus provide ways far short of litigation to encourage, rather than to enforce, compliance with agreements.

b) *If Litigation is pursued, Canada often has a choice of forum.* Once a decision is taken to pursue formal dispute settlement, the Government does have to ask itself a number of legal and policy questions, given the coexistence of the FTA/NAFTA and WTO systems. For example:

> What is the result of the process? Is there a binding result or simply a declaration? Is there a remedy available for non-compliance?
> What is the nature of the case and are there particularities in one agreement or the other that assists Canada's interests?
> Would Canada be assisted or hindered by the participation of a critical mass of other countries? Or is it more appropriate to deal with the issue as a regional matter?
> Does the process allow for a good presentation of the Canadian case? Is there an appeal process?

c) *There is, inevitably, a need to take account of both private and public interests.* The assessment of whether, when, and how to proceed with international dispute settlement is completely discretionary within government. But government does not pursue dispute settlement solely for the sake of principle. The dispute settlement system provides a means for governments to protect and promote the reasonable expectations of traders and investors. Accordingly, commercial interests as well as principle will both figure prominently in any assessment of dispute settlement options.

Permit me to conclude these remarks with a brief look ahead at the new challenges emerging in respect of trade dispute settlement. Yet again, three propositions:

First, trade disputes are no longer just about trade
Increasingly, Canada's trade agenda is more about strengthening markets and less about opening markets. Its focus is the horizontal, domestic agenda of regulatory reform, the creation of non-corrupt governments, working to create a stable, predictable, transparent supervisory structure (i.e., financial services regulation) that ultimately creates a stable environment for trade and investment. And this means that trade matters will increasingly involve domestic, including sub-federal, departments and agencies. It also means that there will be

increased use of expert and scientific evidence in the standards and food safety areas in particular.

In the result, architects of dispute settlement systems will need to balance expeditiousness with competence, since the best evidence and best experts may not be available in the short term, and the timelines imposed on panels may be somewhat tight to allow them to absorb and analyse complicated technical matters

Second, trade dispute settlement must be considered together with domestic avenues

By implementing WTO agreements into domestic law, governments effectively make domestic judicial and quasi-judicial institutions agents to enforce international rules, in such areas as customs procedures, trade remedies and procurement. With more and more issues (e.g., investment, services, intellectual property, standards) now reaching into domestic areas and requiring legislation affecting domestic industries to implement, private parties must consider whether a bit of "self-help", using available domestic avenues, may be more productive than seeking government intervention to address problems.

Third, and in sum, dispute settlement is but one item in the government toolbox; diplomacy and trade policy remain key before, during and following dispute settlement .

As the growing interplay between the domestic and the international unfolds it will have a significant impact on your daily lives as traders, investors and legal professionals; it is advisable to stay current with international legal developments. The best-designed dispute settlement system, supranational or domestic, can only work if the rules themselves respond to business imperatives. The business and legal communities thus play an essential role, not only in helping to write and to enforce the rules, but also in thinking strategically about where we are headed and to keep pace with developments as they unfold. An ongoing dialogue among the legal community, business and government is thus essential to the development of an intelligent response to economic trends.

JONATHAN T. FRIED is the Assistant Deputy Minister, Trade and Economic Policy, Canada and the former Assistant General Counsel, Trade Negotiations Office.

Dispute Settlement: A Practitioner's Perspective

SIMON V. POTTER

Ten years after the advent of free trade between Canada and the United States, and five after its spread to include Mexico, it is a timely juncture to review the innovative[1] dispute settlement mechanisms which the FTA and the NAFTA brought not only to trading relations but also to investment rules and rules regarding the cross-border movement of services and even financial services.

These are the thoughts of a practitioner, who has been involved in the dispute settlement mechanisms under both the FTA and the NAFTA. They are offered with an audience of business people in mind, rather than trade law professionals.

CHAPTER 19: JUDICIAL REVIEW OF FINAL DETERMINATIONS IN ANTIDUMPING AND COUNTERVAIL CASES

The novel and original dispute resolution mechanism for reviewing U.S. and Canadian (and now Mexican) final dumping and countervailing duty determinations, which was offered as a temporary[2] measure in Chapter 19 of the FTA and institutionalized in Chapter 19 of the NAFTA,[3] has proved a highly successful feature of both agreements. It has removed political considerations, or at least their appearance, from such judicial review and has served to reassure exporters that the importing country's rules will be applied in a more or less reliably objective way.

The experience with binational panels under the FTA and the NAFTA clearly suggests that binational panels have offered a judicial review markedly different from that of traditional courts. They have created different dynamics in the review process of antidumping and countervailing cases. NAFTA requires, unlike the FTA, that the roster "shall include sitting or retired judges to the fullest extent practicable." This is a significant change which was originally expected to affect the binational panel process significantly. Indeed, the change was generally seen as an attempt by the United States to dampen what was seen as the activist and interventionist bent of the exclusively practitioner panels created under the FTA's Chapter 19. It is perhaps too early to assess whether there has been any such dampening, and there may be debate as to whether there was any needed to begin with, but I think that the new requirement has not brought noticeably different results from the Chapter 19 panels.

Of course, the goal of the Chapter 19 reviews was never to get to any particular result or to have determinations of dumping or of subsidization overturned more often or less often. It was only to provide assurance to exporters that the importing country's rules would be applied without political influence. The panel's ability to review a final determination is limited to a review of the administrative record before the investigating authority; a panel review is not an appeal or a trial *de novo* and the panel is not free to seek further evidence or to call witnesses. The panel cannot substitute its opinion for the views of the administrative agency whose decision it is reviewing. Even if the administrative agency is found to have reached its decision unreasonably, a panel is not free to substitute its own decision for that of the administrative agency but can only either uphold the determination or remand it to the administrative authority for action "not inconsistent with" the panel's decision (though this in effect allows panels to dictate to the agency concerned the judgment expected on remand, this power has generally been used only, in exasperation, on second remands).

Even though panel decisions do not become precedents binding on other panels or national U.S., Canadian and Mexican courts hearing appeals of antidumping and countervailing duty determinations, they do form part of the trade law jurisprudence and, as the Canada-U.S. experience has shown, they are taken into respectful consideration by other panels and may well soon be taken into consideration by the courts which traditionally hear cases of judicial review.

On the whole, the FTA's Chapter 19 binational panels appear to have functioned as intended and to have been successful. The process of review has proven to be speedier than traditional judicial review of antidumping and countervailing duty determinations and panellists have issued well-reasoned decisions most of which have been unanimous and most of which have evidenced no bias along national lines.[4]

EXTRAORDINARY CHALLENGE

Chapter 19 of NAFTA provides for two mechanisms designed to protect the integrity of the binational review process to which Mexico, Canada and the United States have agreed to subject their domestic antidumping and countervailing duty laws and their application. First, NAFTA has retained the extraordinary challenge procedure set out in the FTA. Though a binational panel decision is not subject to review or appeal, it can be challenged in certain circumstances by one of the governments involved before a three-person Extraordinary Challenge Committee comprising, as outlined in Article 1904(13), judges or former judges from the countries involved. This procedure is not an appeal; it is better described as a safeguard procedure protecting the integrity of the panel process.

A Party can resort to the Extraordinary Challenge under Article 1904(13) when, in its view, the integrity of the binational panel review process is threatened by a member of the panel being guilty of gross misconduct, bias or serious conflict of interest or of violating the rules of conduct, by the fact that a panel seriously departed from a fundamental rule of procedure or where a panel manifestly exceeded its powers, authority or jurisdiction set forth in Article 1904, "for example by failing to apply the appropriate standard of review."

It should be observed that the reference to the "failure to apply the appropriate standard of review" was absent in the FTA and has been added in NAFTA as an example of a criterion for an extraordinary challenge. This is in response, one may reasonably presume, to a request from the United States which advanced the argument, unsuccessfully, in the first extraordinary challenge under the FTA.[5] The amendment to Article 1904(13), explicitly allowing an extraordinary challenge on the basis that the panel failed to apply the appropriate standard of review, was expected to open the doors wider to extraordinary challenge.[6] It did not, and the Canadian negotiators were by all appearances right to think that it changed nothing, but only gave an example of a criterion for a successful challenge, and that the complaining party would still have to satisfy the extraordinary challenge committee that the error as to the appropriate standard of review "has materially affected the panel's decision and threatens the integrity of the binational panel review process," both hurdles not cleared in the *Pork* and *Swine* cases.

The NAFTA also implemented a second safeguard mechanism, in addition to the FTA regime. Under Article 1905 of NAFTA, a NAFTA country may request a "special committee" to determine, if consultations do not resolve the matter, whether the application of another Party's domestic law has prevented the establishment of a panel, prevented a panel from rendering a final decision, prevented the implementation of a panel's decision or denied it binding force, or failed to provide opportunity for judicial review by an independent court applying the standards set out in the country's domestic law. If a committee determines that one of the grounds for the extraordinary challenge has been met, it will vacate the original panel decision and a new panel will be established.

CHAPTER 20: COUNTRY-TO-COUNTRY DISPUTES

The dispute settlement process itself is modelled on the mechanism in the FTA's Chapter 18, which was clearly seen by the Parties to work rather well. Briefly, any Party may insist on Consultations and, failing their success within a period of thirty days, on discussion of the dispute at the level of the Free Trade Commission (ministerial level meetings). Failing settlement there, the aggrieved Party may insist on referral of the matter to an Arbitral Panel of five, named in a prescribed manner (Article 2011). That Panel must examine the problem and issue its final report within a demanding timetable which will ensure (as the FTA has done) resolution of the matter about twice as quickly as can be done under the aegis of the GATT. The third Party can always participate in the Arbitral Panel's proceedings (Article 2013). The Arbitral Panel's report is said by some to be "binding", but it is so in the sense that, should the Parties not come to an agreement that it should be implemented and as to how this should be done, the aggrieved party may suspend "equivalent benefits". (The notion of "equivalent benefits", long known in GATT circles in relation to trade in goods, now finds its application to trade in services.)

The experience under Chapter 18 the FTA suggested that Chapter 20 of the NAFTA would be used relatively frequently. Commentators, including this one, thought that private parties, though themselves without standing before the Chapter 20 Arbitral Panels, would press their governments to put the recourse to work. However, it has been used little.[7] This does not mean it has not served its purpose, or that the parties automatically prefer the WTO mechanisms[8] over the NAFTA mechanisms. It is rather an indication that the parties are more inclined to settle their disputes rather than allow them to reach the stage of submission to a panel, which was precisely the hope of the drafters.

CHAPTER 11: INVESTMENT DISPUTES

Investment is now subject, as are goods and services, to the golden rule of national treatment (Chapter 11): cross-border investors are to receive a treatment as good as the domestic investors receive (Article 1102). No Party will impose on investments from elsewhere in North America requirements as to export quotas, domestic content, technology transfers or the like (Article 1106). No Party will require that investment from elsewhere in North America be managed by senior management of any particular nationality (Article 1107).

The Parties agree to allow all transfers of capital and international payments, including dividends and profits repatriation to be made without delay (Article 1109).

An investor who feels that the equal treatment guaranteed by Chapter 11 of the NAFTA has not been afforded may resort to arbitration (Article 1115). This is highly innovative, in that it allows private parties access to what is essentially a question of a state's compliance with a treaty obligation. Indeed, since it allows foreign private parties to seek by arbitration the enforcement of treaty obligations, it has been said by some to constitute a weakening of the sovereign immunity of states.

Though the NAFTA encourages settlement through negotiation (Article 1118), the disputing investor has the right to submit a claim in arbitration under any of the ICSID Convention (if the investor's country and the defendant country are signatories of that Convention), the Additional Facility Rules of the ICSID (if only one of those countries is a signatory) or the UNCITRAL Arbitration Rules. The investor can seek not only declaratory relief but also damages. The defendant country gives a consent precedent to the arbitration by Article 1122 of the NAFTA. Explicit rules are provided in the NAFTA to allow for the arbitration to proceed smoothly, even in the case of stubborn defendant governments. There is simply no experience anywhere to allow any prediction as to how this ground-breaking feature will perform. All we know so far is that the uncertainty of the process, and the large stakes run by a government in such an arbitration, are an encouragement to settlement. Whether this encouragement will be large enough to prevent arbitrations from reaching judgment in future remains to be seen.

We do know enough, however, to predict that the claimants under Chapter 11 will be imaginative, and that the broad wording given to the definitions of investment and of investor will provide an amusing variety of claims. Claims of disguised "expropriations" have been made in the case of prohibitions on the importation of substances seen as dangerous to the environment, impositions of quota regimes for the export of softwood lumber, requirements for large deposits by appellants in civil cases, outrageously high jury awards which are not reversed, as well as jury findings which are reversed. Threats of claims have been made in the case of threatened plain packaging for tobacco products. None has come to judgment.

FINANCIAL SERVICES

Chapter 14 of the NAFTA, regarding financial services, provides for dispute settlement as well. Article 1414 provides for a mechanism which mirrors Chapter 20's mechanism for country-to-country disputes but requires that the panel members be drawn from a specialized roster.

Article 1415 provides that, in the event of an investor-state dispute under Chapter 11, the issue of the defendant country's justification of an impugned measure as necessary to protect the integrity of its financial system shall be referred for binding determination by a Financial Services Committee made up of representatives of each country's authorities responsible for financial services. Clearly, the parties did not want such an issue left to arbitrators.

SIMON POTTER is a partner in the law firm of Ogilvy Renault, practicing in the areas international trade law, competition law and commercial litigation. He was among the twenty-four Canadians named to the first roster of individuals eligible to serve on binational panels under Chapter 19 of the FTA, and is a member of the NAFTA roster.

NOTES

1 Innovative, but mimicked. The provisions in the FTA regarding country-to-country disputes as to compliance with the requirements of the treaty certainly set the stage for the WTO dispute settlement proceedings which are now, much unlike their predecessors, obligatory and binding and, generally, efficient.

2 Chapter 19 of the FTA established a Working Group whose task was to develop a substitute binational antidumping and countervailing duty Code which would, within five to seven years, replace national antidumping and countervailing duty laws for Canada-U.S. trade. This never came about, thanks in part to distractions from a slowly evolving Uruguay Round, and the NAFTA came with its institutionalized Chapter 19 before the expiry of the seven years.

3 It is also institutionalized in the free trade agreement between Canada and Chile and it is likely that the United States' last-minute and deal-saving concession to Canada, of a temporary Chapter 19 binational judicial review has now become a permanent and unavoidable fixture of any further free

trade agreement to be signed by the United States. That is, Canada's success, at first temporary, has likely become a permanent success for all the hemisphere, once free trade covers the hemisphere.

4 Though splits along national lines do not necessarily indicate bias, a glaring split occurred in *Softwood Lumber Products from Canada,* U.S.A. 92-1904-01, December 17, 1993.

5 Fresh, Chilled or Frozen Pork from Canada, in June of 1991 (U.S.A.-89-1904-11). In that case, the International Trade Commission had issued an affirmative determination that a threat of material injury to U.S. pork producers existed because of imports of allegedly subsidized Canadian pork. During the first review, the binational panel remanded to the ITC for reconsideration of the underlying data; the Commission came back with views on remand containing the same threat of injury result. Upon a second review, the panel unanimously remanded to the ITC with specific instructions, which the Commission read as leaving no choice but to reverse its affirmative finding. In its second views on remand, in February of 1991, the ITC, while reversing its finding, strongly denounced the binational panel (USITC Pub. No. 2362, Inv. No. 701-TA-298 at 19, 1991 FTC LEXIS 95) as having violated both the FTA and U.S. law. In the extraordinary challenge which followed, the committee unanimously concluded that the United States failed to meet the required threshold for seeking an extraordinary challenge and dismissed the request and upheld the binational panel's decision.

6 Some even wondered whether it would transform the FTA's limited extraordinary challenge into an appeal, on the panel's assessment of the law, at least on the question of the standard of review.

7 For example, in *Tariff Applied by Canada to Certain U.S.-origin Agricultural Products,* CDA-95-2008-01, which concerned the application of Canada's WTO tariff equivalence to certain U.S.-origin agricultural goods (dairy, poultry and egg products as well as barley and margarine). Mexico participated in the panel proceedings as a non-disputing third party.

8 Chosen by the United States in relation to Canada's provisions regarding split-run magazines.

Mexico and Dispute Settlement

M.H. YVONNE STINSON

In the last five years we have seen enormous growth in intra-regional trade within the NAFTA countries. Trade was valued at \$482 billion in 1997, with \$157 billion between Mexico and the U.S., \$320 billion between Canada and the U.S., and \$5 billion between Canada and Mexico. This can be compared with the figures for 1994, where trade between the U.S. and Canada was over \$240 billion, while U.S.-Mexico was \$100 billion and Mexico-Canada there was less than one billion. With such a huge amount of trade it is expected disputes of several kinds would be generated at both private as well as public level. It is therefore necessary to find institutions to deal with them.

The main dispute resolution provisions in the NAFTA are related to investment (Chapter 11), financial services (Chapter 14), interpretation and application of the agreement in general (Chapter 20), appeals of unfair trade actions (Chapter 19), failure to enforce environmental laws (North American Agreement on Environmental Cooperation), and failure to enforce labour laws (North American Agreement on Labour Cooperation). In addition, the NAFTA includes commitments to steps that will facilitate resolution of commercial and agricultural disputes in the future.

Despite this huge trading relationship, only a limited number of trade disputes among NAFTA members have reached even the consultations stage either within NAFTA Chapter 20 or the WTO Dispute Settlement Body (DSB). In fact, there have only been two final Arbitral NAFTA Panel Decisions. With regards to the WTO, the NAFTA countries have used the DSB in seven cases: i) Canadian measures affecting the imports of milk and export of dairy products, a complaint made by the U.S.A.; ii) Mexican antidumping investigation of High Fructose Corn Syrup (HFCS) originating from the U.S.A., with the complaint made by the U.S.; iii) Canadian patent protection term, a complaint made by the U.S.A.; iv) a U.S. countervailing duty investigation with respect to live cattle from Canada, a complaint made by Canada; v) in the United States, certain measures affecting the imports of cattle, swine and grain from Canada, a complaint made by Canada; vi) in Canada, certain measures concerning periodicals, a complaint made by the U.S.A.; and vii) an antidumping investigation regarding imports of fresh or chilled tomatoes from Mexico, a complaint made by Mexico.

The NAFTA Chapter 20 mechanism is similar in scope and jurisdiction to the WTO's Dispute Settlement Understanding, However, NAFTA's Chapter 19 incorporates a more limited scope – antidumping and countervailing duty matters – and operates under national rather than regional or international law. The NAFTA mechanism does not contain an autonomy clause such as the WTO incorporated to allow it to advance procedures, e.g , the choice of panellists.

Chapter 20 of NAFTA provides a means for resolving disputes among the NAFTA governments for the application and interpretation of the NAFTA. The steps include consultation between the parties; conciliation or mediation before the "Free Trade Commission" and arbitration; then ultimately, implementation of the arbitral report. This mechanism is a rule oriented system, which incorporates a formal adjudicatory decision – making process and effective enforcement mechanisms to resolve conflicts over the interpretation and application of international agreements. The jurisdiction of NAFTA Chapter 20 dispute resolution mechanism is defined as follows: "Except for the matters covered in Chapter 19 (Review and Dispute Settlement in Antidumping and Countervailing Duty Matters) and as otherwise provided in this Agreement, the dispute provisions of this Chapter shall apply with respect to the avoidance or settlement of all disputes between the Parties regarding the interpretation or application of this Agreement or wherever a Party considers that an actual or proposed measure of another Party is or would be inconsistent with the obligations of this Agreement or cause nullification or impairment in the sense of Annex 2004."

The arbitral panel process contemplates the use of a standing roster limited to thirty persons designated by the NAFTA parties, with experience in "Law, International Trade, other matters covered by this Agreement or the resolution of disputes arising under international trade agreements," who are independent of their governments and comply with an applicable code of conduct. One of the areas where there has been a problem is the naming of the roster. While unofficial lists of candidates exist, no official roster has been agreed by the parties.

A group of five arbitrators will be chosen, normally from the roster, in a reverse selection process; the Mexican government chooses the American panellists and vice versa. In fact in the two cases resolved the panels were composed of two nationals from each of the disputing parties, and a chairperson from a neutral country. Eight of the ten panellists, who have served on the two cases under Chapter 20 to date, have been law professors; partly because they have fewer conflict of interest than a practising trade lawyer. In addition they tend to be more familiar with WTO and GATT, which can be involved in Chapter 20 cases.

This proceeding is only for the use of the government parties who provide written submissions and one or more hearings and provides for panels to seek information and technical advice from experts. The panel must review the submissions of the parties, and clarify their understanding through the hearing process. They then provide the parties with a confidential initial report, findings of fact, a determination of the legal issues, and recommendation for resolution of the issues in dispute. Parties may submit written comments on the initial report. A final report is then issued which normally is made public.

The decision of the panel is not automatically applicable to resolve the dispute; that is, the "disputing Parties shall agree on the resolution of the dispute, which normally shall conform with the determination and recommendations of the panel". If the panel report is not implemented or another mutually satisfactory resolution is not reached, the complaining Party may retaliate, by suspending "the application to the Party complained against of benefits of equivalent effect until such time as they have reached agreement or a resolution of the dispute."

The NAFTA, in order to deal with the expected commercial issues and disputes, creates a "Free Trade Commission" composed of the Trade Ministers of the three NAFTA governments. It also creates a Secretariat made up by national sections to provide assistance to the NAFTA Free Trade Commission and to the panels established under Chapters 19 and 20 as well as their rules for procedure and codes of conduct. It is important to note that these decisions have no precedent that could be applied in other panel reviews.

As of June 1, 1999, four cases have gone under Chapter 20 of the NAFTA; three were in opposition of measures taken by the U.S. government that were considered to be contrary to the NAFTA. In these three cases Mexico requested the Panel. Of these three, only one has been resolved while two are still active, cross border traffic and investment and cross border bus services. The other completed case was against measures taken by Canada, well known as "tariffs applied by Canada to certain U.S.-original agricultural products."

While the only NAFTA mechanism for resolving "government -to-government" disputes generally is Chapter 20, the Chapter 19 dispute settlement mechanism is also relevant because of its subject matter, which is antidumping and subsidies disputes under national legislation. Furthermore, Chapter 19 provides a very narrow basis for government-to-government dispute settlement under article 1903; when a party alleges that the changes in national law made by another NAFTA party are inconsistent with the NAFTA or with the provisions of the WTO. The inconsistency issue may be resolved by a distinct binational process under Chapter 19, not Chapter 20, in a government-to-government action that is controlled by international trade law rather than national law provisions. Under the NAFTA Chapter 19 in article 1902, each party reserves the right to apply its antidumping law and countervailing duty law to goods imported from the territory of any other party. Each NAFTA Party also reserves the sovereign right to change or modify its antidumping and countervailing duty laws.

Chapter 19 of the NAFTA, like Chapter 19 of the CFTA, provides a unique arbitral mechanism designed primarily for private "interested parties" to seek binational panel review of findings of the administrative agencies of the three countries in antidumping and countervailing duties. Chapter 19 thus effectively substitutes panels of trade experts for the federal courts of each Party, for cases involving NAFTA goods. The five person arbitral panels of trade experts are nationals of the two countries involved in AD or CVD actions. Chapter 19 panels have to decide whether the decisions of the administrative agencies were issued in accordance with the applicable national law listed in the standard of review established in the Annex 1911. The panels do not directly apply international law – provisions of the NAFTA, GATT Articles VI or XVI, or the provisions of the WTO Antidumping and Subsidies Agreements – except to the extent these international trade rules are considered part of the applicable national law.

The panel's powers are not co-equal with those of the Federal Courts. For example, a NAFTA panel may uphold a final determination (of dumping or subsidies) or remand it for action not inconsistent with the panel's decision. It has no authority to reverse or dismiss an agency determination. There is no appeal of a panel decision except where there is an allegation of gross misconduct, bias, or serious conflict of interest, where the panel decision departs from a fundamental rule of procedure, or where the panel exceeds its power, authority or jurisdiction. In such instances, an extraordinary challenge procedure is permitted to a especial three person review panel for decision.

THE MEXICAN EXPERIENCE

The five and a half years of experience at applying the Chapter 19 process in Mexico has unveiled several aspects of these resolution mechanisms unique to this commercial agreement.

When NAFTA entered into force on January 1, 1994 and the country members decided to continue applying their antidumping and countervailing laws, the parties just modified their AD/CMD Laws to let the companies choose between national review or binational panel review under NAFTA.

Since 1987, the Mexican Investigating Authority (SECOFI), has initiated 205 antidumping investigations and 18 countervailing investigations against producers involving trade with 42 countries. (If you take each product and country individually you have a total of 884.) Most of the complaints were against the United States with 65 investigations, China with 38 and Brazil with 22; and other countries totalling 44. The investigated industries are mainly in the iron and steel, chemical, and the textile and apparel sectors. The chemical industry represents 29%, while textiles represent 12%. Thirty-six steel sector cases have been initiated, representing 34% of all the investigated cases. The Mexican antidumping system is among the five most used in the world.

The Mexican legislation concerning AD/CVD was enacted in 1986 when the country undertook important structural changes after being a closed market. In 1986, the country agreed to shape its trade policy in accordance to the main regulations of the General Agreement on Tariffs and Trade (GATT). In 1993, Mexico modified the AD/CVD legislation in order to comply with the NAFTA obligations.

Under Chapter 19 of the NAFTA, the parties strengthened their respective regulations to assure objectivity when decisions are issued by a group of qualified and internationally recognized experts. Chapter 19 also establishes an Extraordinary Challenge Committee to preserve the integrity of the binational panel, and a safeguard mechanism to ensure the correct operation of the binational panel.

Of the 53 chapter 19 cases which deal with antidumping cases brought before NAFTA panels, 14 cases are related to the steel sector. This indicates that this sector is the one having the most problems with unfair trade practices.

Now in NAFTA proceedings, Mexico has a docket of nine Chapter 19 cases, all of which deal with the final determinations of the Investigating Authority of Mexico in the matter of Antidumping Duties, and from which six are against the U.S., and three against Canada. It is important to point out that a final determination rendered by the Mexican Investigating Authority contains AD/CVD determinations as well as injury and threats of injury determinations because one single agency deals with both issues as well as causation. (It is as if there were 18 cases.)

Currently in Mexico, five NAFTA panels have decided upon SECOFI's resolutions to impose antidumping duties against imports from U.S. and Canada. Three cases were related to products from the U.S.. One of those deals with solid crystal polystyrene and the others were related to steel products cut-to-length steel plate. and flat-c from United States. The remaining two cases were against Canadian steel products, rolled steel sheet and hot-rolled steel.

Another three cases were terminated by complainants, seamless commercial steel tube from the United States, cold rolled sheet from Canada and hydrogen peroxide imports from the U.S.A.; and there is one active dumping case on high-fructose corn syrup from the U.S.A.

One of the main issues in this review process is the difficulty arising by mixing legal culture between the common law system and the civil law system within the framework of a free trade area. The Mexican legal system is not based on *stare decisis*, that is on precedents of law. However, it has been found that precedents can be helpful in interpreting the application of NAFTA and specific language in the Agreement. The Canadian and U.S. legal systems are not very acquainted with the concepts of legal security and legality contained in the Mexican constitution. As example, even though the panellists from the United States have reviewed the civil law system, it was very hard for them to understand several substantive and procedural points of Mexican law and the way they are applied, such as the so-called "actos de molestia." Panellists engaged assistants who were experts in Mexican legislation and procedure to advise them during the review.

A second issue is that of "developed country vs. developing country."In the case of Mexico there are three areas of friction:

a) In the area of law, there are not only differences of law, but also differences in legal culture. Mexico did not have a legal culture of judicial review of administrative decisions in matters of international trade and unfair practices (TFF). With the coming of NAFTA Mexico was forced to deal with that and find a way to accommodate the new situation in matters related to unfair trade reviews.

b) The different legal procedures, especially the fact that there was a new procedure imposed upon the SECOFI trade ministry, has required a new approach to issues. In the procedure rules under Chapter 19 there are numerous gaps that have to be filled in, either by analogy or by existing procedural law of the country (e.g. when to apply international procedure and when it is necessary to fall back on domestic procedure law). With less procedural law to relay upon panels reviewing Mexican agency findings have had difficulty dealing with unusual procedural questions. No doubt that this review mechanism had brought a lot of changes in the practice of unfair investigation not only in the investigating authority stage, but in the practitioners too.

c) The problem of formalistic approach of Mexican procedure before the more liberal procedures of U.S. and Canadian law (e.g. affidavit).

The third issue that should be taken into account is that of "culture," the way decisions are made, the way people elect the decision, the way the panel treats and interacts with the parties involved, and as well as how the panel meetings operate. Unless you approach correctly the issues to be discussed, it can be a serious impediment since parties are of different nationalities with different experience and training. This issue includes the problem that might be faced due to language differences. Even when they speak the same language, it sometimes proves difficult to get the message across due to differences; and this represents time used just to get the panellists to understand each other. It has been the experience once that was necessary to use the three NAFTA languages in their meetings: Spanish, French and English. It is hard to imagine the difficulties to discuss the issues involved in a review of a sophisticated case such as the ones relating to antidumping and countervailing duties. If being bilingual becomes a requirement then it narrows the group of participants who could be helpful in this process.

M.H. YVONNE STINSON, a former Trade Counsellor of the Mexican Embassy in Ottawa, is an associate of ESANE Consultores in Mexico City, and teaches trade law at UNAM, the National Autonomous University of Mexico.

The NAFTA: From Canada to Mexico

From Canada to Mexico: "A Common Future"

GEORGE BUSH

I'm pleased to be at this prestigious Institute's conference, the *Free Trade @ 10 Conference*. You have a great group of experts here, every single one of them knows more about the details of trade than I do, and then you have those who helped shaped and implement the policies and questions.

And it's great to be here to celebrate the legacy of an agreement that represented the best of international diplomacy. And I say this because whether you're talking about the FTA, the Free Trade Agreement between the U.S. and Canada, or NAFTA between Mexico, Canada and the U.S., each agreement reflected a mutual commitment by the respective countries to build a common future based on shared values, rather than always dwelling on past differences.

And I might also say that I'm pleased to see Bill Reilly here, because as important really in a lot of ways was the environmental cooperation between our countries and the environmental component as a part of NAFTA, but also the separate agreements we have with Canada on the environment.

I was pleased to see this conference not only looking back at what happened, how NAFTA came to be, but also looking forward to the future, to the challenges that clearly remain. My presidential library, of which I'm so proud, at Texas A&M university in College Station, has hosted some conferences. And my dear friend and colleague, Brian Mulroney, was kind enough to participate in one of them, as we took a look at events that led to the end of the cold war and to challenges that lay ahead. The George Bush School of Government and

Public Service at A&M also had a great exchange with Canadian and Mexican students on NAFTA, and I loved being a small part of that.

The point is that conferences like this one offer a great opportunity to look back and forward and, if you'll kindly indulge me in a personal observation, I'm so pleased that several members of my team have participated and will participate in this conference: James Baker, Carla Hills, Clayton Yeutter, Peter McPherson, and of course, Bill Reilly, our environmental expert. I don't believe any American President was better served by the men and women who stood at his side, and I believe Brian Mulroney and Carlos Salinas were equally well served by their teammates. I am very pleased that Jaime Serra, who was instrumental, a key instrument in negotiating the NAFTA agreement, is sitting with us here today.

And one thing is sure, we came together to work at a momentous time in history. We had a rare opportunity to build a new partnership with our hemispheric neighbours in the day the dictator was yielding to a new dawn of democracy and market capitalism. We wanted to help foster this trend. As Vice-President, I supported the Free Trade Agreement with Canada, and as President I was committed to continuing opening markets for American goods, services and farm products. We recognized that exports were a growing element of our economic growth, so we naturally had an interest in finding better access to more markets.

It wasn't without controversy. I remember Don Mazankowski took me on a fishing trip to the west here. We were minding our own business and suddenly an airplane came over, circling low, threatening our very lives, saying "shakes and shingles." I didn't know what that meant, but apparently we had a huge controversy on shingles, and what the heck a shake is, I don't know, but that was upsetting a lot of people too. So it wasn't easy.

We sought to expand free trade through a number of avenues, the Uruguay Round at GATT, bilateral negotiations with Japan, active involvement in the development of APEC, and our Enterprise for the Americas initiative, the Brady plan, these were but a few of the things we tried to do.

Without a doubt, NAFTA became a critical cornerstone in our trade strategy. It doesn't seem possible, but just nine years ago this month that Carlos Salinas and I presented the product of our negotiation, which Canada had been advising on all along, and that Canada promptly joined. And having come into office about the same time, the Mexican president and I had been able to forge a new spirit of cooperation. For my part, I thought it was absolutely essential to my country that we have close relations with Mexico as we had long enjoyed with Canada, and expanding free trade through NAFTA, lowering the barriers between our people, was part of that effort.

With respect to the other more troubling matters linked to President Salinas' tenure in office, I'm not here to be a judge, to pass judgement on somebody, but in dealing with him on NAFTA and a host of other issues comprising the U.S.-Mexico bilateral relationship, I have to speak up for him because his word was always good. A trained economist, and a committed free trader, I think our work together had real merit. And I'm sorry that he has these difficulties, but I think we would be remiss if we did not pay tribute to him for his key role in the NAFTA agreement.

As for Brian Mulroney, with whom I first worked with as Vice-President, after I became President, and as our relationship became closer, my respect for him only grew. I always appreciated his wise counsel, his constructive criticism – he could be very frank with the criticism, believe me – and he'd offer these things up. We'd talk very frankly about U.S.-Canada issues, and also on issues of global import. I learned from him, I learned a lot from your Prime Minister. And perhaps that was indicative of how similarly we saw some of the fundamental issues we faced as leaders of our respective countries. It was also a reflection of the fact that far more often than not, I think the people of Canada and the U.S. shared similar values. In any event, while I expect Brian paid a political price for being perceived at times to being too close to us, maybe to me, I can tell you however close our working relationship was, that Prime Minister Mulroney always had Canada's interest at the forefront of whatever discussion, never yielding on principle as to what was best for his country.

NAFTA was but one good example. After we were both out of office, Brian confided that during the debate over NAFTA, at one point his political support was down to the members of his immediate family, and he was a little suspicious of Mila, as a matter of fact. I know the feeling, I'm an expert on how polls can be here one day, and down there the next. Like Brian I felt the benefits of NAFTA far outweighed the downside for workers and companies, that it would create far more winners than losers, and, moreover, speaking from my perspective, it was in the interest of the U.S. to see Mexico and Canada grow their economies, to say nothing of our own, in ways that created widespread prosperity and thus further enhancing regional stability.

And yet, as clear as the reasons were for fighting for NAFTA, given the increasingly partisan mood prevailing on Capitol Hill, I knew that NAFTA would be a tough sell, and I wasn't disappointed. Leading congressional Democrats, including the top leaders of that party in the House of Representatives, backed by labour, and joined by some in our party, on the right wing you might say, fought us tooth and nail all the way. It was a passion-filled debate. At times the rhetorical barrage coming from the opposition both on Capitol Hill and around the country got a little out of hand. One prominent American, I prefer to leave him nameless, went so far as to predict there would be a giant sucking sound – you know who I mean.

There's no giant sucking sound. You've heard the statistics, those of you attending this conference, but here's just a couple of them. Since NAFTA took effect in 1994, over 16 million jobs were added to the payrolls in North America, 16 million new people with the hope of building a better future. On a parochial note, U.S.-Mexico trade has doubled, growing at 17% annually, and in the process Mexico surpassed Japan as our second largest trading partner.

Meanwhile, U.S. trade with Canada, already our number one trading partner, continues to grow at 10% annually. Also, NAFTA is widely credited with helping to stabilize Mexico following the peso devaluation, in the aftermath of that crisis.

Meanwhile, more recently in the U.S. as the Asian currency problem resulted in a significant drop in our exports to Asia, growth in our trade through NAFTA has protected jobs. Indeed, with U.S. unemployment at its lowest rate in decades, it is simply not credible for anyone to say that NAFTA is costing us in terms of net jobs.

True, the U.S. lost some manufacturing positions last year, a figure that was used was 385,000, but at the same time we gained 3 million new jobs in advanced sectors such as computer programming, management consulting, all kinds of services. Everywhere you look in North America, it seems that the job market is being transformed, and the trends for the most part are in the right direction.

Now, does this mean our work is done? Far from it. And yet regrettably the momentum that so many people worked so hard to build towards getting NAFTA passed has not been sustained. I can't speak on Canada, but I can talk about the United States in this regard. With the Cold War behind us, many countries are still struggling to develop and adopt policies to negotiate the geopolitical landscape still in a state of flux.

In my country, some people are using uncertainty and ambiguity of the moment to create a momentum for turning America selfishly inward, away from the world. Even though they deny it, they advocate policies that amount to protectionism and isolationism. Their slogans: "Come home America," and "America First."

This is selfish, this is beneath the history of my great country, but it's out there, and it worries me, this coalition of left and right. I just simply think that these views are wrong. On trade, that same odd coalition that fought me earlier this decade, the far left joined by the far right, remains in tact, and no doubt these elements were emboldened by our inability, President Clinton's inability, to secure fast-track authority. You all know that fast-track authority is necessary so the President can negotiate a treaty without mindless amendments being placed on it.

The treaty then goes to the Congress and has to be voted up or down. Without that fast-track, it is impossible for any President to negotiate a trade agreement. I believe that loss of fast-track sent a horrible signal to the world, not simply in this hemisphere, but I know it sent a bad signal to Asia and to Europe as to what the heartbeat, as to what the intent of the United States was. Are we backing away from our commitment to free and fair trade?

Meanwhile the world is not waiting for us to muster renewed resolve, as Canada has shown by securing further free trade agreements with Chile and Israel and others. Suffice to say, I hope the United States can find a way to move forward with Chile, and engage the member states of MERCUSOR. As I stated as President, I hope to see the day that our hemisphere is totally united under free trade agreements for the Americas, and I might add that as soon as Mr. Castro leaves the scene, I hope – I know – our hemisphere will be united in democracy.

With regards to the global trading I hope that we can continue to find ways to eliminate, in a responsible, forward-looking way, barriers to trade. I might say parenthetically that I hope China soon becomes a member of the World Trade Organization. It makes no sense at all to keep China on the outside looking in.

I hope that agreements like NAFTA will lead to the elimination of trading blocs, pitting one region against another. I believe the NAFTA and the FTA were not just steps to expanding free trade north and south, but also east and west. I hope that we'll hold up our end of our agreement, and make sure NAFTA is fully implemented by 2008. The complexity of the issues that remain to be ironed out are a testament to the difficulties we've faced in securing the peace, and yet at the end of the day, in spite of all the new challenges that remain, I am more optimistic about the future than at any time in my life. I believe that my grandchildren have the opportunity now to live in a very, very peaceful and productive, harmonious millennium.

I think we all have to work towards that end, but with the superpower confrontation gone, I believe that is going to be a real result. As we near the end of this decade, and look at the challenges and opportunities, much work remains to secure the full promise of peace, justice and growth. Looking around this room at this distinguished gathering, and last night having the opportunity to interact with some of Canada's leading businessmen and academics, I believe we all seek the same thing. And that is a better, more peaceful, more prosperous future for our children and our grandchildren. To do so, it is absolutely imperative that our respective countries continue to work to maintain the kind of partnership that at its core recognizes and values international cooperation as the key component to building the brighter future we all seek.

Brian Mulroney did that. Others in Mexico and in the United States and in Canada, must emulate his commitment to free and fair trade. Sometimes you have to take the political heat to get something majestic done for your country and indeed for the hemisphere.

GEORGE BUSH was President of the United States from 1989 to 1993. The NAFTA was an initiative of the Bush Administration. As Vice-President from 1981–89, under President Reagan, he was also closely involved with the Canada-U.S. FTA.

The Most Comprehensive Agreement Ever

CARLA A. HILLS

I am delighted to participate in this conference to commemorate the fifth anniversary of the North American Free Trade Agreement and the tenth anniversary of the Canada-U.S. Free Trade Agreement. I was so pleased by the prospect of a reunion with John Crosbie, Michael Wilson, Jaime Serra, my counterparts in trade and partners in the quest for market openings. Each has become a friend for whom I have deep respect, admiration, and affection. Actually, I saw this event as an opportunity to share with you less reported occasions, like the time that John taught us the refrain "She's dead but she won't lie down!" Jaime's undying attachment to U.S. baseball. And Michael's fondness for walking paths around the Watergate Hotel.

They got wind of this and to bring substance and order to these proceedings, the organizers sent me a four-point agenda:

1 What was the U.S. looking for in the NAFTA negotiation?
2 What did we get?
3 Was it a good deal?
4 How did the processes of negotiating the NAFTA and the Canada-U.S. Free Trade Agreement influence the World Trade Organization?

So let me address those questions.

First, our goal: The North American Free Trade Agreement was an unusual negotiation in many ways. Apart from a very few exceptions, all three parties agreed at the outset that our goal was to create a free trade region. So while there was hard bargaining, particularly regarding the time that each of us would take to remove our respective barriers, we were partners in the effort to find ways to overcome the obstacles to achieve our goal. What was required most was ingenuity and analysis, and Michael and Jaime, and their respective teams, brought both in generous measure.

Second, what the U.S. got was the most comprehensive trade agreement ever concluded.

The NAFTA:

- Eliminates, not just reduces, tariffs on *all* industrial goods;
- Guarantees unrestricted agricultural trade within 15 years between U.S. and Mexico, the first trade agreement to remove all such barriers;
- Provides the highest standards of protection for intellectual property of any trade agreement;
- Opens a broad range of services; and
- Establishes rules to protect investors, something not yet achieved in any multilateral agreement.

Third, it was a great deal for all three parties, for the NAFTA resulted in explosive growth of trade throughout the region. Between 1994, the first year of the agreement, and today:

- U.S. exports to Mexico have soared more than 50 percent;
- Mexican exports to the U.S. have doubled;
- Mexico's exports to Canada have jumped more than 50 percent; and
- Shipments between the U.S. and Canada have doubled.

Trade of all three parties has grown substantially faster within the region than with the rest of the world. Canada remains our largest trading partner. Mexico has replaced Japan as our second largest.

Removing trade barriers and restrictive regulations enabled industries like the automotive, electronic, chemical, and textile and apparel to integrate their production across a wide region which has substantially strengthened their competitive positions.

And the NAFTA had benefits beyond North America. This agreement demonstrated that nations of very different backgrounds, language, and development levels can sit down and negotiate the means to enlarge opportunities that benefit all of the participants.

Finally, the NAFTA dramatically affected thinking worldwide. The negotiation and ratification by our three countries:

- Encouraged leaders in the Asia Pacific Economic Cooperation Forum (APEC) just a few days after the U.S. Congress ratified the NAFTA to agree to negotiate free trade and investment throughout the vast Asia-Pacific region – the industrialized countries by the year 2010 and the developing countries by the year 2020.
- Breathed new life into the then stalled multilateral negotiations, and few months later the Uruguay Round was concluded and its crown jewel, the World Trade Organization, was created.
- Persuaded all 34 leaders at the Miami Summit just one year later to commit to negotiate a Free Trade Agreement for the Americas by the year 2005.

These trade initiatives, multilateral and regional, have made and will continue to make a positive contribution to our respective economies – proving once again that open trade and investment fuel growth and raise living standards.

Though not on the agenda sent to me, let me mention one problem associated with the NAFTA, which has nothing to do with what was negotiated and everything to do with what has and has not happened in the U.S. since the negotiation was concluded. What has happened is that opponents of NAFTA have used it as a club against opening markets. Ironically, "no more NAFTAS" continues to be used as a rallying cry in the U.S. by the very labour unions whose workers have benefited very substantially from the agreement.

What has not happened is that proponents have not conducted a sustained campaign to set the record straight. President Bush envisioned the NAFTA as a first step in creating a hemisphere without barriers. Instead, despite the agreement's very positive outcomes and our robust economy, we have not yet implemented that vision. We still do not have fast track authority necessary to move forward. Our challenge is to galvanize opinion makers to talk about the good things that have come from the NAFTA and why opening markets constitute a proven way to tap into new and larger opportunities that make us more competitive, which in turn increases our productivity and raises our standards of living. Because this conference contributes to that end, it adds to my pleasure in being here.

CARLA A. HILLS, United States Trade Representative in the Bush Administration (1989–1993), negotiated the NAFTA on behalf of the United States. She is Chair and CEO of Hills & Company, Washington D.C.

NAFTA and the Mexican Economy

JAIME SERRA PUCHE

It's a pleasure for me to participate in this important conference, which marks the fifth anniversary of the NAFTA, and allows us to evaluate the progress our three countries have achieved, and the progress we have yet to make.

It's also a pleasure, as always, to be here with Carla Hills and Michael Wilson, veterans of the long march to the NAFTA agreement, and particularly fellow survivors of the long, hot summer of 1992.

I might say that I returned again in the summer of 1993, to another Washington hotel, to conclude the side deals on the environment and labour standards, but by then Carla and Michael had moved on. If you'll permit, I want to pay tribute and say a word of thanks to the negotiating teams of all three countries, who set the highest standards of professionalism throughout negotiating process. Each delegation represented the national interest of its own country, but each also took the larger and longer view of the benefits that would result from an agreement.

The NAFTA trading area is today the largest regional economy in the world, accounting for some 22% of global output. It's a market of nearly 400 million people, some 90 million in Mexico.

The NAFTA represented the first regional trade agreement in the Americas, and significantly was the first negotiation and agreement between two developed economies and a developing one, between two firmly established trading nations and one whose export economy has emerged only in the last 15 years, and grown remarkably in the five years of the NAFTA.

I've brought along power point material which makes these points very clearly.

First, on the effects of adhering to trade organizations and trade agreements on the degree of openness in the Mexican economy, measured as exports plus imports, divided by GDP. As you can see, there is a significant increase in openness after Mexico joined the GATT in 1986, and a spike after NAFTA implementation in 1994.

It's interesting to look at the growth of Mexican exports since the last pre-GATT year of 1985. This is illustrated by Chart 2. In 1985, Mexican exports were only $21 billion U.S., and by 1998 they had increased nearly six times to $117.5 billion, and we had become America's second largest trading partner, ahead of Japan and behind only Canada.

But look at the breakdown of those exports, then and now. In 1985, nearly two-thirds of Mexico's exports were in oil and mining, only 30% in manufacturing, and the remainder in agribusiness products. In 1998, 90% of exports were manufactured goods, with only 5% in oil and mining. Expressed in dollars in Chart 3, non-oil exports, which amounted to less than $10 billion in 1985, increased by a factor of more than 10 to $110 billion last year.

Again, in Chart 4, we see the contribution of exports to total GDP growth on a quarterly basis in the five years since NAFTA implementation. On average, exports have contributed about half of GDP growth over the period.

Looking at the U.S. market in Chart 5, we can see the growth of imports from Canada and Mexico, as well as the rest of the world, since 1991. In the first three years, Canada was within the FTA framework while Mexico was not yet within the NAFTA, and Canada experienced measurable export growth, even in the deep recession of 1991 when Mexican exports flatlined. But since 1994, Mexican exports to the U.S. grew by nearly 25% in a single year, 1996, while Canadians exports continued to experience stronger growth than the rest of the world.

On a regional basis of U.S. imports from Latin America, in Chart 6, imports from Mexico have increased by 184% since 1990, as compared with 59.8% from the rest of the Latin American nations, a gap that has grown since NAFTA implementation in 1994.

In addition to trade flows, it's also important that we examine and evaluate investment flows, since the NAFTA is also an investment agreement. Chart 8 gives us a historical overview of the evolution of Foreign Direct Investment (FDI) in Mexico.

Going back to 1980, FDI in Mexico was less than $2 billion U.S. After we joined the GATT in 1986, it surged to $4 billion in 1987. But the real growth, explosive growth, comes after the NAFTA.

Chart 1*
Degree of openness in Mexico

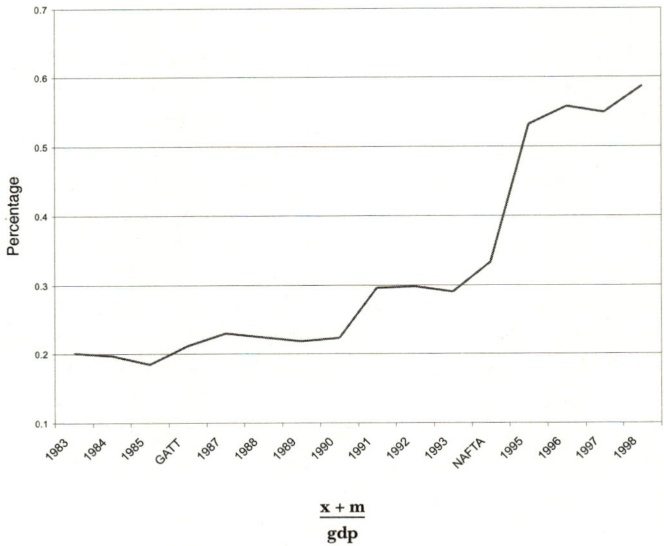

$$\frac{x + m}{gdp}$$

In the last pre-NAFTA year of 1993, FDI was around \$5 billion, but immediately doubled to \$10 billion in 1994, and after the 1995 recession grew to \$13 billion again by 1997. Over the five years of the NAFTA, FDI in Mexico is some \$47 billion.

The final chart shows the breakdown of FDI in Mexico, with 58% in manufacturing, and another 25% in commerce and financial services. The implications for employment creation are obvious. Investment creates jobs. That's what we had in mind from the beginning.

To summarize, Mexico has benefited from NAFTA. Trade and investment flows have increased dramatically, improving overall economic growth, building a more open and competitive economy, and creating new jobs.

DR JAIME SERRA PUCHE, former Minister of Trade for Mexico, negotiated the NAFTA on behalf of his country. He is now a senior partner in the firm of SAI Consultores in Mexico City.

* All charts in this presentation are from SECOFI, Mexican Trade Ministry

Chart 2
Composition of Mexican Exports

1985 : 21.6 billion dollars

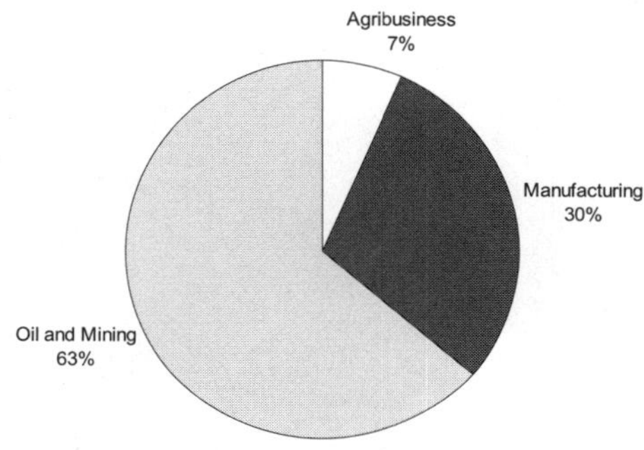

1998: 117.5 billion dollars

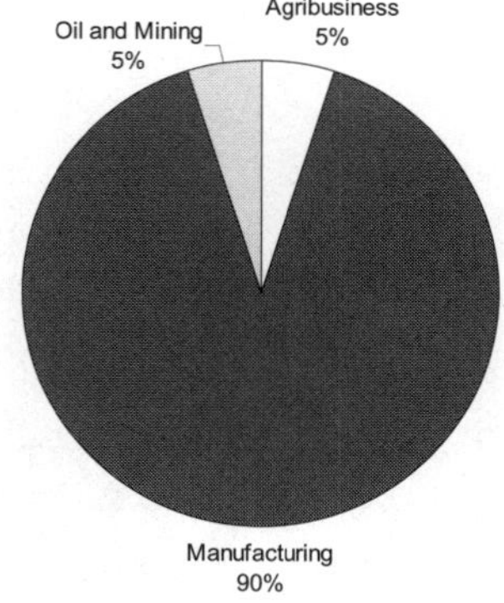

Chart 3
Evolution of non-oil exports in Mexico

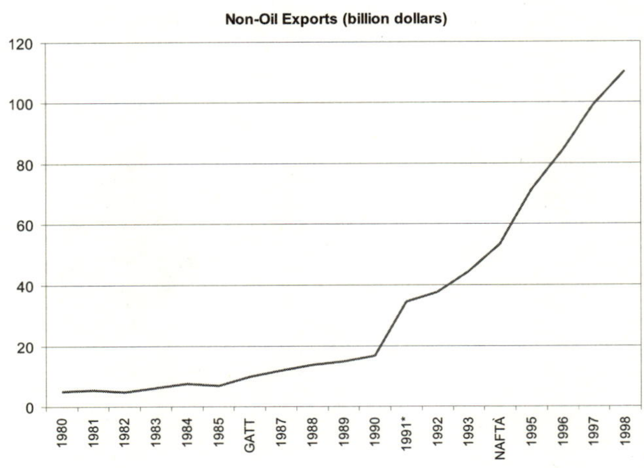

Chart 4

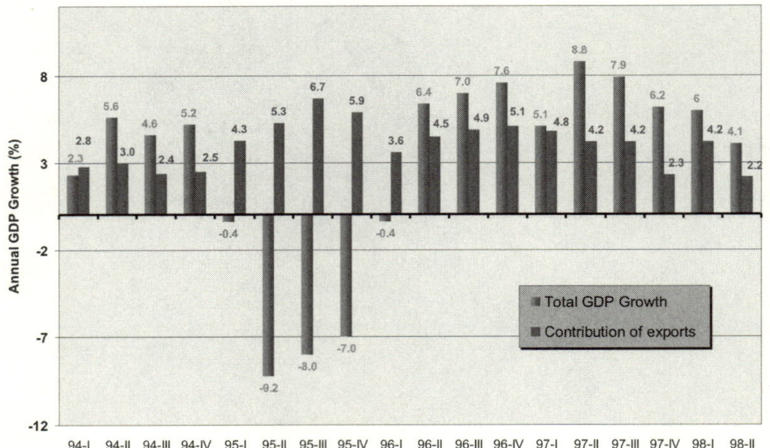

Chart 5
Exports and the US market

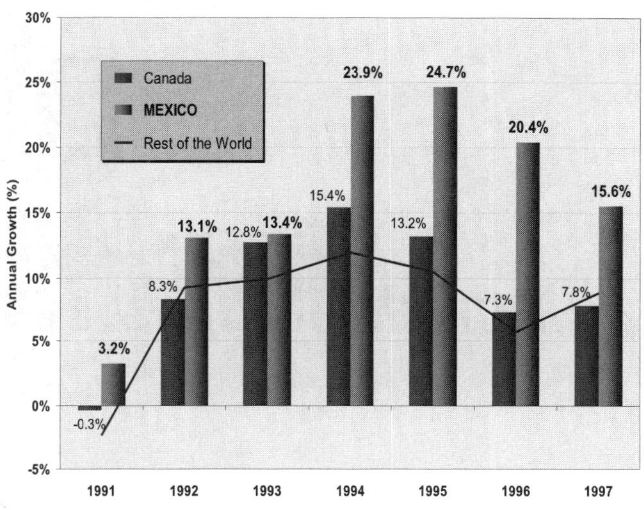

Chart 6
Latin American exports to the US market

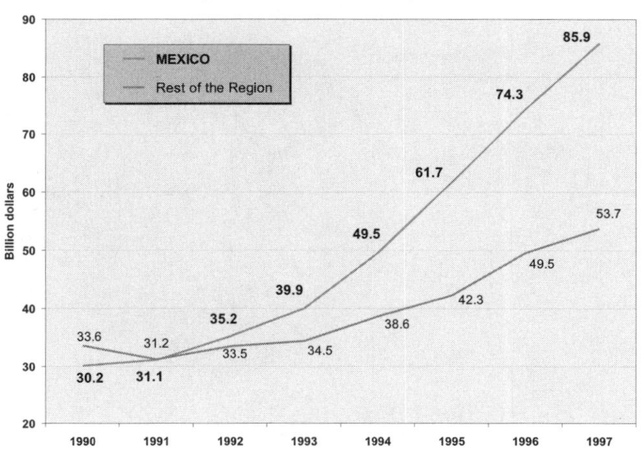

Chart 7
Historic evolution of foreign direct investment in Mexico

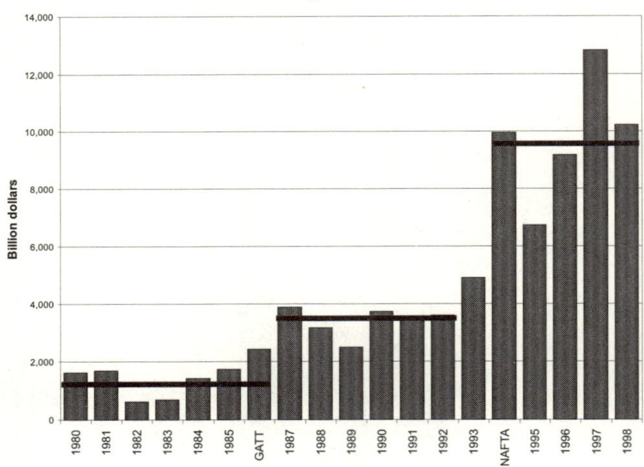

Chart 8
Foreign direct investment by recipient sector

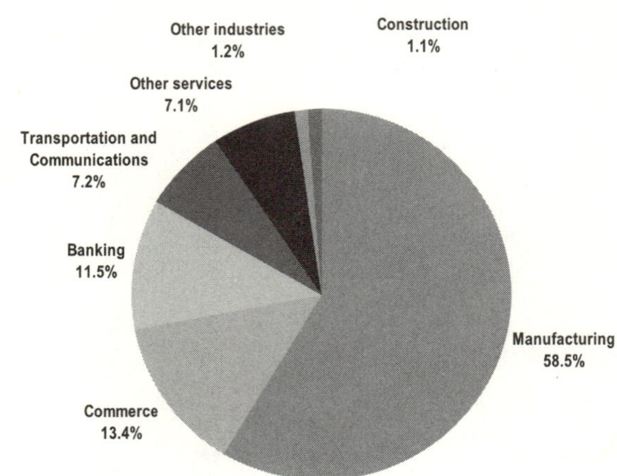

Free Trade: Then and Now

MICHAEL H. WILSON

With your permission, I'd like to take both a 10-year look back and a five-year retrospective on both the FTA and the NAFTA, since I was privileged to be present at the creation, so to speak, of both.

In the first instance, I was Minister of Finance, and was involved in the final three-day crunch in October of 1987 in Jim Baker's boardroom at the Treasury Department in Washington. In the second, I was at the table for Canada as Minister of International Trade from 1991 through the final negotiation of the NAFTA in 1992. I have many warm memories, literally, of a long hot month of August at the Watergate Hotel in Washington where, more than once, we had to send out for new shirts. I also have warm memories of my colleagues Carla Hills and Jaime Serra, and it is always a pleasure to find myself in their company again.

Looking back to the 1988 election campaign, it's pretty clear that the rhetoric on both sides was overheated. The opponents of free trade claimed Canada would be relegated to the status of a client state. There would be a significant loss of sovereignty. Our social programs would be endangered. Even water was said to be part of the deal. The proponents claimed that free trade was a panacea that would solve all our problems. History has demonstrated that neither position was correct.

What did we set out to achieve in the free trade negotiations? We had four main objectives, and you could consider each one as a deal-breaker.

- First, we wanted access to the U.S. for a wider range of goods and services.

- Second, we wanted an effective dispute settlement mechanism to deal with inevitable problems, and to bring discipline to the process.
- Third, we wanted preservation of essential Canadian programs, in health and education, and we wanted an exemption for cultural industries.
- And fourth, we wanted to enhance the trading relationship in a way that improved the fundamentals of the economy, particularly in productivity as a key to our competitiveness in the merging global economy.

Where are we now? The trade numbers speak for themselves. From $101 billion of merchandise exports in 1988, the last year before implementation, Canada exported $271 billion of goods to the U.S. in 1998, the tenth year since implementation. That's an increase of 169%, and as noted by John McCallum in the Royal Bank impact study, that represents "an explosion" of trade that can hardly be a coincidence. Inflation has been near historic lows throughout the period, so those constant dollars are not far from being current dollars. As for the supposed impact of exchange rates and the declining Canadian dollar, it is interesting to note that U.S. imports have risen from $86 billion to $203 billion, in spite of the higher exchange rates on U.S. dollars. With trade in services, two way trade is now $535 billion, or about $1.5 billion a day.

In my province of Ontario, where the branch plant economy was supposedly most threatened by the FTA, exports to the U.S. are now 40% of GDP, as compared with 20% in 1989. And the U.S. now accounts for 82% of Canadian exports, as opposed to 71% at the time of implementation.

And while you can't attribute this growth entirely to free trade, the fact remains, as noted by the Royal Bank of Canada (RBC) study, that exports of FTA-affected goods increased 140% versus 65% for non-affected exports, while imports from the U.S. increased 103%, versus only 38% for goods not covered by the FTA. Similarly, bilateral trade in services has more than doubled. So I think it's fair to conclude that we have obtained access to the U.S. market for a much broader range of goods and services.

As for dispute settlement and free trade, the FTA and NAFTA panels aren't a perfect solution, but they have introduced disciplines and by and large are perceived as fair. There is a common perception, or misperception, that trade disputes are a result of free trade. Quite the opposite, they usually occur in areas where parties were not prepared to negotiate free trade. The most visible examples have been softwood lumber and, most recently, magazines.

Our original objective was to eliminate all anti-dumping and countervailing duty law and replace them with rules enforced by binding dispute settlement. Thus, our aim was a rules based system, not subject to the vagaries of domestic politics and interest groups. This was not achieved, but because of the FTA and NAFTA dispute settlement panels, disputes today are more likely to be settled on the basis of principle, precedent and the rule of law.

As for preserving Canadian essentials, this was also a deal breaker for us, as any politician knows, or will learn quickly in negotiating any international trade agreement. Health care, education and environmental standards are non-negotiable to Canadians. But none of these things can be guaranteed without the economic essentials to support them.

Happily, governments have moved in this direction, in a virtuous cycle of balancing budgets and economic growth, to be followed, one hopes, by tax cuts, which among other things will improve our competitiveness in terms of both disposable incomes and human resource management.

The question is, are we better off now than we were before free trade? The answer is Yes. Was there short term pain in making the adjustment? The answer is Yes. Is there still work to be done? The answer is Yes.

On productivity, for one thing. Improvements are still needed. But I would argue that the FTA/NAFTA market frameworks provided the first important spur to productivity growth in Canada. Work remains to be done on other fronts: taxation levels, regional disparities, education and training, in order to maintain and improve Canada's ranking in world competitiveness, the key to growing markets in the global economy.

As for the NAFTA, it was a different negotiating dynamic, with three parties at the table rather than two. And it marked the first time two fully industrialized economies, two G-7 countries in fact, joined in a trade agreement with a developing economy.

But let me answer the question posed for this panel. What was Canada's objective in joining the NAFTA talks? It was not a defensive manoeuver. We were not just looking to protect what we had won in the FTA, we wanted to enhance the FTA and grow into a continental market. What we got was a comprehensive agreement that eliminates tariffs on all industrial products, includes a broad range of services and addresses important investment issues.

The deal has been a win-win-win for all sides, despite the 1995 currency crisis in Mexico. Mexico is now the second largest trading partner of the U.S., and Canada is now Mexico's second largest customer. Imports from Mexico have more than doubled from $3.7 billion in

1993, to \$7.6 billion last year, while exports have increased by two-thirds to \$1.4 billion. There is real room for Canadian business to grow in Mexico, as their economy increasingly de-regulates. It is a platform to the U.S. market, especially California and Texas, and a strategic gateway to Latin America, where we hope to conclude the FTAA by 2005.

MICHAEL H. WILSON, Deputy Chairman of RBC Dominion Securities, was Minister of Finance during the FTA round, and Minister of International Trade who negotiated the NAFTA on behalf of Canada.

Desmond Morton, Director of the McGill Institute for the Study of Canada, accompanies former Prime Minister Brian Mulroney at the *Free Trade @ 10* Conference in Montreal, June 4–5, 1999. (Jack Goldsmith)

Donald S. Macdonald, former Minister of Finance in the Trudeau government, and Chairman of the Royal Commission that recommended the "Leap of Faith" of free trade, with the former prime minister. "It is clear that Canada would have been at a substantial disadvantage in the subsequent expansion of worldwide commerce that has occurred," Macdonald observed in his keynote address, "if we had not undertaken that first, bold 'leap of faith,' as a people, to meet international competition." (Jack Goldsmith)

Simon Reisman, by his own admission a "pretty tough customer" as Canada's free trade negotiator with the Americans, father of the Auto Pact, and veteran of Canada-U.S. trade talks since the Mackenzie King era. "If it weren't for you, we could have had a deal a year earlier," U.S. Trade representative Clayton Yeutter told him at the time of the FTA agreement. "Yeah," Reisman retorted, "if we settled on your terms." Reisman meets with students and media. (Jack Goldsmith)

Derek Burney (*left*), who closed the free trade deal for Canada over three momentous days in Washington in October 1987, greets former Treasury Secretary James A. Baker III, later U.S. Secretary of State, who would "plead guilty" to being a dealmaker. (Jack Goldsmith)

Michael Hart (*left*), former adviser to the Canadian Trade Negotiations Office and author of *Decision at Midnight,* moderates the plenary session addressed by Jim Baker and Derek Burney. (Brian Morel)

John Crosbie, Trade Minister from 1988–91, who had the tough task of selling the FTA to Canadians despite suggestions of economic absorption by the Americans. "I'd like to see an American that could absorb me!" said Crosbie, in a Team Canada-Team USA plenary session that reconstructed the making of the free trade deal. (Brian Morel)

Jean Charest, Quebec Liberal leader and former federal environment minister, listens to an intervention from the floor in the workshop on NAFTA and the environment, while session chair, former Quebec Premier Pierre Marc Johnson, looks on. Despite problems with the NAFTA Commission on Environmental Cooperation, Charest noted that it was the only body of its kind, "worth keeping and worth improving. "There is", Charest said, "a clear need to raise the profile of NAFTA and the environment." (Brian Morel)

Bush is greeted by Hydro-Québec Chairman Jacques Ménard, also Chairman of the Montreal Expos, who, in thanking the former president following his keynote address, presented him with a personalized Expos warm-up jacket. (Jack Goldsmith)

Agreeing to disagree. Mulroney chats with Gerald Larose, outgoing president of the Conseil des syndicats nationaux (CSN). "It's all very well to recognize that Canada has recorded record trade surpluses with our number one partner," Larose noted, "but it would be more exact to see this as the result of successive monetary devaluations than as the success of the FTA." (Jack Goldsmith)

McGill Principal Bernard Shapiro (*left*) and Tom d'Aquino, president of the Business Council on National Issues, chat with Bush and Mulroney at a head table reception preceding the former president's keynote speech. (Jack Goldsmith)

McGill University Chancellor Richard Pound, also Vice President of the International Olympic Committee, presides over the Bush luncheon, as the former president chats with Mila Mulroney. (Jack Goldsmith)

Mulroney closes the *Free Trade @ 10* Conference: "Democracies," he concludes, "are inspired by the collision of great ideas and the vigourous disagreements and debates they provoke." (Jack Goldsmith)

Five Windows for the Future of NAFTA's Environment Commission

PIERRE MARC JOHNSON

NAFTA's Commission for Environmental Cooperation (CEC) is in many ways a unique institutional experiment in trade and environment related initiatives. Created under the North American Agreement on Environmental Cooperation (NAAEC), a parallel agreement to NAFTA, it has been instrumental in: strengthening continental cooperation on environmental issues, supporting local conservation projects, preventing environmental disputes between trading partners, and fostering the development of a regional environmental community by linking together government officials, specialists, consultants, academics and elements of a broad public around its work.

During its first five years (1994–99) the CEC experimented with and developed initiatives and procedures in a number of areas with its very broad mandate. It developed tools and took action on a wide variety of issues, including: the control of pollutants, public participation, investigation and reporting on pollution, capacity building, enforcement and environmental law, the relationship between trade and environment, harmonization of specific standards, and the prevention of disputes. For a new organization, these tasks were undertaken rigorously and effectively, all on a budget of $U.S.9 million.

Differences between the countries created challenging conditions for this unique North American institution. Quite apart from the highly political nature of its birth and the great breadth of its mandate, differences in language, culture, government systems, democratic sensitivities, public service interests and administrative practices all created a series of hurdles for the three responsible ministers and the Commission's first executive director, Victor Lichtinger, a respected Mexican economist-diplomat.

Still, given the difficulties it faced, the Commission's output was impressive. Between 1995 and 1998, the CEC completed 65 projects in six program areas. It issued 27 publications and it established a North American web site (www.cec.org) that includes an environmental law data base with hundreds of legal references, extensive list-served contacts and a regular newsletter. In addition, the Commission released reports on three independent investigations of environmental issues and received 20 petitions from the public. For its part, the North American Fund for Environmental Cooperation (NAFEC) created under the CEC funded 95 projects in a three-year period. Finally, the Joint Public Advisory Committee (JPAC) of the CEC held public consultations each year in the three countries, organizing more than 30 international meetings in four years.

The Commission came to a crossroads in 1998 with the departure of Victor Lichtinger and the fulfilment of an obligation in the NAAEC to conduct a five-year review of the agreement, which was undertaken by an independent review committee. These two events can be seen as marking the end of an era of experimentation in which the young institution worked to establish itself as a significant player on the North American scene, and the start of a drive toward maturity in several aspects of its work.

The three countries reiterated their support for the CEC at the annual meeting of the commission's governing council (made up of the three countries' environment ministers), which was held in Mérida, Mexico, in June 1998. This came with a commitment to offer a clear vision to the Commission Secretariat for the elaboration of its annual programs by designing and annually updating a three-year work plan for the Commission.

This paper explores five windows of opportunity and challenge that the CEC will face over the next few years. These are all areas in which the CEC has already developed significant expertise and can bring concrete value-added to the process of North American integration. How the CEC focuses on these issues, seizes opportunities, and meets expectations, will largely determine its future relevancy as a central player for North America and, eventually, for the whole hemisphere.

The first window of opportunity for the CEC results from its proven expertise in adding to our knowledge of a wide range of continental environmental issues. The Commission has developed a considerable body of research and issued a number of major publications in its first five years. Among other things, it has produced: a continental map of North American eco-regions, an information network on biodiversity in North America, a similar network on North American birds and an inventory of important areas for the conservation of bird species in North America. It also published annual reports on the release and transfer of pollutants in North America and set up a web site that examines air quality in the three countries.

In addition to its annual work plan, under article 13 of the NAAEC the CEC can initiate independent investigations and report on various issues that fall within the scope of its very broad work program. Such a report was prepared in 1995, responding to a massive bird kill at the Silva Reservoir in the State of Gunajuato in Mexico. A second report on pathways for air pollutants was released in 1997. A new initiative is underway to assess issues related to water use in the San Pedro Riparian Conservation area along the Arizona-Mexico border.

Trade and the environment are at the core of the CEC's mission. Its initial efforts in this area were concentrated on developing an analytical framework for assessing the environmental effects of NAFTA. A second draft of this framework was released in early 1999, with a final framework due in 2000, in time for a North American conference on NAFTA and the environment. The Commission has also produced an evaluation of the environmental potential and performance of NAFTA's institutions, and it has developed projects on ecological products and services, on trade in endangered species and on ecotourism.

An important challenge in this area is to find ways for the CEC to complement the Word Trade Organization and other organizations that are studying trade and environment issues. As the multilateral trading system moves into another round of negotiations, the CEC's output could be an important input into efforts to assess the environmental effects of increased trade, including agricultural trade.

Of particular interest in the next three years is a project on new environmental trends as early warning mechanisms on environmental degradation. Tools for identifying trends and devising policy responses will be developed, based on indicators devised by other international organizations.

Documenting and researching issues is key to the development of a common understanding of specific policy challenges. It opens doors for trilateral strategies and minimizes the likelihood of disputes. The three NAFTA partners have recognized this by identifying the CEC in the triennial work plan as an information hub and an important body for research and policy analysis. But developing knowledge is only one part of the challenge. Another is dissemination and raising awareness, which opens a second window for the Commission.

The CEC is a unique organization in its openness to groups and individuals from all sectors and regions in the three countries. During its first five years, the Commission developed mechanisms for public participation and built public outreach as a major component of every project it undertook. The CEC's web site, which provides the documents and tools produced by various CEC work projects free of charge, is at the core of the organization's strategy to reach individuals and groups all over North America. In addition, an extensive communications network has been developed, with a listserver that reaches over 2,000 people in the three countries.

The Joint Public Advisory Committee (JPAC) that is built into the Commission's structure is instrumental in fostering public participation. Each of the three countries appoints five members to the Committee, which is designed to provide the Commission with significant input from non-governmental organizations and the private sector. Each year the JPAC holds public consultations on various issues, including the annual work plan of the Commission. It reports directly to the ministerial Council, the highest decision-making body in the CEC structure.

Despite the CEC's impressive efforts at fostering public participation, in 1998 the Independent Review Committee (IRC) pointed to what it considered the haphazard functioning of this process and the lack of a framework to integrate participation. The proliferation of unrelated meetings, together with frustration about the low productivity of some public meetings, led the IRC to conclude that the Commission should design a new participation strategy, and organize more efficient and productive meetings.

In response, the CEC has produced a draft framework for public participation that is based on six principles: equity; efficiency and timeliness; transparency and accessibility; inclusiveness; resourcing and accountability; and, finally, evaluation. While these principles are unobjectionable, the document still falls short of a clear strategic vision on public participation. The CEC will have to identify and focus on certain groups and segments of the population in each issue-area. Meetings should be organized in a structured way to ensure their productivity, but should also conserve the flexibility required for meaningful participation. The organization could also use make more effective use of the visibility created by its presence in North America to publicize and disseminate its work, thereby strengthening its ties with civil society in every region of the continent.

If the CEC is to have an impact on the ground, the ability to collect views and suggestions from – and deliver information and knowledge to – groups and communities directly affected by specific issues is critical. In the new triennial work plan, the Council specifically recognizes the Commission's role as a convenor. To ensure appropriate and productive involvement of stakeholders and the general public, a clear strategy will have to be developed and necessary resources made available. If this is done appropriately, it would serve to open a third window for the CEC, that of capacity building.

In fact, capacity building has been another priority for the Commission since its creation in 1995. Particular attention has been given to enhancing capacities for pollution prevention, environmental monitoring and law enforcement in Mexico. Elements of capacity building are present in one form or another in almost every CEC project, through initiatives that include data sharing, training, and the exchange of best practices. A paper on the demand for environmental education and training in Mexico was produced. A capacity-building task force on the sound management of chemicals undertook several initiatives, including the transfer of technical tools, and exchange programs for specialists. Another project aims to reinforce Mexico's capacity for pollution prevention.

As part of the overall capacity-building effort, the North American Fund for Environmental Cooperation (NAFEC) was created in 1996, with a budget of $U.S.1.5 million, reduced to $1 million in 1998. The NAFEC supports local community-based initiatives for various issues related to environmental protection. Several projects involve continental cooperation or collective action on transnational issues, such as a Mexico-United States roundtable on transboundary waters and a community bird conservation project between Mexico and Canada. In 1998, the IRC concluded that the dispersion of NAFEC funds to too many unrelated projects was the result of an excessively broad mandate. It suggested that the fund's mandate be made narrower and linked more closely with the CEC's work program. The goal would be to increase projects' impact by concentrating efforts on specific issues and developing synergies with the Commission.

In its report, the IRC recognized that capacity- building activities such as training and data sharing are particularly important in ensuring the effective implementation of environmental law. It suggested that the CEC cooperate more closely with the World Bank, the Inter-American Development Development Bank and other funding agencies to finance capacity-building projects in Mexico. Systematic cooperation of this nature would multiply the potential impact of the CEC at the community level.

Effective law enforcement is a pivotal element in efforts to prevent environment-related disputes between trading partners. Not surprisingly, effective enforcement of environmental laws is at the core of the NAAEC. Not only is it an important component of the CEC's work but the three countries are required by the agreement to produce an annual report on the fulfilment of their enforcement obligations.

In addition, in cases of persistent patterns of failure to enforce environmental laws, Part V of the NAAEC provides for government-to-government consultations and outlines a dispute resolution mechanism, although none of the three countries has yet invoked these articles.

A unique aspect of NAAEC is that it allows citizens or groups to file submissions with the Secretariat of the CEC alleging that a country is failing to effectively enforce its environmental law. Such a process of direct public petitioning is rare in international institutions. Under the NAAEC, it can eventually lead to the drafting of a factual record on the alleged non-enforcement, which can be made public. Ultimately, no legally binding obligation can be imposed on the country that is the object of the petition, yet the process facilitates the application of public pressure on that country, by making officials uncomfortable, and may prevent similar cases in the future.

In the last five years, the CEC has established a body of principles and interpretations that will govern the analysis of future petitions. As of May 1999, 20 petitions had been filed. Four of these were rejected for not meeting the threshold requirements set out in the agreement; three were closed after a short investigation, one was withdrawn; 10 are being processed, and one has been terminated following the preparation and release of a factual record. Many voices have expressed the need to strengthen the process and reinforce its end results. Some have argued for binding legal obligations, though that would require the reopening of NAAEC, which seems unlikely. There are many other ways to strengthen the process by modifying existing practices without amending NAAEC, however.

The CEC has already moved to separate the legal team responsible for processing petitions from the team that manages the enforcement cooperation program. This "Chinese wall" is a first step in the right direction. Many other steps could be taken to consolidate the petition process, making it more relevant and giving it more impact. The entire process should be accelerated so as to mitigate possible harm to the environment or to petitioners. Factual records should be made publicly available and should go further in condemning non-enforcement. They could also propose alternative remedies, as provided by article 13.

Over the past five years, the CEC has promoted effective enforcement of environmental laws and regulations, particularly in Mexico. The Commission created a North American Regional Enforcement Forum and developed a project on enforcement and compliance capacity building. It produced a review and analysis of North American initiatives to promote voluntary measures to ensure environmental compliance. It also began work toward the harmonization of standards in environmental labouratories in the three countries to facilitate mutual recognition and prevent disputes from arising on technical grounds. Finally, it developed data bases on environmental law and transboundary agreements. Indicators of effective environmental enforcement will be developed by 2001, and these could become an important tool for the prevention of disputes.

Law enforcement and dispute avoidance will require deepening co-operation among the three countries and the other NAFTA institutions. The IRC suggested that links between the CEC and the NAFTA Free Trade Commission be strengthened. It also suggested that environment and trade ministers from the three countries meet annually. In addition, the CEC should be encouraged to provide technical advice to other NAFTA organizations, including the Free Trade Commission, with mandates touching on the environment. This need for strengthened cooperation between the three countries constitutes a fifth and last window on the future of the CEC.

The promotion and consolidation of continental cooperation is a fifth promising area for future action by the Commission. The CEC has developed many cooperative initiatives over the last five years and the Council recognizes its role as a catalyst in the triennial work programme. A biodiversity conservation strategy was developed which elabourated regional action plans and monitoring mechanisms. A program of stewardship for shared terrestrial and marine ecosystems and transboundary species was created, including a joint implementation of the Global Programme of Action for the Protection of the Marine Environment from Land-Based Activities, namely in the Gulf of Maine and the Bight of the Californias. A North American Network of Protected Areas was also established as suggested by the international Union for the Conservation of Nature. A cooperation project was developed on issues related to air quality in North America, an important initiative in the context of engagements for reductions in greenhouse gas emissions under the Kyoto Protocol. The three countries are currently working on a North American agreement on transboundary environmental impact assessment, an interesting initiative that will have to be designed so as to avoid overlap and duplication with other trans-boundary organizations.

The Commission developed an extensive cooperation project on the sound management of chemicals. The project targeted hazardous substances such as PCB's, pesticides, chlordane and lindane, and metals such as lead and mercury. The project allowed the three countries to develop a common policy and expertise that are now being used in negotiations on a globally binding instrument on Persistent Organic Pollutants (POPs) and in various other related international activities.

A common approach to international agreements at the continental level is another promising area for future action by the CEC. Projects have been or are being developed that are related to the elimination of CFC's, trade in endangered species, and the continental protection of biodiversity, which coincide with the objectives of major international agreements such as the Montreal Protocol on endangered species and the UN Biodiversity Convention. The Commission has also moved to define instruments for a common approach to the UN Convention on Climate Change's Kyoto Protocol with strong support expressed by the Council at its Mérida meeting in 1998. An experimental project will be developed in the next three years.

To reinforce and renew its relevancy, the CEC will have to meet public and official expectations. Having struggled with an overly broad mandate during its first years of existence, it will have to concentrate on issues and sectors in which it has a comparative advantage and to which it can bring real value-added. Its success or failure in doing so will condition the support and funding it receives over the course of the coming decade.

The Council made clear its expectations for the Commission in the triennial plan. The CEC should, by 2001:

- solidify its role as an information hub and policy analysis centre for key North American environmental issues;
- demonstrate North American leadership in accelerating the implementation of regional and global initiatives;
- establish a North American network of professionals, academics, NGOs and businesses on selected issues of regional environmental importance;
- prove its value as a forum for avoiding environmentally-related trade disputes;
- contribute significantly to the reduction and elimination of pollutants in North America;
- enhance the protection of North American ecosystems and biodiversity.

The demands on the CEC are compounded by the ongoing negotiations on hemispheric free trade. With the official target date for a free trade zone from Alaska to Patagonia set at 2005, the CEC has little time left to demonstrate its ability to address the difficult trade and environment nexus, which is where it can become most relevant as a model for hemispheric cooperation beyond NAFTA. How it seizes this opportunity will determine whether it continues to be a key player in this field, or is marginalized and relegated to the role of a minor regional organization.

It remains to be seen whether the CEC model can be extended from three to almost 30 players and still retain its capacity to reach the public of all the Americas, address key environmental issues, and to demonstrate its ability to sketch areas of consensus. The challenge will be to identify ways of extending elements of the model while ensuring that a hemispheric CEC does not crumble under its own weight.

PIERRE MARC JOHNSON is senior counsel in the offices of Heenan Blaikie. A former premier of Québec, he is author of *The Environment and Nafta: Understanding and Implementing the New Continental Law* (Washington DC: Island Press, 1996). Mr. Johnson sits on various corporate boards and is a member of the Council of the International Union for the Conservation of Nature (IUCN).

NAFTA and the Environment: Five Years After

VICTOR LICHTINGER

My comments pertain to the CEC, the Commission for Environmental Cooperation, established by the NAFTA side agreement and reporting to the Council of the three NAFTA countries. I was privileged to serve as the first executive director of the CEC, based here in Montreal, and my observations reflect that experience.

NAFTA is the first trade agreement that takes environmental considerations into account and promotes sustainable development.

After five years of experience with the CEC we can now understand the areas in which the Agreement has worked and the areas in which there is much work to do.

The CEC has been successful in promoting understanding and creating opportunities for cooperation. Within the CEC there have been important agreements of the three nations that imply explicit commitments that reduce toxic substances in the North American environment, induce changes in priorities for conservation and promote public participation.

Another area where the CEC has proven its value is in the generation of up to date information and its dissemination, especially on environmental issues that are common to the three parties to the Agreement.

There are a couple of experiences in the first five years of the CEC that show certain avenues of specialization for the Commission. I am referring to the "Presa de Silva" and the "Rio San Pedro" cases (both of them Article 13 issues). These two show potential comparative advantages for the CEC in mediation exercises at the local level, with potential implications for the regional or global environment. In some respects these two experiences could be seen as success stories and taken as examples of what the CEC could do best. Article 13 should be strengthened in this respect.

On the other hand the CEC has proven to be quite slow and unsuccessful in one of the most important objectives of the agreement, which is effective enforcement of environmental laws.

After the first five years of the functioning of the provisions contained in Articles 14 and 15 of the Agreement, it is obvious that the Council does not want this mechanism to function correctly, or at least as intended at the beginning of the operation of the CEC. Without the support of Council, this mechanism is quite ineffective, as has been demonstrated in the few cases where there has been a factual record.

The Cozumel case (relating to the environmental permits for the construction of a pier on Cozumel Island), the first case, was a clear example of why the mechanism is not effective without the unlikely will and leadership of the other two members of Council. Even though the final record on the case points out indirectly – since it cannot do it directly as a decision, determination or recommendation – to obvious omissions in the application of environmental Mexican regulations, the Council did not want to make any kind of recommendations to the Mexican government.

The Mexican environmental authorities did not change these practices and omissions in the application of the law as a consequence, and they have not even discussed the possibility of modifying or adapting the regulations to close certain imprecisions that allow for this kind of interpretation. The same situation occurred with the second case. This case involved the practices and lack of enforcement of environmental regulations in Canada, British Columbia in particular, related to the generation of electricity and the protection of aquatic ecosystems.

I believe that the mechanism contained in Articles 14 and 15 of the Agreement is wrongly designed and probably does not fit comfortably in an environmental cooperation agreement. The Secretariat must receive instructions from the Council for the rest of the programs of the CEC and support the interests of the three members of Council.

At the same time, it has to investigate the wrongdoing of the same governments that comprise the Council and that decide each year the budget for the Commission. It is a double task that implies tension and conflicted interests in the functioning of the CEC as a whole. The secretariat is the least interested in receiving meaningful complaints from the public and developing investigations, since it puts it in a situation of conflict with one or more of the members of Council.

The members of Council (especially Mexico and Canada), on the other hand, tend to protect each other and work together to make the procedures bureaucratic, slow and ineffective. This commonality of interests in at least two members of Council to support each other – either to stop the investigations, or not to get any direct recommendations from Council at the end of the process – is a situation that ensures failure.

A a matter of fact, a mechanism of this sort, and especially the dispute mechanism in part five of the Agreement, is not concerned with the environmental quality as such and with the impact this might bring on the environment or degradation of natural resources. This fact is a negative incentive for environmental authorities of the three governments to apply it seriously and correctly.

Actually, these mechanisms might be more appropriate for a trade agreement. They are mostly concerned with the lack of effective enforcement of environmental laws, which is seen as an unfair practice to support industry or other economic activities for exports (considering the lack of enforcement of environmental laws as a kind of unfair subsidy). Probably, the fact that these mechanisms are part of an environmental cooperation agreement is due to the fact that trade negotiators saw it as a disruptive factor in NAFTA and in the multilateral trading system.

The mechanism that the CEC has to carry out according to the Agreement is neither practical nor adequate and the institutional design that supports it is a source of internal conflicts, with minimum potential for improving enforcement of environmental laws in the three countries. The CEC as a watchdog is something that the media created when President Clinton promised to change the situation at the border. In reality this promise was not very realistic. The mechanisms that exist are neither apt for this goal nor has the Council ever agreed with the CEC becoming a watchdog.

If the analysis of the experience of the CEC would be based on the demonstrated effectiveness vis a vis the distinct functions and objectives in the Agreement, the conclusions would be very different on where to strengthen the CEC's work.

On the other two objectives of the Agreement that are of the highest importance the Agreement has also demonstrated to be quite weak in its implementation and development. These two issues are the following:

- evaluate the environmental impacts of free trade
- agree on a specific mechanism to deal with transboundary environmental issues.

The Council of the CEC has relatively neglected both of these matters. In the case that requires the Council to evaluate the environmental impacts of NAFTA there has been a clear intention by Council to maintain it as an academic exercise – so that it does not influence in any way policy decisions or public opinion on the benefits and costs of NAFTA. In the case of agreeing on a mechanism to deal with transboundary issues, the U.S. government has not accepted to have any kind of formal mechanism that commits the federal and state governments to notify of any border projects that might have transboundary effects. In general there has been a lack of political will by governments and the result is quite unsatisfying.

In the coming years, there will be new challenges for the CEC. Article 1114 (Environmental Measures). The article states: "The Parties recognize that it is inappropriate to encourage investment by relaxing domestic health, safety or environmental measures". In this sense, there have been diverse complaints from NGO's that allege that regulations and environmental standards in different parts of North America have been going down as a result of competition and the desire to attract investment (the cases of the Canadian provinces of Alberta and Ontario). There is no clear criteria on how to understand what this chapter refers to or what to do in different situations. It is also not clear what role the CEC might play in these matters. This issue is important since it is directly related to the reasons behind the creation of the CEC and the expectations that it created.

VICTOR LICHTINGER, now a prominent environmental and economic consultant in Mexico City, was the founding executive director of the NAFTA Commission for Environmental Cooperation in Montreal from 1994 to 1998.

NAFTA and the Environment:
A Review of the Basic Issues

DAVID K. SCHORR

At the time of NAFTA's adoption more than five years ago, sharp disputes developed over the relationship between trade and environment, and over the environmental implications of NAFTA itself. Fears and promises on all sides were expressed, sometimes without perfect regard for moderation. Today, as new negotiations gather steam in the Americas and at the global level, debate continues over the rudiments of linking environment with trade and investment agreements. Indeed, controversy around this linkage contributed to the demise last year of a proposed multilateral treaty on investment that in many respects was modeled after the investment chapters of NAFTA itself. Twelve weeks ago, senior trade and environmental officials from around the world gathered at the WTO for a symposium which Sir Leon Brittan hoped would "break the logjam" that the trade and environment controversy has suffered – an outcome that remained sadly elusive, despite the level of political attention accorded to the meeting.

In short, half a decade has done little to resolve the tensions that exist between the trade and environmental policy agendas, even as the need to do so has become increasingly apparent. And yet, many of the necessary elements for achieving a productive relationship between these two vital disciplines were included in the rules and institutions of the NAFTA system.

As a contribution to this conference, this short paper reviews some of the key issues raised by environmentalists in the context of the NAFTA debate, and offers a brief catalogue of how the NAFTA system was crafted in response. The paper closes with a few comments on the experience we have had to date with this system and takes the stubbornly optimistic view that, despite the significant environmental shortcomings of the NAFTA system, there is more reason to hope than to despair that the NAFTA model will ultimately prove its environmental worth – if governments are willing to renew their dedication to fostering trade and environmental policies that are truly mutually supportive.

THE UNDERLYING CONCERNS

The concerns expressed by many environmentalists around the advent of NAFTA (and around other trade and investment systems, including the WTO) have a solid grounding in reality. The commercial life of our species is currently based on patterns of production and consumption that simply cannot be sustained over time. We are overtaxing our renewable and nonrenewable natural resources, we are dangerously altering our climate, we are continuing to expose ourselves and our ecosystems to unacceptable levels of toxic pollutants, and we are rapidly depleting our planet's biodiversity through an unprecedented wave of human-caused species extinctions. One need be neither an alarmist nor a doomsayer to recognize the legitimacy of fears about expanding the global economy based on the way we are doing business today.

This does not mean, of course, that economic growth is inherently bad. On the contrary, many environmentalists recognize that poverty is among the environment's worst enemies, and that sustainable economic growth is a necessary goal. But it is important to recognize that environmentalists did not come to the trade and investment policy arena in search of new techniques for exercising political leverage (as some muddled critics continue to suggest), but rather with a set of concerns for how rapidly advancing liberalized trade would affect environmental values. The fact that many in the trade community feel equally defensive around trade and environment issues reflects a certain mutual paranoia that has played a significant role in producing the logjam we now face. To make progress, policy-makers will need to deal squarely with these defensive concerns, as well as to move decisively beyond them.

The "defensive" environmental concerns in question are of three basic kinds, each partly addressed in the NAFTA accords, and each still central to discussions of trade and environment policy today.

Direct Environmental Impacts

First, international trade and investment policies (including tariff and non-tariff measures) contribute to the market signals that shape how we produce and consume, and so can have direct environmental impacts. Unfortunately, despite lofty references to sustainable development in various preambles, trade and investment treaties are negotiated without attention to how the resulting market incentives will affect the sustainability of international commerce. Certainly, these impacts are not necessarily all negative. But neither are they all positive. In the days prior to NAFTA's conclusion, for example, WWF found that some landowners in Mexico were converting forest land into citrus groves in anticipation of new U.S. markets for citrus products. The expected change in a tariff rate was thus the proximate cause of at least some deforestation.

Proponents of "free" trade may find no flaw in this, arguing that trade liberalization has inherent benefits, and that maintaining trade barriers is a bad way to serve environmental goals. If you don't want the forests cut down, they might say, pass a forest conservation law, but don't maintain an economically inefficient tariff. But environmentalists find this an insufficient response. In the absence of robust environmental policies, the conditions for a healthy market–and thus for policies designed to accelerate market activity–have not been established. Moreover, it is hard to escape the observation that extraordinary levels of political will and leverage are often employed to achieve market openings that are marginal (apart from the benefits they may bring to particularly powerful commercial interests), while wholesale failures to establish economically necessary environmental policies go unattended.

A clear illustration of such environmentally skewed priorities is the traditional approach to liberalization in natural resource based sectors. Not only are sectors such as fisheries, forestry, and agriculture subject to what might be called high elasticities of environmental impact in response to price changes, they are also often environmentally underregulated and plagued with trade distorting policies (*e.g.*, subsidies, quotas, *etc.*) that can have dramatic negative environmental effects. In these sectors (as well as in energy- or pollution-intensive sectors), the case is especially strong for taking account of the environmental implications of proposed changes in the terms of trade, and for giving high priority to reducing environmentally harmful trade barriers first. But even in these sectors, today's trade policies focus almost exclusively on opening international markets, rather than on setting the conditions for their long-term economic health, with liberalization efforts driven largely by quasi-mercantilist commercial interests rather than a view toward the public good. The current proposal for rapid liberalization of the forestry sector within the WTO has this unfortunate character.

Normative Impacts

A second "defensive" environmental concern is that trade and investment agreements can have direct impacts on international and national environmental norms and rules. For example, basic clauses of the NAFTA (and the GATT) are in tension (if not outright conflict) with trade-related provisions in some international environmental treaties. And the treatment of domestic environmental regulations as potential "non-tariff barriers" to trade is the best-known source of conflict at the trade-environment interface (and of claims that trade rules infringe the "sovereignty" of national governments). Environmentalists first heard of international bodies like the GATT when they were confronted with trade challenges to existing or proposed environmental regulations. The *Tuna-Dolphin* case was the first highly visible example.

Here again, trade policy-makers are often unapologetic. Trade rules do not attack environmental standards because they are high, they argue, but only where they are needlessly trade-distorting. But the facts on the ground have not always supported this view. The legal burdens and tests imposed under current international trade law often allow trade bodies to sit in judgment of the adequacy of the environmental arguments they hear, or to impose their own brand of "rationality" test on how an environmental policy was carried out. Rather than simply being employed against protectionism, these rules are increasingly used to require a kind of "trade policy purity" from environmental lawmakers that effectively gives greater value to trade policy goals than to environmental goals. No trade policy has ever been subject to the requirement that it open markets in the "most environmentally beneficial" manner possible, as unassailably "rational" (and symmetrical) as such an approach might be.

One result of this normative overreaching is that trade and investment arenas are increasingly beset with controversies that go way beyond their true competencies. In fact, environmentally related issues are beginning to destabilize trade systems not as a result of acceding to environmentalists' demands (as is so often feared), but as a direct consequence of ignoring environmentalists' warnings. A contemporary example illustrates this point. The EU and the U.S. (among others) are heading for a showdown over the mass introduction of genetically modified organisms into the environment and into commerce. At issue are deeply held beliefs and preferences regarding an unprecedented and boldly experimental manipulation of our shared biosphere. To say this debate has more the character of a basic religious dispute than a commercial one is not much of an exaggeration (if it is an exaggeration at all). The depth of the scientific questions involved is also profound. But, driven by the special interests of a powerful commercial elite, and – more to the point – by the unique availability of the mechanisms of international trade law, it is now being seriously suggested that this fundamental social policy issue be decided by a trade institution applying trade rules.

Unfortunately, the range of these "normative impacts" is growing. Recently developed or newly proposed areas for trade rules – such as rules governing intellectual property, government procurement practices, labeling and commercial speech, services, and investment – are already creating potential flash points at the trade-environment interface.

Institutional Impacts

As just noted, international trade and investment bodies themselves have become the loci of significant policy-making, whether through adjudicative or quasi-legislative processes. A third "defensive" environmental concern relates to the character of these institutional arrangements, and particularly with their openness to public scrutiny and their responsiveness to public concerns. Another contemporary example – drawn straight from the heart of the NAFTA experience – illustrates this point. Over the past couple of years, a series of cases has been brought by private companies against one or another of the NAFTA parties alleging expropriations contrary to the investor guarantees in NAFTA's Chapter 11. These cases have been distinguished by the claim that the expropriations in question resulted from regulatory activity (in some cases, environmental regulatory activity) by the defendant governments. These are, in the jargon of U.S. constitutional law debate, allegations of "regulatory takings." The public values at issue in these cases are important ones. Not only have the challenged regulations been of significant public concern (one, for example, dealing with restrictions on a toxic fuel additive), but the "regulatory taking" legal theory itself has been the center of a long-standing legal debate at the core of environmental politics in the United States. These cases thus may have significant public policy impacts in the NAFTA countries; yet they are carried out under the rubric of a rule system designed mainly to protect investors, through a closed-door process modeled after standard international commercial arbitrations.

ENVIRONMENTAL PROVISIONS OF THE NAFTA SYSTEM

NAFTA's environmental provisions are contained partly in the NAFTA text itself, and mainly the "side agreement" known as the North

American Agreement on Environmental Cooperation ("NAAEC").
The following is an abbreviated review of how NAFTA and the NAAEC
address the environmental concerns described above.

Addressing Direct Impacts

At the heart of NAFTA's environmental provisions is a basic requirement: each party agrees to enforce effectively its domestic environmental laws. There is also a soft and vague commitment by the parties to
having high environmental standards. In addition, NAFTA contains language forbidding the relaxation of environmental standards in order to
attract investment. The NAAEC also lays out a broad set of commitments to cooperate to solve regional environmental problems. Finally,
the NAAEC mandates cooperative steps to monitor and respond to
NAFTA's environmental impacts.

Of these provisions, only the commitment to enforce environmental
laws comes with any real enforcement mechanism. The obligation is
backed by two sets of procedures: one which allows NAFTA governments to seek monetary penalties and possible withdrawal of NAFTA
concessions in the event of another government's non-compliance;
and a separate procedure by which citizens can petition for fact finding investigations of alleged failures to enforce. The first of these procedures has been the subject of lasting resentment by some business
leaders and government officials who harbor an extraordinary allergy
to the use of trade sanctions to enforce environmental obligations. It is
regrettable that this debate over "sanctions" became one of the most
contentious parts of the NAFTA environmental dialogue. It is not
uncommon for business leaders to remember virtually nothing else
about the NAAEC, other than its granting the hated right to use trade
sanctions. As explained in the appendix to this paper, however, the
likelihood that sanctions will ever be imposed under the NAAEC are
very remote. Even assuming a NAAEC party had the will to bring a case,
the length of the process and the limits on the availability of the penalty would strongly discourage an outcome that included significant
use of the sanction mechanism.

The citizen's petition process (the so-called "Article 14" process) is
another matter. So far, eighteen submissions have been filed, although
only one has gone through a complete investigatory process (in part because the CEC Secretariat has been circumspect and legally rigorous in
determining which petitions qualify for review). The mechanism has
clearly functioned as intended: it allows citizens to have recourse to the
international level to vindicate certain rights under the NAFTA treaty
system (a weak analogue to the "investor-state" arbitration provisions

described above); and it has given local groups a lever for generating national attention to their enforcement complaints. Naturally, the process has also generated controversy. Governments have never been fully pleased to be the objects of the petition process, while some environmentalists have decried the limited applicability of the system. For example, the Article 14 process cannot be applied allegations of violations of NAFTA's provision prohibiting "competitive deregulation" to attract investment.

The other major tool for addressing NAFTA's direct environmental impacts – the mandate for the CEC to monitor them – has had a troubled history. Viewed in some quarters as an invitation to bash NAFTA, implementation of this provision was not warmly embraced by the NAAEC parties. Moreover, the monitoring function was quickly caught up in the debate over how to identify an environmental effect caused by NAFTA. With governments mandating a narrow approach, the outcome has been disappointing. Rather than treat the monitoring function as an opportunity to review the relationship between international commerce and environmental pressures around the region, with an eye towards identifying environmental policy needs, governments have given the impression of wishing to avoid any conclusion that NAFTA may be related to negative environmental outcomes. A broader approach – extending, for example, to the improvements in regional environmental infrastructure – would have allowed a more balanced and useful outcome that would likely reveal many positive consequences of NAFTA.

Addressing the Normative Impacts

The technical relationship between NAFTA's trade rules and international and national environmental laws is complex, and has still not been thoroughly tested in practice. In a ground-breaking effort to reduce conflicts with multilateral environmental agreements ("MEAs"), NAFTA exempts three major MEAs from its trade disciplines. NAFTA's effects on all other environmental treaties remains uncertain. From an environmental perspective, NAFTA's "specific exception" approach is an important step towards establishing the principle that MEAs should not be subject to *de facto* amendment by trade agreements. But until that principle is established more generally, NAFTA's approach remains incomplete.

NAFTA gives less leeway to domestic environmental laws. The "standards" sections, which specially affect health and environmental laws, include language reenforcing the rights of the parties to choose their own levels of environmental protection, and to discourage downward harmonization. Nevertheless, the burdens and legal tests are in general similar to those undeer the WTO, which have proved problematic from an environmental perspective, as described above. Meanwhile, the Chapter 11 expropriation cases, also described above, are among the starkest examples of normative conflicts between trade and investment agreements and domestic environmental rules.

Addressing Institutional Concerns

NAFTA's institutional provisions represent its most dramatic advance toward integration of trade and environment. The principal accomplishment is the establishment of the Commission for Environmental Cooperation ("CEC"), which consists of a ruling Council–the environmental ministers of each NAFTA party–a Secretariat, and an international citizens advisory panel. The CEC has three basic functions:

(i)   The CEC *promotes enforcement of environmental laws* through two mechanisms: 1. adjudication of intergovernmental disputes over "persistent patterns of failure to effectively enforce" environmental laws; and 2. factual investigation of complaints submitted by any resident of a NAFTA country alleging that a party fails "to effectively enforce" its environmental laws;
(ii) The CEC is charged with helping monitor and respond to *NAFTA's environmental impacts*; and
(iii) The CEC has *a broad mandate to foster environmental cooperation* among the NAFTA parties.

Whether the CEC is considered a success so far depends on whether one prefers to call a glass half empty or half full. In many ways, for a young international entity, born amidst controversy into a world where international environmental governance is famously weak, it has been a notable success. It has brought forward several cooperative initiatives that have positively influenced environmental outcomes in the region, and it has done a decent job within its means at encouraging environmental law enforcement. It has fallen shortest on the second prong of its mandate – responding to NAFTA's environmental impacts – as noted above.

From the outset, the success of the CEC has depended on three factors. First and foremost is the willingness of the three governments to take the CEC seriously, and to use it to promote significant environmental outcomes. Here again, one's satisfaction with what has happened so far depends on one's original expectations. Perhaps one starting place is with the realization that the CEC was created at the behest of one government, and practically against the will of at least one of the other two, and yet has received real support and "buy-in" from all three. The second key to the CEC's potential has been the vigor and independence of its Secretariat. The three governments had the courage and the wisdom to appoint an independently-minded environmentalist to act as the first executive director of the CEC. And even the CEC's harshest critics acknowledge the caliber of the environmental professionals who make up the Secretariat's staff. While the CEC has passed through periods, and dealt with specific issues, that have tempted the governments to micromanage the institution, by and large it has shown a remarkable degree of independence, given its fundamentally intergovernmental nature. If anything, the CEC suffered in its first years from giving too little attention to the overriding environmental goals of its governmental masters. Finally, the CEC has begun to develop a degree of direct interaction with public constituents that is unusual for an intergovernmental environmental body.

None of this is to say that the CEC has fully realized its institutional potential. It is deeply disappointing, for example, that no real working integration has been achieved between the CEC and the intergovernmental mechanisms responsible for administering NAFTA's trade and investment provisions. The fact that the CEC has so far been essentially uninvolved in the problems surrounding the "regulatory takings" cases under NAFTA Chapter 11 is the most obvious example of this failure, although others could also be given (and, in fact, have been partly outlined in a publication brought forward by the CEC itself in 1997).

CONCLUSIONS

The foregoing discussion reveals that the NAFTA system made some substantial–but incomplete–progress on each of the basic environmental concerns described in the first section of this paper. The ultimate value to the environment of these advances, however, remains to be achieved. Among the most important contributions that NAFTA was expected to make was to act as a prototype for the integration of trade and environmental policies in future regional market integration agreements. It has been a profound disappointment that this has not yet proved to be the case. Indeed, as the WTO increasingly struggles with the best means to reconcile environmental demands with the objectives of the trading system, the NAFTA/NAAEC model provides the form of a solution whose fuller implementation on the regional level worldwide would help create circumstances in which environmental concerns about the WTO could be reduced.

What is perhaps the most interesting potential for the NAFTA/ NAAEC model is that it points the way towards transcending the purely defensive aspects of the trade and environment agenda. By taking the first steps towards establishment of basic environmental infrastructures in parallel with market liberalization, the NAFTA/NAAEC system represents the most advanced experiment in the *pari passu* pursuit of the environmental policies needed for sustainable international commerce. In the end, it is the weakness of this parallel effort, and not the direct frictions between trade systems and environmental values, that is the deepest cause of remaining conflict between trade and environmental agendas.

APPENDIX

Penalties & Sanctions in the NAAEC

When allowed:
If a NAAEC arbitral panel finds a "persistent pattern of failure to effectively enforce its environmental law," the offending government must negotiate an "action plan" to solve the problem, or the panel can impose one. Failure to implement an action plan may result in monetary penalties imposed by the panel. If penalties are not paid within 180 days, the complaining party may impose sanctions by withdrawing equivalent NAFTA benefits.

Penalties and sanctions are available *only* in government-to-government disputes under Part Five of the treaty. Private party actions *cannot* lead to penalties or sanctions under NAAEC, unlike in trade disputes under various provisions of U.S. law, such as the famous Section 301.

The difference between penalties and sanctions:
"Penalties" – technically known as "monetary enforcement assessments" – are fines paid by an offending government to a fund created under the NAAEC. Nothing under the NAAEC would transfer the burden of penalties to private parties.

"Sanctions" are the withdrawal of NAFTA benefits through the raising of tariffs (or denial of other advantages) on NAFTA trade. The cost of sanctions falls initially on private traders, and may or may not include "cross retaliation" on "innocent" sectors.

Penalties & sanctions are sharply limited under the NAAEC:
• Penalties are limited to approximately $20M per case per year;
• Sanctions are limited to the amount of penalties actually owed;

- Sanctions cannot raise tariffs above pre-NAFTA or current MFN rates;
- Cross-retaliation is explicitly discouraged.

It takes a long time, and a lot of process, before penalties or sanctions apply:
There are a dozen significant procedural steps that must be accomplished before penalties and sanctions go into effect, including: several rounds of governmental "consultations," several special meetings of the NACEC Council, a two-thirds Council vote to arbitrate, a full arbitration proceeding, negotiation (and subsequent failure) of an "action plan" to redress a violation, the assessment of penalties (if required), the lapse of a significant payment period, and only then the imposition of sanctions affecting private traders. Given the times allotted for each step, it would likely take a minimum of 580 days (one year, seven months) before penalties were imposed, and at least another 180 days (for a total of more than two years) before sanctions could apply in a given case.

DAVID K. SCHORR is Director of the Sustainable Commerce Program at World Wildlife Fund (WWF-US) in Washington D.C.

Challenges for the Environment and NAFTA

JEAN CHAREST

The basic NAFTA agreement was concluded in 1992 without the companion accords on the environment and labour standards that were negotiated in 1993 at the request of the Clinton Administration. President Clinton was basically supportive of the NAFTA, but needed to bring the environmental and labour constituencies onside in the U.S. The side deals, as they were known, were finalized only in the summer of 1993 and the enhanced NAFTA entered into force on January 1, 1994.

NAFTA includes in its preamble a basic commitment of the parties to sustainable development, to environmental protection and conservation, and to the enforcement by the parties of their environmental laws, despite economic competition between them.

The NAFTA acknowledges the authority of a number of important international environmental agreements, including the CITES convention, the Montreal Protocol and the Basle Convention.

The NAFTA encourages harmonization of standards and the application of international standards, and specifically prohibits downward harmonization.

There are six key objectives to the North American Agreement on Environmental Cooperation (NAAEC).

- First, to foster the protection and the improvement of the environment, and to promote sustainable development, within North America.
- Second, to support the environmental goals of the NAFTA.

- Third, to strengthen trilateral cooperation in improving environmental laws and regulations.
- Fourth, to enhance enforcement of and the compliance with environmental laws.
- Fifth, to promote pollution prevention policies as well as economically efficient and effective environmental measures.
- Sixth, to promote transparency and public participation in the development and improvement of environmental laws and policies.

The Commission for Environmental Cooperation (CEC), which has its headquarters here in Montreal, was mandated to carry out the policies and promote the objectives of the NAAEC. There is also a commission on labour standards headquartered in Dallas, and an overall NAFTA commission, which was to be established in Mexico City. At the time, Canada saw the CEC as the key commission, the one on the cutting edge of public and economic policy. Its location in Montreal has proven to be beneficial to both the city and the environment.

The CEC's presence here has created a critical mass of expertise on the environment, and stimulated environmental studies in Montreal's university community, particularly at McGill. Since the CEC located here in 1994, the United Nations secretariat on biodiversity has also established its headquarters in Montreal. These are "brain gains" for Montreal and Quebec, and all of Canada, and provide leadership benchmarks in environmental policy.

The CEC has focused its work on four main areas: Conservation and biodiversity; pollutants and health; environment, trade and the economy; and finally, law and public policy.

As concerns effective enforcement of environmental laws, there are two remedies that the agreement provides where there is an alleged failure to effectively enforce environmental law. The first mechanism is submission on matters of enforcement. The agreement provides that citizens and NGOs can make submissions to the CEC Secretariat that a party is failing to enforce its environmental law. The CEC Secretariat must consider these submissions. The Secretariat may request a formal response to the submission by the party may recommend that the CEC Council prepare a factual record, namely an inepdendent presentation of the facts by the Secretariat. As of now, 20 such submissions have been received, eight of them directed at Canada, and the first factual record is being prepared that addresses the enforcement of Canadian environmental law.

The second process is consultation and dispute resolution. The NAFTA agreement provides for party to party consultation and dispute resolution. If consultation and mediation efforts fail, then an arbitral panel may be established to consider the allegations. Arbitral panels have the authority to require remedial action plans and impose fines for failure to implement such plans.

That's the structure of the NAFTA commission on the environment. In terms of enforcement and dispute resolution, it is meant to promote a common commitment to the environment, without raising difficult issues of sovereignty. The problem is that environmental issues don't respect borders. They are usually transboundary issues, whether in the atmosphere or in lakes, rivers and other bodies of water such as the Gulf of Mexico.

I have some first hand experience of this on the issue of acid rain between Canada and the United States, which particularly effected the maple syrup and Christmas tree producers of the Eastern Townships of Quebec, around my own riding of Sherbrooke. Many of those pollutants came from the industrial heartland of the U.S. Midwest. After years of debate, the issue was finally addressed by both governments in the 1991 Canada-U.S. accord to reduce emissions by 50 percent over the next decade, and restore the health of our lakes, rivers and forests. (As Environment Minister in the Mulroney government of the day, I was privileged to participate closely in those discussions, which demonstrated that there is no substitute for the political will to move a file forward.).

But, as the experience of the CEC has reminded us, bureaucracies in the three NAFTA countries are like bureaucracies everywhere, very protective of their turf, very risk averse, and very good at covering the rears of their political masters. Every international agreement implies some degree of diminution of national sovereignty, for the sake of achieving common objectives that will improve the standard of living and the quality of life. For the CEC to achieve its goals, it must command the confidence of all three national governments not only as to the transparency of its process, but the integrity of its work.

In Canada, there needs to be strong commitment to the NAAEC and CEC by the federal government, and a highly developed degree of co-operation with the provinces. To repeat, environmental issues respect neither national borders, nor provincial or state boundaries; but they can be successfully addressed by both levels of government.

In the United States, there is a clear need to raise the profile of the NAFTA and the environment. The fact is that both the NAAEC and the CEC have an extremely low profile in the U.S. The resistance of state governments, and the reluctance of Washington, in engaging with the CEC, can be overcome only by reinforcing its legitimacy and building its reputation with the general public.

In Mexico, the need is to make Mexico feel at home in the NAAEC. The fact is that Mexico continues to feel that the NAAEC was a tax imposed on it in order to get the NAFTA. And that continues to be an issue with Mexico. Changing Mexico's view of the NAAEC is a key challenge for the future. Mexico's attitude to the environmental side deal, and particularly the enforcement-related commitments and focus on the environment and trade relationships, lead to high transaction costs in order to reach any agreements.

Mexico is one of the leading opponents of linking environment and trade commitments. If Canada and the U.S. want to make progress on the trade and environment file in the global context, they will need to show that they have been able to make Mexico comfortable in the CEC. In this regard, the CEC should be seen by both Canada and the U.S. as a critical environment and trade laboratory.

The global trade and environment debate is going nowhere multilaterally. It is stalled in the WTO and going nowhere in the context of the FTAA. In fact, the CEC is virtually the only place where we have an example of a free trade agreement with parallel environmental commitments involving both developed and developing countries. In that sense, the NAAEC and the CEC may yet prove to be models for future discussions and eventual agreements in both the hemispheric and global contexts. In that sense, the CEC is not only worth preserving, but also worth improving.

JEAN CHAREST, Leader of the Quebec Liberal Party, was previously federal Minister of the Environment, and led the Canadian delegation to the 1992 Earth Summit.

Where Do We Go from Here?

New Policies for a New Century

THOMAS d'AQUINO

Let me begin with a salute. A salute to Presidents Reagan and Bush for their leadership and vision in advancing the cause of free trade in North America and the hemisphere. We are delighted that President Bush is here with us today, as convinced as ever of the importance of trade liberalization to the advancement of global economic prosperity. A salute to the Mexican leadership – political and private sector – for boldly reversing history and for opening the Mexican economy to North America and the world. No single Mexican more clearly represents this spirit of opening – of *apertura* – than my friend Jamie Serra. A salute to Brian Mulroney who pursued the goal of free trade in Canada with extraordinary courage and conviction and who won a decisive mandate from the people of Canada in the election of 1988 – signaling a mammoth transition in the economic history of Canada. To the former Prime Minister I would say this: I have no doubt that in time historians will be much more appreciative of your efforts and of your contributions than have been some of your contemporaries. And finally, a salute to the business leadership of Canada who in the early 1980s abandoned a century of opposition to free trade, who articulated a vision of Canadian and global competitiveness that is very much with us today, and who in those early days provided the necessary encouragement to politicians and officials alike to think the unthinkable and, in Donald Macdonald's own words, to "make the leap of faith."

My task is to look ahead and to offer some thoughts on where we go from here. I will couch my remarks in a double context – the first, global, the second with a focus on Canada.

The global picture is deeply disturbing to me. The global economy is far from healthy. Japan, the world's second largest economy, is still mired in recession. A serious recovery in Asia will be impossible without Japan's return to good health. European growth is lacklustre, with the German economy lagging badly and the Italian economy in recession. Russia is in chaos and facing an uncertain future. In Latin America, the jury is still out on Brazil, and the prospects for the continent are far from rosy. The super-charged United States economy continues to offer up stunning performance, but there are serious dangers lurking. The savings rate of Americans is in negative territory, the trade deficit is exploding, and the stock market continues to defy gravity.

Against this backdrop, we are seeing a backlash against globalization and, with it, a dangerous escalation of protectionism. Global trade volumes reflect this malaise. In 1997, we saw 10 percent growth. In 1998, growth dropped to less than 3.5 percent. For all these reasons, the world needs now, and for the 21st century, a powerful re-affirmation of rules-based market policies throughout individual economies. The world also needs, urgently, a revival of the principles of open trade. This means moving ahead quickly with the next round of World Trade Organization negotiations and with reforms to the WTO itself.

The agenda must be an ambitious one and must include further reductions to tariffs on industrial goods; it must address non-tariff measures; curb the abuse of anti-dumping, countervail and safeguard actions; extend the coverage of the rules on trade in services; open up agriculture to free trade; expand the rules to adequately reflect the importance of intellectual property, e-commerce and the Internet; move forward with investment liberalization; and explore ways to ensure that trade respects environmental, labour and human rights issues.

In addition and extremely important, in my view, the WTO must ensure that its rulings are implemented and enforced and that private restraints such as cartels, refusals to deal, and other unfair business practices are dealt with. The WTO itself must play a much more effective role in integrating and co-ordinating the international monetary and trading systems. It must be truly representative of the global economic community. In this regard, every effort should be made to have major players such as China join at an early date and play a responsible role.

The agenda I have described is ambitious. Its execution is urgent. Urgent, because without significant action, the world could easily lapse from financial crisis to trade crisis and to a new and dangerous global disorder. The WTO would do well to set its sites on a three year action plan and to the achievement of early and significant results. Business will not wait while the politicians squabble. Nor will the world.

Let me turn now to Canada. Canadian economic performance in a number of key areas has been quite outstanding. The federal government and most provincial governments are running fiscal surpluses, inflation has been virtually eradicated, our export performance has been stellar and, contrary to conventional wisdom, the productivity improvements in larger Canadian firms have been healthy. The World Economic Forum ranks Canada as the 5th most competitive economy in the world.

There is not the slightest doubt in my mind that the Canada-United States Free Trade Agreement has been a powerful catalyst in improving our economic performance. You have heard a number of my CEO colleagues from the aerospace, transportation, power, information technology and telecom businesses attest to this fact.

But Canada does continue to face some serious impediments to fully unleashing the potential of the Canadian economy. High levels of taxation, public debt and unemployment, and shortfalls in overall productivity and innovation are the key impediments, and we must waste no time in addressing them. Canadian business leaders are determined to do their part and this is why my own organization, the Business Council on National Issues, recently launched the *Canada Global Leadership Initiative.*

In pursuing remedies to the weaknesses in Canadian economic performance, trade strategy must continue to be an important card. The attainment of an effective set of global rules under the umbrella of the WTO must be our top priority. Under that umbrella, we must continue to reach out aggressively for strategic markets in Europe, Japan, China and Latin America.

The other dominant priority on the trade strategy front must be the United States. Here we must make fresh efforts to engage Americans in a common cause. For starters, we must seek every opportunity to eliminate impediments at the border; but in addition, we should consider moving beyond the NAFTA rules to common standards; to non discrimination in government procurement; to further liberalization in services; and yes, even to common rules about competition and subsidies. The effect of such a move would be to bolster Canadian growth, productivity, innovation and investment.

Some of you may be startled that I am suggesting a bilateral initiative here rather than a NAFTA negotiation. If a trilateral negotiation were feasible, I would be the first to support it. But given widespread skepticism about the NAFTA in the United States and Mexico, I fear that the appetite for such a negotiation involving the three countries would be very difficult to develop – particularly in the United States.

Canada should take the lead just as we did in the formative stages of the process leading to the Canada-United States Free Trade Agreement.

First, we must build a consensus for such an initiative in Canada, and then we must convince the Americans of the wisdom of such a course of action. As Canada prepares to enter the 21st century, the opportunities are extraordinary. Two factors will be critical to achieving our full potential – a strong and effective, rules-based global trading system, and an even more open, two-way economic relationship between Canada and the United States.

THOMAS d'AQUINO is President and Chief Executive of the Business Council on National Issues (BCNI), an organization composed of 150 chief executives of major enterprises in Canada.

The Future Work of the FTA, NAFTA and the WTO

PETER S. WATSON

INTRODUCTION

1999 serves as a useful year to take stock of the progress of the FTA, NAFTA and the WTO, in order to determine the agendas to move beyond their many current limitations. While the FTA and NAFTA are clearly more advanced than the WTO in terms of adopting disciplines needed in this era of increasing international economic integration, they share the need of the WTO for new instruments in the areas of investment protection, competition policy, and regulatory reform. Indeed, reforms in these areas would help achieve the vision of the world trading system originally intended to be incorporated into the post World War II International Trade Organization, through the *Havana Charter.*

In short, fundamental to the *Havana Charter* is its adoption of former U.S. Secretary of State Cordell Hull's understanding that domestic, as well as external, measures can restrict and distort the international movement of goods, services and capital, and that such distortions must be eliminated or significantly limited. However, today we are still trying to determine whether we wish to incorporate into the FTA, NAFTA and the WTO system a fundamental underpinning of the ITO – that governments should obligate themselves, not only to providing MFN and national treatment to other Members, but indeed to constructing a domestic economy without access barriers, through undertakings on restrictive business practices, the providing of services, and investment protection. The paradox, is, of course, that due to the realities of integrated markets, a greater need exists today than at the time of the ITO for disciplines in these areas, but with less consensus existing on if, and how, to proceed to adopt them.

IMPROVEMENTS TO THE FTA & NAFTA

While the FTA and NAFTA do indeed have disciplines facilitating cross-border investment, many exceptions to the same need to be revisited. For example, certain areas were carved out of NAFTA; generally, NAFTA countries have rights to limit investment in certain "public" sectors where the government is the major provider of services. NAFTA provisions do not cover some types of investments in any member country, including maritime and basic telecommunications investments, and Mexico and Canada retain some screening rights of foreign investment.

Progress is not easy in this area. The U.S. has reacted negatively at the recent Quad and OECD meetings to formally include investment disciplines in the next WTO Round.

The need for NAFTA and the WTO to adopt effective competition and regulatory reform policies is becoming more apparent as restrictive business practices and inappropriate regulations increasingly affect cross-border trade. The need to have regional and multilateral disciplines deal with these in-country practices in a comprehensive fashion is needed as globalization has transformed domestic policies and regulations into potential trade barriers.

Modern companies need to integrate production processes and support services located in many countries into a unified production system, and require some uniformity in technologies, standards, business relationships, and support systems – all of which can be affected by distortion to competition, and government regulations and sectoral policies. In short, the internationalization of production subjects production decisions to influence by internal restraints on trade, and domestic regulatory policy.[1]

How much support exists for new disciplines in these areas is unclear. For example, the U.S. has frustrated all attempts to have competition rules formally introduced either into the NAFTA, or the WTO, in large measure as this is seen by it as an attempt to water down the existing anti-dumping instruments. Clearly, it is timely to further examine the merits of a mutlilateral agreement on Trade related Anti-Competition Measures, or TRAM's, just as currently exists with TRIM's and TRIP's. Such a TRAM's agreement would assist in achieving the objective of true contestability of domestic markets.

THE NEW WTO AGENDA

Meanwhile, border problems, such as burdensome customs procedures, and other technical barriers to trade and investment facilitation bedevil the FTA. While NAFTA and APEC have been useful in advancing proposals to address such technical barriers to trade, such initiatives can be advanced in parallel at the FTA level, and also at the WTO. In the short term, one way of advancing the FTA construct is to seek the conclusion of a deeper integration agreement between Canada and the U.S., possibly ultimately leading to a full customs union between the two countries, as advocated by Michael Hart, and others.

Meanwhile, the progress at the WTO level must continue. We need to see progress in several areas, in addition to that of the TRAM's, as follows:

- to further liberalize trade in services;
- curb substantial protectionist measures impeding trade in agricultural products;
- further reduce and eliminate tariffs, especially in industrial goods;
- push forward the process of creating within WTO multilateral rules to liberalize and protect foreign direct investment, including longer-term equity capital;
- develop WTO-consistent criteria for the use of trade measures contained in multilateral environmental agreements;
- elaborate comprehensive multilateral rules to simplify and modernize trade procedures, and especially inefficient and costly customs procedures;
- extend the membership, sectoral coverage, and transparency provisions of the existing plurilateral agreement on government procurement.

GAINS FROM A NEW WTO ROUND

Already the Government of Australia, in its recent publication *Global Trade Reform 2000: Maintaining Momentum,* has set out three major reasons for a new WTO trade round. First, the global welfare benefits from a new round would be huge. Welfare gains from the Uruguay Round (1986–94) are likely to exceed U.S.$200 billion annually according to the OECD (1998a). The Uruguay Round, however, left heavily protected sectors in many economies. The global community would gain substantially from further multilateral trade reform. Analysis commissioned for the Australian report shows that further liberalization could generate even larger welfare gains than the Uruguay Round. Welfare gains from having trade barriers are estimated at around U.S.$400 billion annually. Eliminating barriers entirely would generate gains of around U.S.$750 billion annually. Earlier and more comprehensive market opening generates larger gains than later and less comprehensive liberalization. Estimates in the study are conservative because they take a cautious approach to estimating the potential value of gains in the services sector, and do not capture economies of scale and all the dynamic effects of trade liberalization. Furthermore, the "announcement effect" arising from forthcoming global trade reforms will itself generate earlier gains as markets and firms adjust for anticipated market opening.

Secondly, a comprehensive round would give bigger gains and greater opportunities for success. As a result of decisions taken at the end of the Uruguay Round, the so-called Built-in Agenda, negotiations in two key sectors – agriculture and services – are already mandated to start by early 2000. Reforms in those sectors alone would provide substantial benefits for the global trading community, including for developing countries. In the case of agriculture, the new analysis suggests gains of around U.S.$90 billion from having protection and around U.S.$150 billion from its elimination. Having trade distortions affecting services would generate global gains of around U.S.$250 billion. While gains from the Built-in Agenda are large there are powerful arguments why a new round should capture all market access sectors, including industrial products. One reason is that tariffs on industrial goods remain high in many economies, impeding further gains from trade for many countries, especially developing countries. The full benefits of trade reform identified by the modeling in this study will only be available with a comprehensive coverage of protected sectors. Many governments have been undertaking unilateral market reform, sometimes in response to global financial instability. As a practical matter, a new round would enable these governments to receive negotiating "credit" for those reforms. A second reason for the inclusion of industrial products relates to the political management of trade reform. Further market opening in some agriculture and services areas will be sensitive in some economies. Agreeing on a broader menu of market access for negotiation would enhance the scope for governments to achieve a balanced outcome on their market access commitments. Developing and emerging countries in particular would benefit from a broader coverage than the Built-in Agenda. While the new modeling shows all economies benefiting from a package involving agriculture, manufactures and services, developing regions in Asia, Africa, the Middle East and Latin America gain the most in proportion to GDP.

Crisis-affected economies would be particularly big winners. Gains from trade reform would be greater than could realistically be achieved by other means, including financial assistance. For instance, to make Thailand as well off from financial aid flows as from free trade would likely require a transfer of over U.S.$50 billion a year over five years – a huge sum. If the negotiations on agriculture and services, mandated to start by early 2000, are unlikely to result in conclusion of balanced outcomes for many governments, there is added urgency to ensuring that any decision in Seattle on a new round includes agreement to extend its coverage to include the industrial sector. At the same time, to keep a new round manageable, and its timeframe short, the agenda must be clearly focused on core market access issues which deliver the greatest gains. While other concerns are important, the scope and ambition of the negotiating agenda should be set carefully so that the key market access gains are not delayed.

Thirdly, a new round will help governments avoid backsliding on their market access commitments. The East Asian economic crisis, which began in mid 1997, has had a pronounced effect on global trade patterns. The sharp currency depreciation of crisis-affected countries, coupled with a severe contraction in demand, led to an immediate collapse of imports in affected countries. While currency devaluation improved the competitiveness of exports, financial and corporate sector problems, and weaker external demand, have prevented competitive gains being fully translated into resumed growth in exports.

Nevertheless, the effect of import contraction on trade balances has been significant, with most crisis-affected economies recording large trade surpluses. Recent indications suggest that the worst of the crisis, in terms of economic contraction, may now be past, but there are many factors, which could derail the recovery process. Ensuring that there is no retreat from engagement with the global economy will enhance the speed and sustainability of recovery from the crisis. Increased exports will be vital to maintain balance of payments stability as domestic demand, and imports, grow once more. A new round now will help keep markets open and underpin recovery in the crisis-affected countries. It is clear, however, that protectionist sentiment against import competition is growing in many wto economies. The most effective way to counter those pressures is to keep global trade reform moving forward. And the most effective way of doing that is by launching a new comprehensive wto round as soon as possible.

In conclusion, much needs to be done in the above areas before either the fta, nafta or the wto can be truly seen as effective vehicles that support the realities of the emerging market place. Collectively, reforms in investment protection, restrictive business practices, and regulatory reform are fundamental prerequisites to the more orderly operation of the international trading system.

PETER S. WATSON, former Chairman of the U.S. International Trade Commission (1994–1996), is counsel in the law firm of Winthrop, Stimson, Putnam & Roberts, Washington, D.C. He is the principal author of *Completing the World Trading System: Proposals for a Millennium Round,* Kluwer publishers, 1999.

NOTES

1 In respect to the above, see Geza Feketekuty, *The New Trade Agenda* (Group of Thirty Occasional Paper No. 40). Feketekuty identifies the following principles for disciplines relating to regulatory reform: transparency, due process, predictability, nondiscrimination, objective, performance-based criteria, minimizing the regulatory burden, transparency of regulatory burden, use of market mechanisms, and minimizing the scope of regulations.

The New Economic Environment

BRIAN MULRONEY

As you know, we are rarely able to evaluate within a few years the real impact of important decisions of public policy. Most often, it takes a great deal of time, even decades, before all the consequences of an important initiative are apparent.

In the recent history of our country, there have been several major policy decisions whose impact is still not completely known. One such initiative was the Canada-U.S. Free Trade Agreement. Few events in the short history of our country have aroused such passions and controversy. The debates were often bitter and indignant, and it took a general election to convince Canadians to ratify the FTA.

The adversaries of free trade didn't mince their words. It meant the end of our social programs, of health care, of regional development programs and of our cultural identity. Even our sovereignty was threatened.

The proponents of free trade were equally convinced. We would become more competitive, our exports would increase by leaps and bounds, and with growing prosperity, we would have the confidence in ourselves to be world competitive in the increasingly challenging context of globalization.

Who was right? Only time will tell in a definitive manner. Yet it's possible, 10 years later, to examine the results and directions flowing from free trade.

Let me put this in context by taking you back 15 years. At one point in the early 1980s, the British weekly magazine *The Economist* had carried an editorial headline which read as follows: "Wildcat Canada Resigns from the World". The headline summarized the economic and fiscal policy against which my party, in Opposition, waged political battle, culminating in the election of 1984. The reference to "resigning from the world" was a bow to the phenomenon we have come to know as globalization.

This new economic environment is so different, the change so great and the transition to it so wrenching, that some historians compare its impact to that of the Industrial Revolution some 200 years ago. At such a time, people are gripped by anxiety and insecurity. It was no different in the 1980s. A resurgence of protectionist sentiment and policy arose in the Congress of the United States. And as *The Economist* noted, the previous federal government had designed its own Canadian version of Fortress America.

Canada had to alter course. We had to make fundamental policy changes: a Free Trade Agreement with the United States. The NAFTA. Abolishing the 13.5% manufacturers' sales tax and introducing a 7% consumption tax (the GST) to spur exports. Eliminating FIRA. Abolishing the National Energy Program, including the PGRT. Privatizing Crown assets, from Teleglobe, to Air Canada, to Canadair, and de Havilland to (partially) Petro Canada. The Patent Act was re-vamped to strengthen the pharmaceutical industry and attract billions of dollars in new investment. On the fiscal side, the average rate of growth of program spending was cut by 70%. Government spending on programs moved from $1.23 for every dollar in total revenues to $0.97 by 1993. An operating deficit of $16 billion per year was transformed into a $6.6 billion surplus. As a percentage of GDP, the federal deficit was virtually cut in half, from 8.7% in 1984 to 4.6% in 1990–91. The worldwide recession took a serious toll on that number, driving it up to 5.9%, but public finances were still left in a position significantly stronger than where we found them.

The groundwork was laid for a strong, export-driven recovery, which has now come to pass. The day I signed the FTA with President Reagan, exports accounted for approximately 23% of our GDP. Today, that number is over 40% and rising swiftly. By the time my government left office in 1993, the prime rate was at 6%, the lowest in 20 years; our inflation rate was 1.5%, the lowest in 30 years, and the United Nations had just reported that in terms of quality of life, as you have repeatedly heard, Canada was the No. 1 country in the world. It needs to be emphasized that these policies, whether of free trade or of fiscal management, are not an end in themselves. They are a means to an end, which is the achievement of greater opportunity, higher incomes and better living standards for all Canadians.

Canada and the U.S. are in the vanguard of industrialized nations building a foundation of economic growth and prosperity in which justice and freedom can flourish both at home and around the world. For generations, the United States and Canada have made common cause for both. More than three million jobs in each country depend directly on trade with the other. And that trade has been growing steadily, from both countries, to both countries, since we implemented the Canada-U.S. Free Trade Agreement.

Since the FTA, our exports to the U.S. have skyrocketed by 180% and our total commerce exceeds $1.5 billion per day – almost $600 billion per year – the largest such trade between any two nations in world history.

Canada buys more U.S. products than the fifteen countries in the European Union combined. In fact, the U.S. exports more to Ontario than it does to the nation of Japan. Trade creates jobs – good jobs, high paying jobs, durable jobs. Every $1 billion in trade abroad means approximately 12,000 new jobs at home. And that's what the NAFTA debate has been about – jobs and the future.

At about this time, the new President of Mexico began articulating his vision for the modernization of the Mexican economy. The cornerstone of that great initiative was to be a Free Trade Agreement among Mexico, the United States and Canada. In Mexican terms, the concept was revolutionary and marked a dramatic break with many past policies. In global terms, the concept was unusual in that it marked the first attempt to link, within a free trade zone, the economies of two mature, wealthy, trading countries (both G-7 nations) with that of the equivalent of a developing nation, with relatively limited democratic achievement in terms of politics, public policy, the judiciary and business leadership – when compared with the U.S. or Canada.

NAFTA was successfully negotiated and signed in San Antonio in October 1992, by the Presidents of the United States and Mexico and myself. Based on the Canada-U.S. experience, NAFTA has opened up the Mexican market of 100 million people, creating the largest, richest, single market in the world – 400 million people accounting for one-third of the world's output. The future looked brilliant as Mexicans opened their economy for the first time and trade expanded by 25% during the first twelve months. But, the enemies of democracy knew that political instability would damage the cause of social justice. I was in Mexico City the day Luis Donaldo Colosio was assassinated. This was an enormous tragedy for Mexico.

Later, powerful tragedy struck again, almost suffocating in its wake the great economic advances and structural changes of recent years. In fact, Mexicans are beginning to emerge from a period of tremendous anguish – from the peso collapse, to new political assassinations. But, because of the strength of the Mexican people and the resolve of their nation, they will survive this and other challenges and Mexico will pursue a course towards greater democracy, justice and prosperity.

Since the Miami Summit and the decision to expand free trade throughout the hemisphere by 2005, a $13–14 trillion market now awaits North America's entrepreneurs and business community. But, there is a cloud on the horizon. The momentum under American leadership is in the process of being lost. Chile, which was to be the next NAFTA partner, has been stiffed and the pledge of fast track negotiations disappeared in the vapor of election-year politics. President Clinton was in fact denied fast track authority last year by members of his own party in the House of Representatives. As a consequence, Latin American countries are now making major trade deals that exclude the United States.

A customs union known as MERCUSOR has emerged among Brazil, Argentina, Uruguay and Paraguay. Their economies produce almost $2 trillion, 70% of South America's total. In spite of present difficulties, MERCUSOR is prospering. It has signed a free trade agreement with Mexico, is discussing one with Canada, which has just signed an FTA with Chile, and with Europe by the year 2005. This trend away from American leadership is ominous and must be reversed. To handcuff the President of the U.S. at the very moment that international trade sweeps forward as the greatest liberalizing and modernizing force the world has known, is to do an enormous disservice to the U.S. and the goal of increased prosperity and social justice around the world.

And, what of the future? As directed by the Miami and Santiago Summits, work will proceed among the 34 partners and the CBI countries, to achieve "concrete progress" toward the FTAA by the end of 1999. This should include agreements this year on concrete and mutually beneficial business facilitation measures. These could include a code of conduct for customs integrity; improved customs procedures for express shipments; transparency and due process in government procurement; or mutual recognition agreements in the licensed professions.

From there, 2005 will be targeted as the year to complete a rigorous, comprehensive trade agreement, expanding trade, accelerating growth, attracting investment from all over the world and cementing our strategic position in the hemisphere. Its benefits for all of us will be immense. One day, NAFTA's successor – the Free Trade Area of the Americas – shall include 34 countries and 800 million people and the U.S. and Canada will have defined powerful roles for themselves at the very heart of a new free trade zone, stretching from Point Barrow to Patagonia, Hawaii to Recife, Easter Island to Nunavut.

We need to raise living standards. Families will benefit from a wider availability of goods and services, with better quality and lower prices.

Domestic firms in each FTAA member country will become more efficient as they more easily import capital and informatics goods – and employ the higher technologies that become available when intellectual property protection improves.

We should encourage competition, transparency, and impartial regulation in and continued deregulation of the service industries – financial systems, telecommunications, insurance, construction, the professions and more. We should develop enhanced means of resolving trade disputes. We should become more effective in addressing our mutual trade concerns with trading partners outside our region. And finally, we will strengthen the values of openness, accountability, and democracy which themselves make the FTAA possible.

Canada's economy has undergone massive restructuring and modernizing over the last dozen years. The results are evident and persuasive. We are growing into a competitive country whose lifeline is exports and international trade. This new growth and wealth have enabled us to eliminate the deficits – both provincially and federally – and begin the process of paying down our debt, while cutting taxes in some jurisdictions for our citizens. The controversial and painful measures introduced to achieve this – principally the trilogy of free trade, GST and high interest rates to eliminate inflation – have clearly made us stronger and enabled Canada to dramatically improve the state of our public finances.

This new economic strength has in turn significantly enhanced Canadian sovereignty – because such sovereignty is merely an illusion without the financial clout to back it up and the economic opportunity it offers to growing numbers of our citizens.

Canada, like other privileged nations, is often extremely resistant to change. Deep and important structural changes are indispensable, however, to maintain a growing economy and can only be brought about by a firm expression of political will. For a generation raised on the bizarre proposition that leadership should be equated with popularity, measured and published weekly, this can be a daunting challenge. In fact "transforming leadership" – leadership that makes a significant difference in the life of a nation – recognizes that political capital is acquired to be spent in great causes for one's country.

Prime Ministers are not chosen to seek popularity. They are chosen to provide leadership. There are times when Canadians must be told not what they want to hear but what they have to know. And what they have to know is a quotation from the Book of Proverbs inscribed on the Peace Tower in Ottawa: "Where there is no vision, the people perish."

Leaders must have vision and they must find the courage to fight for the policies that will give that vision life. Leaders must govern not for easy headlines in 10 days but for a better Canada in 10 years – and they must be ready to endure the attacks and the opprobrium that often accompany profound or controversial change, while they await the distant and compelling sounds of a verdict that only history and a more reflective nation can render in the fullness of time.

It was a great and genuine privilege to serve as Prime Minister at a time of remarkable challenge and convulsive change, at home and around the world. Many of you here today participated in that journey in differing ways, for which I express deep gratitude and personal admiration. The service of one's country is the noblest one of all.

Democracies are inspired by the collision of great ideas and the vigorous disagreements and debates they provoke. In this great debate all the participants from all parties and all parts of the political spectrum – in government or out – have served Canada well, and I feel honoured to be in your company.

BRIAN MULRONEY was Prime Minister of Canada from 1984 to 1993. His government negotiated both the Canada-U.S. Free Trade Agreement and the North American Free Trade Agreement.

Two Cheers for the FTA: Ten-Year Review of the Canada-U.S. Free Trade Agreement

JOHN McCALLUM

Canada can count many positive economic achievements in the decade since the signing of the Canada-U.S. Free Trade Agreement (FTA). In the past decade, Canadian exports to the United States have increased by 169%, while imports have gone up by 149%. We have enjoyed very strong employment growth during the past two years (838,000 new jobs created). We've moved sharply upwards in competitiveness rankings according to international agencies. While our economy has been less buoyant than the United States, we have also avoided the large increases in income inequality that have taken place south of the border. We are still the "best country in the world" according to the United Nations. We have conquered inflation. Having tamed fiscal deficits, Canadians can look forward to large and growing fiscal dividends in coming years.

However, in a number of respects, the Canadian economy has done worse than the U.S. economy since 1989. The Canada-U.S. productivity gap in manufacturing has probably been moving in the wrong direction. Our unemployment rate is almost double the U.S. unemployment rate. Between 1989 and 1998, our living standards, as measured by inflation-adjusted personal disposable income per person, have declined by 5%, compared to a 12% increase in the United States. Between 1990 and 1997, our estimated share of the world's inward stock of foreign direct investment (FDI) declined from 6.5% to 4.0%, while our share of the inward stock of FDI in North America fell from 21% to 14%.1. While the U.S. stock market, as measured by the S&P Index, is up 340% from a decade ago, the TSE has managed a gain of only 95% (in U.S. dollars).

Chart 1

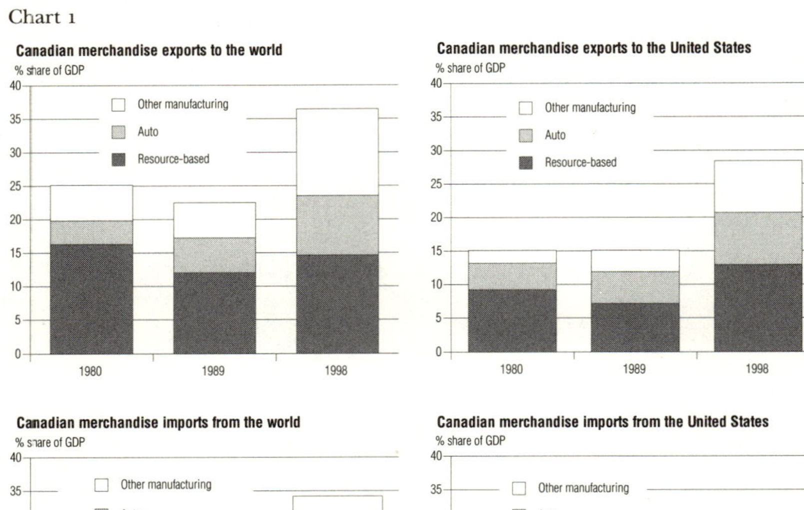

How is an economist to assess the impact of the FTA, given all these other things that have been happening in the past decade? The short answer is: with difficulty. What we want to know is whether the FTA made a bad situation worse or a bad situation better. Certainly, there is no shortage of other candidates to explain Canada's relatively poor performance in the 1990s. For example, while there is no doubt that we are benefiting today from low inflation and fiscal dividends, there is equally no doubt that the path to where we are today has been painful. In addition, our currency and living standards have suffered because of the Asia-induced decline in global commodity prices, while Canada's high tax burden, in both absolute terms and relative to the United States, is often cited as a problem.

The organization of the paper is as follows. We begin with descriptive charts showing the evolution of Canada-U.S. trade by province or region and by major sector. Next, and in the major body of the report, we survey the existing literature to ask how the FTA has affected Canada in the following areas: currency, trade, productivity, foreign direct investment, jobs, and access to the U.S. market, or the success or failure of dispute resolution mechanisms. Finally, we draw conclusions.

Chart 2

Atlantic Canada

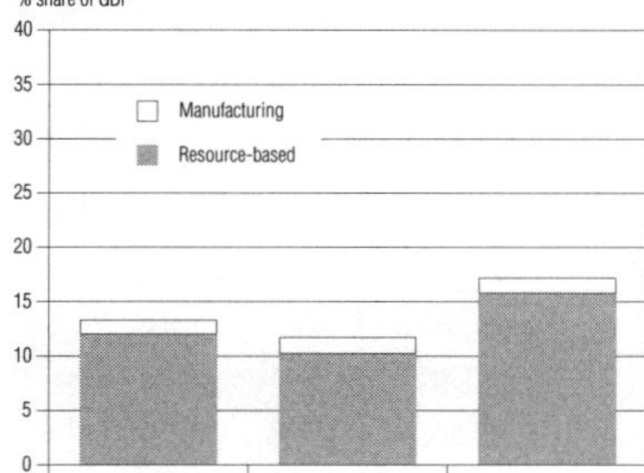

Quebec

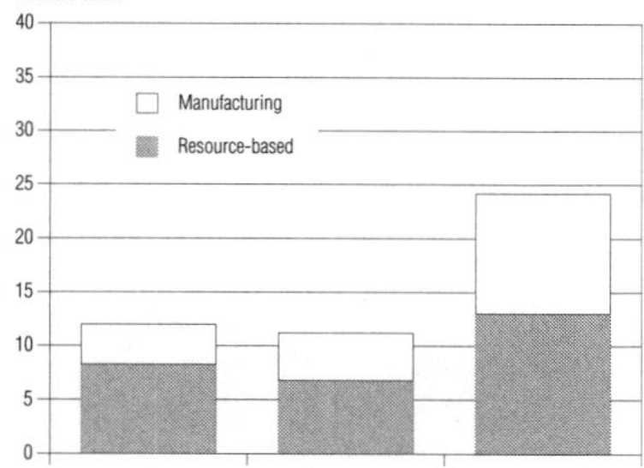

Ontario

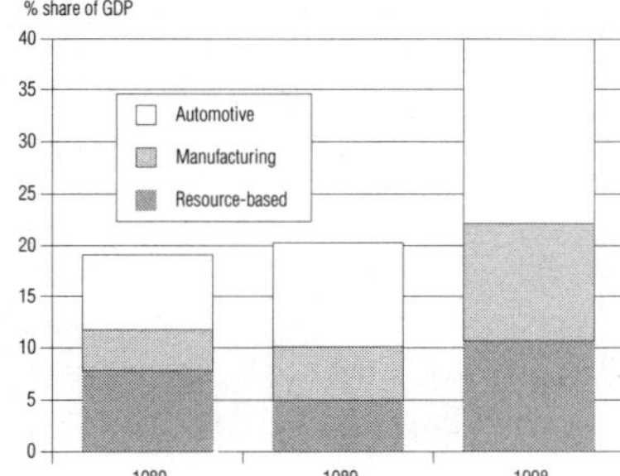

Manitoba

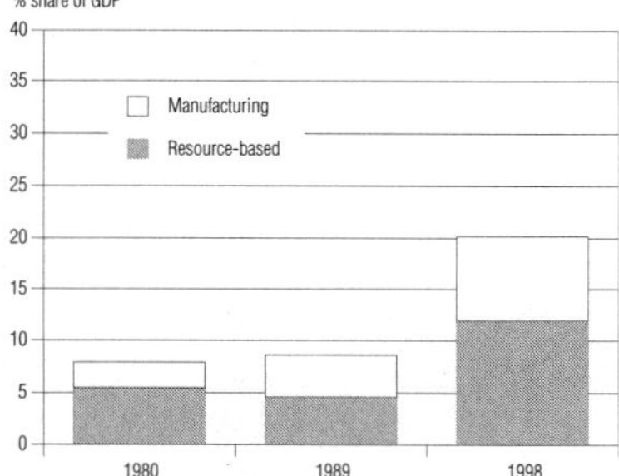

Saskatchewan

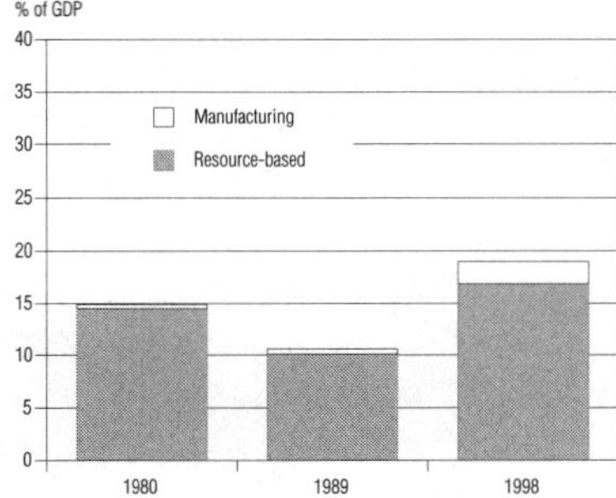

Alberta

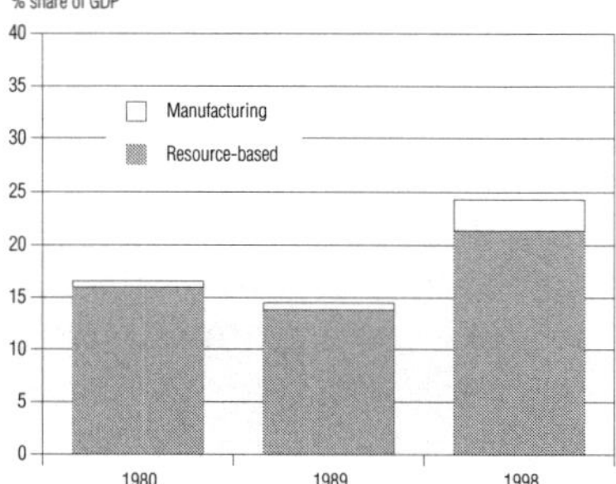

British Columbia

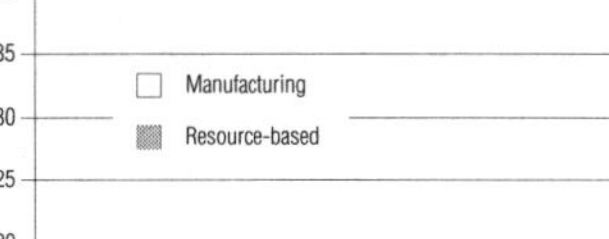

EVOLUTION OF CANADA-U.S. TRADE
BY PROVINCE AND SECTOR

Merchandise trade

For each of the years 1980, 1989, and 1998, Chart 1 plots Canadian exports by major commodity class (resource-based, auto-related, and other manufacturing), as well as Canadian imports. The chart covers both Canada-world trade and Canada-U.S. trade. Chart 2 shows exports to the United States from Atlantic Canada, Quebec, Ontario, Manitoba, Saskatchewan, Alberta, and British Columbia. In all cases, exports and imports are measured as a percent of nominal gross domestic product (GDP).

Beginning with exports, in most cases there was not a great deal of change between 1980 and 1989, although the relative importance of resource-based exports declined in all cases. Then, between 1989 and 1998, what can only be described as an explosion of Canada-U.S. trade took place. For the country as a whole, exports to the United States rose from 15% of GDP in 1989 to 28.4% in 1998. While all three sectors increased, in relative terms the largest increase was in the "other manufacturing" component, which increased from 4.3% of GDP in 1989 to 9.1% in 1998. The explosion was greatest for Canada-U.S. trade, as the share of Canadian merchandise exports going to the United States increased from 71% in 1989 to 84% in 1998.

Among the provinces, Ontario is uniquely dependent on the United States, with exports to that country accounting for an astounding 40% of GDP in 1998, as compared with 20% in 1989. The three sectors shared more or less equally in this doubling of GDP shares. Next to Ontario are Quebec and Alberta, each with about one-quarter of GDP devoted to U.S. exports. Quebec has enjoyed huge growth in manufacturing exports to the United States, while Alberta's exports are still dominated by resource-based goods. Next come Manitoba and Saskatchewan with one-fifth of their GDPs devoted to U.S. exports, although Saskatchewan is still resource-dominated while Manitoba has a more balanced diet. Finally, Atlantic Canada and British Columbia, perhaps because of their locations at the extremities of the country, remain the least dependent on the United States, with exports amounting to 17% and 15% of GDP, respectively.

In all cases, however, the 1989–1998 growth of exports to the United States as a share of GDP was huge, ranging from lows of around 50% for Atlantic Canada and British Columbia to highs of well over 100% for Manitoba and Quebec. In the case of imports, it can be seen that there

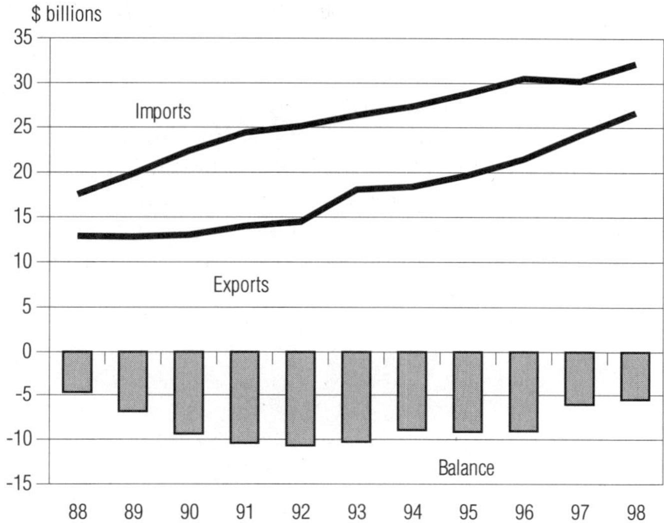

Note: Statistics Canada does not record Canada-Mexico trade in Services to the same degree as Canada-U.S. services trade, and similar numbers for Mexico are not available. Source: Department of Foreign Afairs and International Trade, December 1998

has also been a large jump in Canada's imports from the United States in the past decade, although somewhat smaller than the jump in exports.

Trade in services

The Canada-U.S. FTA provided for a partial liberalization of trade in services which was subsequently expanded by the North American Free Trade Agreement (NAFTA) to include virtually all aspects of cross-border trade. Canadian exports of services to the United States have increased in areas including computer and information services, architecture and technical services. Import gains have also featured computer services, as well as management and advertising services. As shown in Chart 3, total Canada-U.S. trade in services almost doubled in the decade to 1998, rising from $30.4 billion to $58.9 billion.

IMPACT OF THE FTA ON CANADA

We come now to the impact of the FTA on the currency, trade, productivity, foreign direct investment (FDI), jobs, and access to the U.S.

market. It will be seen that the first two of these six topics provide the clearest conclusions.

Currency

At the time of the FTA negotiations, there was a conspiracy theory alleging that Canada had secretly committed to maintaining the dollar at its current exchange rate, then around 89 U.S. cents. With the benefit of hindsight and given that the Canadian dollar now stands at around 69 U.S. cents, we can safely say that one of two conclusions must be true: either this conspiracy theory was never true, or it was very poorly executed. Unfortunately, conclusions on other aspects of the impact of the FTA are less clear-cut.

Trade

It would be quite a coincidence if the explosion of Canada-U.S. trade after 1989 had nothing to do with the implementation of the Canada-U.S. Free Trade Agreement in that year. The fact that Canadian imports from the United States exploded almost as much as Canadian exports to the United States indicates that this is not just an exchange rate story.

The most powerful evidence pointing to a direct role of the FTA in the expansion of Canada-U.S. trade is the fact that trade in goods that were liberalized by the FTA grew faster than trade in goods that were unaffected by the FTA. According to Schwanen (1997), between 1988 and 1995 Canadian exports to the United States of goods that were liberalized by the FTA increased by 139%, as compared with 65% for goods that were not liberalized by the FTA. Corresponding figures for imports from the United States were 103% and 38%, respectively (see Chart 4). This finding seems highly robust, as several other studies using different industry classifications and time periods come to broadly similar conclusions [Statistics Canada (1993), Clausing (1996), Trefler (1999), and Helliwell, et. al. (1998)]. As further evidence of the positive impact of the FTA, Schwanen notes that Canada's trade with other countries also grew less quickly than Canada-U.S. trade in goods that were liberalized by the FTA.

These studies suggest that something like one-quarter of the increase in Canada-U.S. trade can be directly attributed to lower tariffs, an amount that implies a very large change in imports in response to a given tariff reduction. Moreover, the overall increase in Canada-U.S. trade was much larger than predicted by most pre-FTA studies – Harris

Chart 4

Canadian exports and imports by FTA status
1988-1995

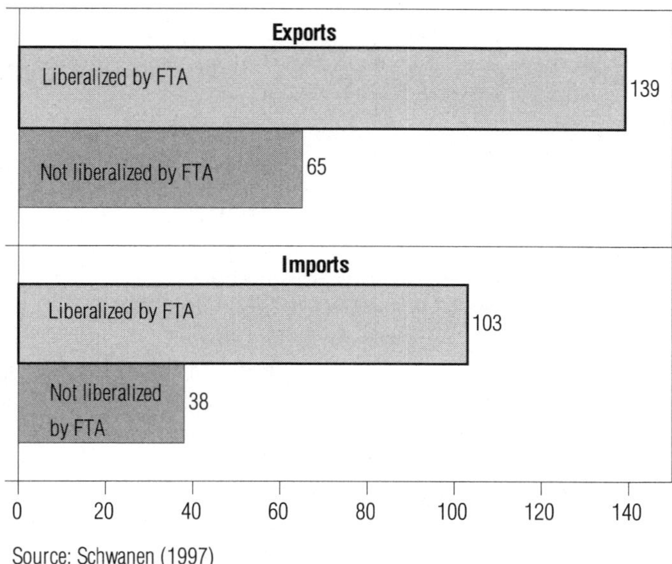

Source: Schwanen (1997)

(1985) seems to be an exception – and the reasons for this remain something of a mystery. Presumably the FTA accelerated an ongoing trend in the direction of a rationalization of North American production facilities, implying an increase in intra-industry and intra-firm trade in intermediate goods. A similar phenomenon was observed in the auto industry following the Auto Pact, and it is also true that there is a rising trend in the share of intra-firm exports in total exports.

Productivity in manufacturing

If the FTA overdelivered on trade, then, at least on the surface, it appears to have underdelivered on productivity in the manufacturing sector. The measurement of Canadian productivity and its comparison with that of the United States is extremely complex and difficult. In recent months, we have witnessed a deluge of new and often conflicting numbers on this topic. While the more recent statistics tend to cast Canada's performance in a somewhat more favourable light than the older numbers, all of the numbers that I have seen point to a widening gap between Canadian and U.S. manufacturing productivity in the post-FTA period. Whether that gap was 28% in 1997, as suggested by Bureau of Labour Statistics (BLS) numbers, or something a bit smaller, it was nevertheless: (a) substantial and (b) probably larger than it was at the time the FTA was signed. This last statement is qualified because the widening of the gap occurred only in the two most recent years, and if history is a guide, there will probably be substantial revisions in the future.

It is hard to believe that the explosion of Canada-U.S. trade that was caused by (or at least associated with) the advent of free trade should not have had a positive effect on Canadian manufacturing productivity. Indeed, Trefler (1999) does find that Canadian industries experiencing larger tariff reductions under the FTA did, in fact, experience higher productivity growth. He estimates that the FTA added 4.1% to Canada's manufacturing productivity. While it would seem that this estimate is not terribly robust, its credibility should be enhanced by several other factors that help explain why Canadian productivity performance has been poor for reasons not related to the FTA. Two such factors especially deserve mention.

A first reason for thinking Daniel Trefler may be right is that, when we look at productivity growth by industry over the period 1989–97, we see that the U.S. lead over Canada arises entirely from super-high productivity growth in two industries – industrial machinery and equipment and electronic and other electric equipment (see Chart 5). In 11 of the other 17 industries, Canada's productivity growth exceeded that of the United States. This suggests that a good chunk of Canada's relative underperformance can be explained by some combination of measurement error in the U.S. statistics and Canada's under performance in the "high-tech," "Silicon valley," computer-related industries. Neither of these factors is FTA-related.

Second, some have argued that Canada's weak currency has reduced pressures on Canadian manufacturers to reduce costs and raise productivity. To the extent this controversial hypothesis has any merit, it would help explain why our productivity performance has been weak in spite of free trade.

In summary, Trefler's finding that the FTA helped boost Canadian manufacturing productivity is consistent with economic logic and with pre-FTA expectations. It is further supported by a number of other non-FTA-related forces that may have contributed to our poor productivity performance. These include relative underperformance in the new computer-related industries, measurement issues, and a possible link between productivity and the currency. To the extent these factors con-

Labour productivity in manufacturing

1989-1997, average compound % growth rate

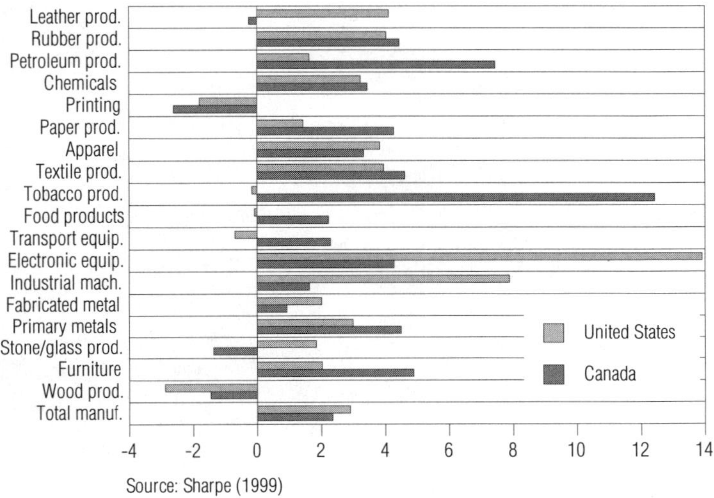

Source: Sharpe (1999)

Canada's inward share of FDI

% of GDP

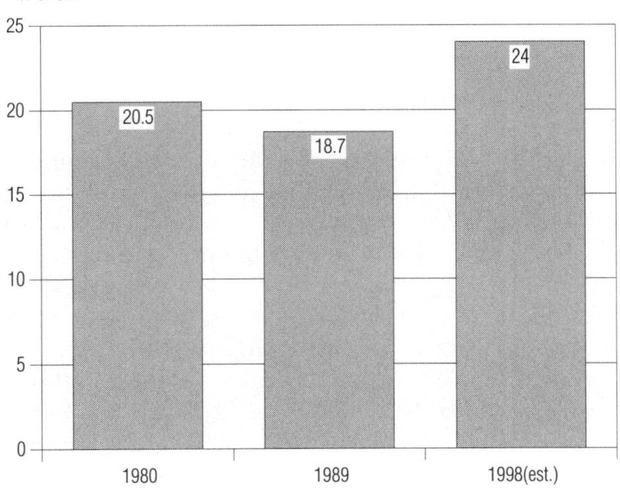

Source : United Nations, World Investment Report, 1998, and Daniel Schwanen

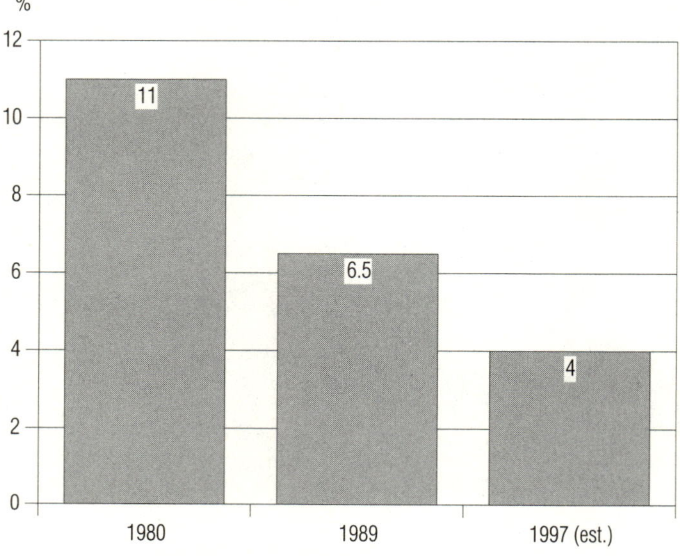

Source: United Nations, *World Investment Report, 1998*

tributed to poor productivity, they do not imply that we don't have a productivity problem, but they do help us understand why the FTA could have had a significant positive effect on productivity even though overall performance was weak.

Foreign direct investment

Many economists will register considerable resonance with Mark Twain's comment on lies, damn lies, and statistics. Nowhere is this more the case than with foreign direct investment (FDI). If we want a rosy picture, we can consider Canada's inward flows or stock of FDI relative to either total investment or GDP (see Chart 6). If we want a gloomy picture, then we turn to Canada's share in the total inward stock of FDI in the world or North America (see Chart 7). Between 1989 and 1998, Canada's inward FDI stock has increased from 19% of GDP to an estimated 24%. On the other hand, between 1980 and 1997, our share of the total world FDI stock has gone from 11% to 4%.

From the point of view of evaluating the FTA, I am not aware of any research that has evaluated the impact of the FTA on FDI into Canada. From a conceptual point of view, the impact could go either way. On the one hand, the dismantlement of the tariff wall set up by John A. Macdonald in 1879 allows American and other firms to supply the Canadian market from outside Canada. This would argue for less FDI. On the other hand, the FTA allows Canadian-based firms to serve the entire North American market, and, given our lower costs in every industry (according to KPMG [1999]), this should favour more FDI into Canada. In the absence of original research in this area, and given that original research is beyond the scope of this report, we cannot comment much further on this matter, except to note that, post-FTA, the inward stock of FDI has both increased relative to GDP and declined less abruptly relative to the world stock than was the case during the 1980s. So, pending further research, it would be difficult to argue that the FTA has resulted in a reduction in FDI into Canada.

More generally, however, the trends that are seen in the charts do represent a worry. It is not just a question of Canada's ability to attract FDI. It is also a matter of Canada's ability to retain its own major corporations and most skilled citizens in this country. The risk is that, as the Canada-U.S. border comes down in economic terms, our deficiencies in terms of tax regime and non-appearance on the radar screens of multinational companies could exact a mounting toll. Canada's desire to become a favoured location for both domestic and foreign investors to serve the North American market could also be thwarted by the continuation of Canada-U.S. border impediments.

Jobs

On the question of jobs, we have a debate between, among others, Schwanen (1997) and Trefler (1999). The former argues that the FTA did not negatively impact manufacturing employment because the performance of sectors most sensitive to the FTA has not deteriorated relative to total manufacturing employment. The latter, using a different classification of industries, comes to the opposite conclusion. Trefler's regression analysis suggests that about a half of the 19% 1988–95 reduction in employment in the manufacturing sector can be attributed to the FTA, although this result does not hold for all his specifications. Also, Trefler states that "the fact that manufacturing employment and output have largely rebounded since 1995 suggests that some and perhaps most of the reallocation has been to high-end manufacturing." Although this debate seems unresolved, it is very likely that there were some transitional job losses as tariffs fell, in some cases from more than 20% to zero in the short space of a decade. On the other hand, jobs were undoubtedly created by the FTA-induced export expansion, although credit for the export boom has to be shared with our depreciating dollar and other forces. Overall, I don't think that we know whether the FTA led to a rise or a fall in total jobs.

Access to the U.S. market

A primary objective of the Canadian negotiators was to secure access to the world's largest market and to replace a power-based dispute resolution mechanism with a rules-based mechanism. The original Canadian objective was to eliminate all anti-dumping (AD) and countervailing duties (CVD) laws and replace them with a system of rules that would be enforced through binding dispute settlement. An alternative objective would have been to negotiate a more limited, common AD/CVD system that would have been enforced through binding dispute settlement. This would have been the most effective means of achieving a rules-based method of dispute resolution, not subject to the vagaries of domestic politics and interest groups. In any event, these objectives were not achieved, as U.S. negotiators were unwilling to have domestic U.S. law supplanted by a new body of international law.

As a result, the dispute resolution mechanisms under the FTA and NAFTA were definitely second-best outcomes from a Canadian standpoint. Without reviewing these mechanisms in detail (see Alvarez et al. [1995]), Schwanen [1995], Howse [1998] for detailed analysis), we make a few general observations. On the positive side, the consensus seems to be that the Chapter 19 panels under NAFTA have functioned well in low profile cases, and Schwanen suggests that the panels have resulted in a significant reduction in the level of disputed exports from Canada to the United States. However, in the notorious softwood lumber dispute, following an adverse ruling by a NAFTA panel, the United States changed its law so as to conform to an earlier decision by the U.S. International Trade Administration. This had the effect of nullifying the force of the NAFTA panel finding and is a major weakness of the Chapter 19 process. Also, because panels are not bound by earlier panel decisions (and, indeed, must follow rulings of domestic courts, not earlier panels), decisions on similar cases have been relitigated and have resulted in widely varying decisions. Another issue involves the questionable constitutionality of the Chapter 19 process under U.S. law, although Alvarez, et al. argue that Chapter 19 should withstand a constitutional challenge.

NAFTA: CANADA-MEXICO TRADE
AND INVESTMENT

Since the signing of the North American Free Trade Agreement (NAFTA), Canada-Mexico trade and investment relations have ex-

Canada-Mexico merchandise trade

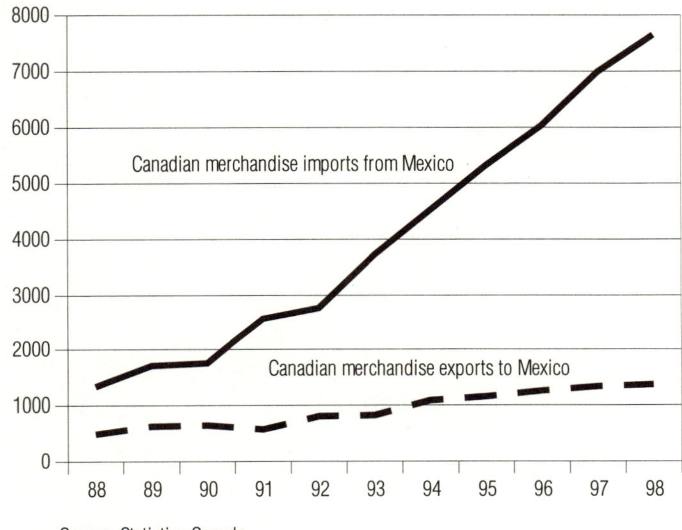

Source: Statistics Canada

Canada-Mexico foreign direct investment

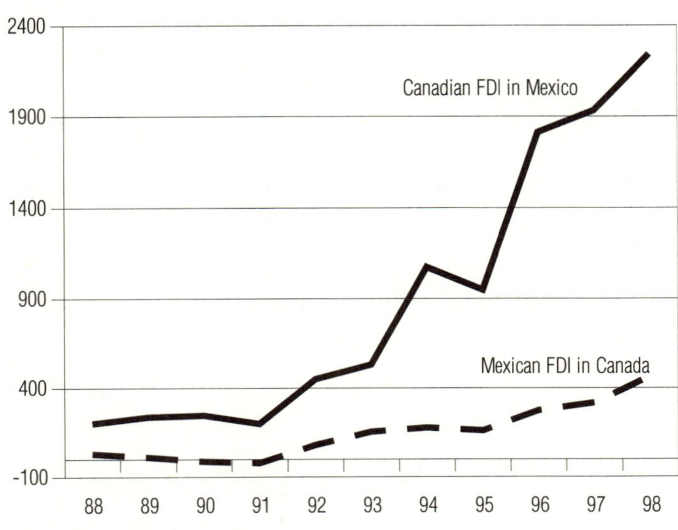

Source: Statistics Canada

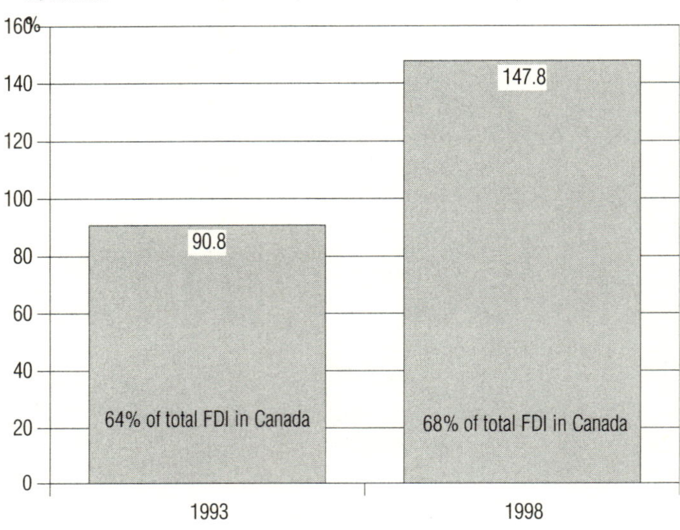

panded rapidly, albeit from a small base. Between 1993 and 1998, Canadian merchandise exports to Mexico increased from $800 million to $1.4 billion, notwithstanding the 1994–95 financial crisis, while imports more than doubled from $3.7 billion to $7.6 billion. Foreign direct investment also registered large increases in both directions. Critics will argue from the growing Canada-Mexico deficits in both trade and investment that Canada has been the loser. While such arguments can be debated both ways, the major point is that Mexico and the United States were going to form a free-trade area, with or without Canada's participation. Given that fact, it was definitely in Canada's interests to become a signatory to NAFTA rather than allow the United States to develop a "hub and spoke" model in which the United States would be at the hub of a number of bilateral free trade agreements. Indeed, Canada has signalled its enthusiasm for hemispheric free trade by signing a bilateral deal with Chile in advance of the Americans.

CONCLUSION

There is no doubt that the FTA resulted in a substantial increase in Canada-U.S. trade. There seems little doubt that the FTA gave something of a boost to productivity in the manufacturing sector. Several other factors, unrelated to the FTA, help explain Canada's poor productivity performance during the past decade. We do not know whether the FTA had a positive or negative impact on FDI, although Canada's performance in this area has been somewhat stronger in the past decade than in the decade preceding the FTA. No doubt there were some transitional job losses, although we do not know how many because it is very difficult to distinguish between FTA-related job losses and losses due to the recession of the early 1990s and the then-strong currency. Moreover, there were also jobs created by export expansion for which the FTA should receive partial credit. Finally, modest progress has been made in settling trade disputes by rules rather than by political power. All in all, then, I would conclude that the FTA has made a positive contribution to the Canadian economy, but a contribution meriting two cheers rather than three.

At the level of trade liberalization in general, the fact that Canada has experienced a difficult decade should not diminish our support for continuing multilateral trade liberalization, as well as regional initiatives like the incorporation of South American countries into NAFTA. Since the signing of the FTA, Canada's stake in a liberalized global trade order has gone up rather than down.

JOHN MCCALLUM is Senior Vice-President & Chief Economist of the Royal Bank of Canada. This study was initially published in RBC's *Econoscope.*

REFERENCES

Guillermo Alvarez et al. 1995. "NAFTA Chapter 19: Binational Panel Review of Antidumping and Countervailing Duty Determinations" in Leycegui et al., 24–42.

Richard Harris. 1985. "Summary of a Project on the General Equilibrium of Canadian Trade Policy." In John Whalley (ed.) *Canada-United States Free Trade, Background Study Number 11 of the Royal Commission on the Economic Union and Development Prospects for Canada* (Toronto: University of Toronto Press).

John F. Helliwell, Frank C. Lee, and Hans Messinger. 1998. "Effects of the Canada-U.S. FTA on Interprovincial Trade." mimeo.

Robert Howse. (1998). *Settling Trade Remedy Disputes: When the WTO Forum Is Better Than the NAFTA* (Toronto: C. D. Howe Institute).

KPMG. 1999. "The Competitive Alternative: A Comparison of Business Costs in Canada, Europe and the United States," Prospectus Inc.

Beatriz Leycegui et al. 1995. *Trading Punches: Trade Remedy Law and Disputes under NAFTA* (Washington: North American Committee, National Planning Association).

Daniel Schwanen. 1995. "When Push Comes to Shove: Quantifying the Continuing Use of Trade 'Remedy' Laws between Canada and the United States." In Leycegui et al., 161–82.

–. 1997. *Trading Up: The Impact of Increased Continental Integration on Trade, Investment and Jobs in Canada* (Toronto: C. D. Howe Institute).

Andrew Sharpe. 1999. "New Estimates of Manufacturing Productivity Growth for Canada and the United States." Centre for the Study of Living Standards. mimeo.

Statistics Canada. 1993. "Trade Patterns: Canada-United States, the Manufacturing Industries, 1981–1991." *Statistics Canada Catalogue* 65–504E.

Daniel Trefler. 1999. "The Long and Short of the Canada-U.S. Free Trade Agreement." mimeo.

Ten-Year Figures for Canada-U.S. and Canada-Mexico Trade

In 1998, total three-way trade among Canada, Mexico and the United States rose to about $752 billion, with Canada-U.S. and Canada-Mexico trade accounting for $484 billion (sources: Statistics Canada, U.S. Department of Commerce and SECOFI). Since the implementation of the NAFTA, Canada's trade with the United States has risen 80% while trade with Mexico has doubled.

Canada's NAFTA exports have likewise grown substantially, and have been particularly successful in high value-added sectors such as automotive equipment (trucks, cars, and parts), machinery and parts, and industrial goods. In 1998, the growth alone in Canada's exports to our NAFTA markets was roughly equal to the total value of our exports to Japan and to the 15 nations of the European Union (EU) *combined*. The growth in our NAFTA exports last year also more than offsets the drop in exports to other important international markets, attributable to the financial crisis and its aftermath. Reflecting this trend, the share of exports to NAFTA partners in Canada's total exports has increased from 80.8% in 1993 to 84.3% in 1998.

Imports to Canada from NAFTA members have also increased significantly over the past five years – particularly for machinery and equipment, communications equipment and automotive equipment. The

Department of Foreign Affairs and International Trade, April 1999 share of imports from the NAFTA partners in Canada's total imports reached 69.4% in 1998.

Following already impressive growth since the FTA came into effect on January 1, 1989, Canadian exports to the United States have increased by 80% in the NAFTA's first five years, rising from $151 billion in 1993 to $271 billion in 1998. Since 1993, Canada's two-way trade with the United States is also up 80% to $475 billion in 1998. Canada and the United States currently exchanges nearly $1.5 billion in goods and services each day.

The graphs demonstrate that trade in machinery and transportation equipment continues to be at the core of trade between Canada and the United States. Since the FTA and subsequently the NAFTA were implemented, Canadian exports to the Unites States for manufactured and industrial goods, with their higher value-added components, have steadily increased. Similarly, Canada continues to be the main destination of exports from the United States, with Canadian imports from the U.S. reaching $203 billion in 1998, an increase of 11% over 1997 and 78% during the first five years of the NAFTA.

TEN YEAR FIGURES FOR CANADA-U.S. TRADE

Following already impressive growth since the FTA came into effect on January 1, 1989, Canadian exports to the United States have increased by 80% in the NAFTA's first five years, rising from $151 billion in 1993 to $271 billion in 1998. Since 1993, Canada's two-way trade with the United States is also up 80% to $475 billion in 1998. Canada and the United States currently exchanges nearly $1.5 billion in goods and services each day.

TEN YEAR FIGURES FOR CANADA-MEXICO TRADE

An important benefit of the NAFTA for Canada has been the much improved access to the Mexican market. Canadian firms have been able to expand sales in sectors that were previously highly restricted, such as automotive products, financial services, trucking, energy and fisheries. Also, Canadian exports have become steadily more diversified, with value-added manufactured products accounting for the largest share of total exports to Mexico in 1998. Mexico is now Canada's thirteenth largest export market and fourth largest import source.

Despite the economic adjustments required in Mexico as a result of the financial crisis of December 1994 and its aftermath, Canadian

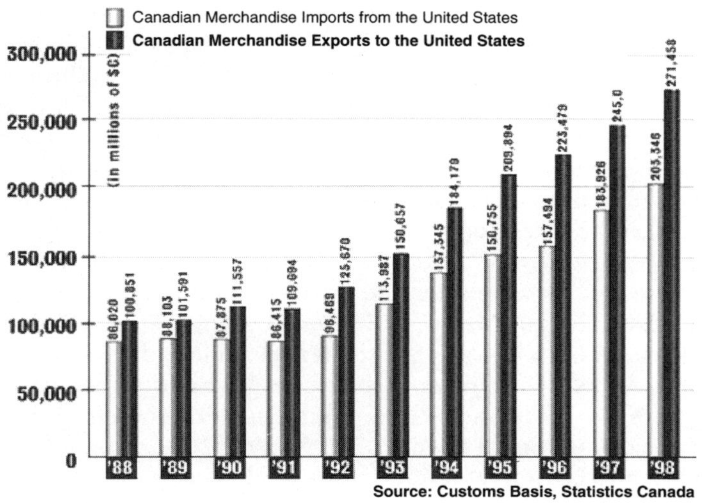

Canadian Merchandise Imports from the United States
Canadian Merchandise Exports to the United States
(in millions of $C)
300,000
250,000
200,000
150,000
100,000
50,000
0
86,020
100,851
88,103
101,591
87,875
111,557
86,415
109,694
96,469
125,670
113,987
150,657
137,345
184,179
150,755
209,894
157,494
223,479
183,926
245,0
205,345
271,458
'88
'89
'90
'91
'92
'93
'94
'95
'96
'97
'98
Source: Customs Basis, Statistics Canada

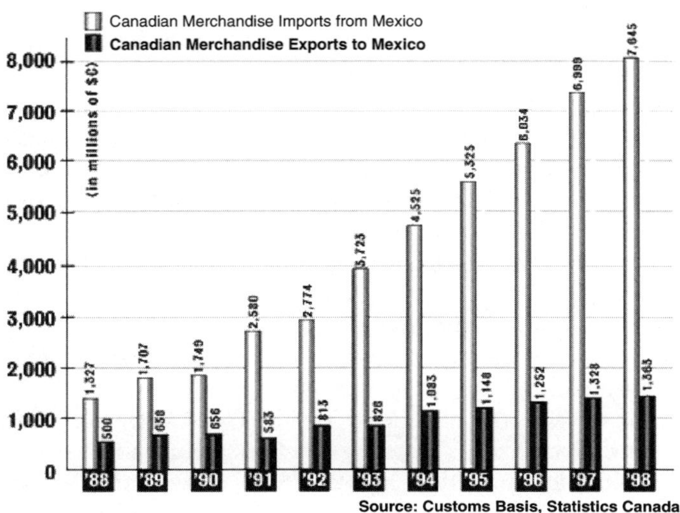

Canadian Merchandise Imports from Mexico
Canadian Merchandise Exports to Mexico
(in millions of $C)
8,000
7,000
6,000
5,000
4,000
3,000
2,000
1,000
0
1,327
500
1,707
658
1,749
656
2,580
583
2,774
813
3,723
828
4,525
1,083
5,325
1,148
6,034
1,252
6,999
1,328
7,645
1,563
'88
'89
'90
'91
'92
'93
'94
'95
'96
'97
'98
Source: Customs Basis, Statistics Canada

exports to Mexico have risen consistently since the implementation of the NAFTA, reaching $1.4 billion in 1998, an increase of 65% over the Agreement's first five years. Canadian imports from Mexico have more than doubled since 1993, increasing to $7.6 billion by 1998. Overall, two-way trade between Canada and Mexico has shown impressive growth over the NAFTA's first five years, doubling to $9 billion in 1998. t is important to note that existing statistics are believed to significantly under-report the true magnitude of Canadian exports to Mexico given the high estimated volume of transshipment via the United States. This in turn results in considerable variance in our respective national trade statistics (with Mexican figures showing bilateral trade at $11 billion and Canadian exports to Mexico at more than $3 billion in 1998). The statistical agencies in the three NAFTA countries are cooperating with a view to reconciling discrepancies between them, and this work is continuing in 1999.

Ongoing market liberalization efforts in Mexico, particularly in the energy, banking, telecommunications and transportation sectors, continue to create opportunities for Canadian exporters. As the Mexican economy evolves and strengthens, its demand for Canadian goods and services will continue to increase.

TEN YEAR FIGURES FOR CANADA-U.S. TRADE IN SERVICES

The NAFTA expanded the extent of coverage under the Canada-U.S. FTA to include virtually all aspects of cross-border trade in services. The Agreement also provides or enhanced access and for fair, transparent and non-discriminatory treatment in the provision of cross-border services between the NAFTA members. As well, the NAFTA ensures that Canadian business travelers can count on improved access to the United States and Mexico in order to pursue the business opportunities created by the rest of the Agreement. It sets out the governing principles and rules under which citizens of each country may have temporary access to the other countries to pursue business opportunities without meeting a labour market test.

The value of the two-way trade in services (such as travel, freight and shipping and commercial fees) between Canada and the United States has almost doubled since the Canada-U.S. FTA was concluded in 1988, growing to $58.9 billion in 1998. Over the five-year period following NAFTA implementation – ending on December 31, 1998 – Canadian service exports to the United States rose by 64% to $26.7 billion, while imports from the United States increased by 24% to $32.2 billion. In 1998, exports of Canadian services to the United States and Mexico

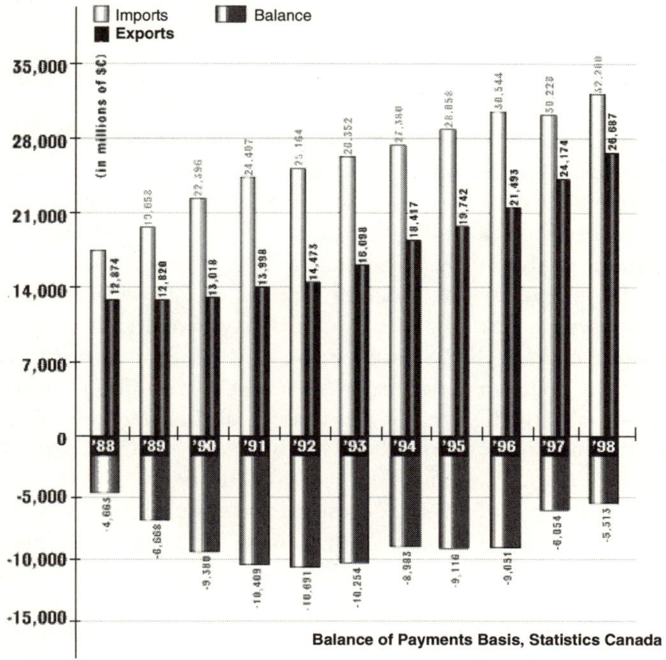

continued to show small increases, moderating Canada's traditional deficit in this sector.

The fastest-growing component of services trade has been in the computer and information services area, in which there is a high degree of specialization. In fact, bilateral trade between Canada and the United States in informatics services has emerged as one of the fastest-growing sectoral relationships in the world. Exports to the United States have also increased in such areas as communications, architecture, engineering and other technical services. Imports of services to Canada from the United States, meanwhile, have increased in areas such as management and advertising services.

Although trade in services is on the rise, it currently corresponds to only 12.4% of Canada's total merchandise trade with the United States.Given the large contribution of services to Canada's gross domestic product (GDP) (services currently make up almost two-thirds of GDP), the rapid growth of the services sector in both economies and the NAFTA's provisions to liberalize services trade between the NAFTA parties, this trade is expected to increase in the future.

CANADA-MEXICO TRADE IN SERVICES

Services trade with Mexico, though not calculated to the same level of detail by Statistics Canada, has also been on the rise since the implementation of the NAFTA, due in large part to the increased participation of Canadian firms in the Mexican economy. Canadian firms have been actively involved in the transportation sector through the provision of consultation services in the privatization of Mexican railways and in the management of the newly privatized railways. Canadian charter companies will benefit from greater liberalization in bilateral air services. In the energy sector, Canadian consultants have participated in Mexico's privatization of natural gas distribution and transmission. On the agriculture side, Canadian service suppliers are contributing consulting and training services in the area of food safety, and expert advice and assistance in the implementation of the Hazard Analysis and Control of Critical Points (HACCP) system. Furthermore, the development of distance learning programs, the projected establishment of private health clinics, and the provision of telecommunications services all point to the increasing diversity of Canada's participation in Mexico's services sector. Mutual recognition agreements negotiated under the NAFTA in areas such as legal consulting and engineering will, once implemented, further increase Canadian participation in Mexico's service industries.